Principles of Ecology and Management:

International Challenges

for Future Practitioners

Alan Sitkin

 Goodfellow Publishers Ltd

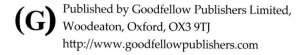 Published by Goodfellow Publishers Limited,
Woodeaton, Oxford, OX3 9TJ
http://www.goodfellowpublishers.com

British Library Cataloguing in Publication Data: a catalogue record for this title is available from the British Library.

Library of Congress Catalog Card Number: on file.

ISBN: 978-1-906884-23-9

 Design and typesetting by P.K. McBride, www.macbride.org.uk

Printed by Marston Book Services, www.marston.co.uk

Cover design by Cylinder, www.cylindermedia.com

Contents

Foreword

In recent years, a number of serious and highly competent authors have written books advising companies on how to engage with the ecological challenges facing the world today. Yet for business students seeking to embark on a corporate career, this corpus has – on the whole – been of limited use. One reason is because the overwhelming majority of green business books on the market today target current managers rather than students. The present text, on the other hand, is expressly designed as an educational tool helping students to incorporate environmental considerations into their business thinking. Secondly and above all, with extremely few exceptions today's green business texts exist to communicate devoted environmentalists' visions of what green companies could look like in the future. The problem is that utopian green visions have existed for many years now without most companies implementing the initiatives needed to reshape their activities along greener lines. The present text, on the other hand, addresses this dilemma by focusing primarily – and uniquely – on the obstacles hampering companies' transition to a greener future. Some consideration will also be given to potential solutions, crystallised, for instance, in the summative 'Obstacles and Pathways' features found at the end of each chapter. However, it is crucial not to repeat the mistake that many worthy green business authors make of confusing hope with reality – an approach that might also (and less generously) be called cheerleading. Ecology and management can only advance as a discipline if sufficient respect is paid to the factors hindering its development.

Of course, green business authors do deserve full praise for their enthusiasm. The present book wholeheartedly shares their view that an ecological imperative does exist, and that it is incumbent upon all business students to take stock of its implications when planning for the future. The environmental crisis is very real and unless it is resolved, nothing else will matter. Yet this dilemma has been widely publicised many years now. The real question is why companies have not responded more strongly to its frightening implications.

Preface

The ambition behind this book is simple – until now, no one has written a university textbook specifically targeting business school students interested in learning how the growing ecological constraint is going to affect the future of the companies for which they plan to work after graduation. Environmental studies have been taught in higher education for decades now, but such programmes tend to be delivered either as standalone (albeit interdisciplinary) topics or else lodged in departments such as geography, politics, economics or biology. Thus, it is from these disciplines' perspectives that existing textbooks apprehend ecology. This is, of course, eminently commendable, but the fact is that business students have been left in the lurch. Indeed, many have felt quite estranged from a discipline that has, up until now, been dominated by the kinds of 'hippies and Green Party activists' that business students often tend to belittle (rightly or wrongly). Given the pressing and potentially catastrophic consequences of not addressing the ecological imperative, however, this kind of false opposition is wrong and needs to be rectified. It helps no one when an existential challenge as crucial as the very future of Planet Earth is being marginalised because the voices debating it most loudly at present cannot or do not speak to the real obstacles facing the corporate sphere that may be our best hope of finding a solution. In essence, it is high time for the mainstream to reclaim something that – unbeknownst to many of main protagonists – has in fact always been a mainstream problem.

This then is the approach taken by the present book, and one that renders it unique in my opinion. There is also the fact that my main area of professional and academic expertise is actually in international business and not environmental studies. I have university degrees in both areas but have spent more of my professional life in business (without ever abandoning my environmentalist outlook). Thus, unlike other green business authors, I am approaching the topic from a business perspective, not a green one. This seems crucial in a business school context where students need a realistic view of the factors (and skills sets) affecting their future career choices. Some of these factors are internal to companies but others are external, explaining why this book is divided, like any good BA/MA level module, between an early macro section detailing the context within which (green) business takes place, and a subsequent micro section focused on corporate functions. The one particularity of this book is the choice to conclude with three future-oriented chapters but this decision seems justified by the relative novelty of the ecological imperative, and by the fact that business students seeking to understand this new area of study are making plans for careers that will play out over quite a few decades to come. It is to be hoped that this textbook will help them in that endeavour.

Councillor Alan Sitkin

Chair, Environmental Scrutiny Panel, London Borough of Enfield
and Pathway Leader, MA in International Business, European Business School London (Regents College)

■ Acknowledgements

In line with this book's international theme, the many people who have supported me so handsomely over the years come from all across the world. My deepest thanks to them and apologies to anyone there was no room to mention here or in my first book.

Yannick, Philippe, Rémi et Richard Zizou, *sous les pavés la plage*. Domecqs, Too Many Cooks and Wordsmiths, going down the country. Nick, Matt, Jeff, Barbara and Achilleas, Harry's Army. Not to forget Doug, Chris, Del and everyone else fighting so hard in Enfield. Or the Sweets, Bear and other Gauchos of my youth, doing whatever good they can.

Lastly, a special mention for beloved family members who have shaped my values and vision. Dear Dolans. Rainer (und Rolf), *immer dabei*. Patty and Roger and all ranch Sitkins past and future – *mi pueblo unido*. Helga and Larry, to whom I owe everything. Jim and Sue Sue, who I am so thankful to have by me always. Above all, boo Lea and md Dani, who have made my life so blessed; and Verena, who is the best.

About the author

Alan Sitkin combines his position as Senior Lecturer and Pathway Leader for the MA in International Business at the European Business School London (Regents College) with his other responsibilities as Councillor for London Borough of Enfield, where he serves as Chair of the Environmental Scrutiny Panel. The same duality is also reflected in his educational background, which includes an MBA from HEC France with a degree in Environmental Studies from the University of California Santa Barbara. Similarly, Alan's professional careers include 15 years in international banking plus more than a decade of economic and business translations. This is Alan's second textbook, after *International Business: Challenges and Choices*, published by OUP in 2010.

The book is accompanied by full online support:

- Student online resource centre featuring advanced materials for advanced study, additional case studies with questions, revision tips and further references

- Tutor online resource centre featuring case study answers, seminar schemes ('requiring preparation' plus 'in-class activities') and lecturer PowerPoint slides

To access these resources visit: http://www.goodfellowpublishers.com and follow the links to *Principles of Ecology and Management*.

1 Introduction to Ecology and Management

Contents

The ecological mindset
Early strands of ecological thinking
Rise of a mass movement

Basic science for managers
General principles
Earth sciences

The estrangement of management and ecology
Managerial incentives
International business effects

Learning objectives

After reading this chapter, you will be able to:

■ Situate environmental thinking in a historical context

■ Apply basic concepts in environmental science

■ Identify factors impeding managers' adoption of an ecological approach

■ The ecological mindset

Since the dawn of history, most cultures have devoted considerable intellectual resources to the question of humankind's connection to its natural environment. In prehistoric times, before advances in technology and science gave thinkers more rational means for analysing this relationship, the predominant attitude was to fear nature's power and potential for harming human populations through natural disasters (floods, droughts and fires), dangerous animals or starvation (crop failure). Such fears were compounded by general ignorance of the physical processes underlying events over which ancient humans had little if any control. Early animists would often attribute a spirit to a place – its so-called 'genius loci' – and view natural elements as moody gods with the power to nurture or destroy humankind. Precautionary tales about nature's revenge were present in many ancient civilisations, exemplified in Greek mythology by the tales of Prometheus or Icarus being punished or killed because they sought, respectively, to steal fire or fly close to the sun. More than living in harmony with the natural world, early populations felt it wise to obey it.

Over time, most societies would assume a more aggressive stance towards nature even as some voices continued to advocate humility. In the Judaeo-Christian Bible, this ambivalence is witnessed in the contradictory statements from the book of Genesis that humans should 'work and preserve the land' (2:15) but also 'be fruitful and multiply; fill the earth and subdue it; rule over the fish of the sea and the birds of the air and every living creature moving on the ground' (1:26). Eastern religions also offered mixed messages, with many of Hinduism's Vedic scriptures expressing reverence for the elements even as others doubted the reality of the physical world. Without purporting to review the sum total of historical attitudes towards nature, it might be generalised that as different civilisations would gain confidence in their ability to control aspects of nature, the physical world lost its mystical properties and began to be seen as an object for potential subjugation – all the more so given widespread belief in the inexhaustibility of natural resources (and the Earth's capacity to withstand the by-products of human activity).

Ultimately, the combined effects of population growth, industrialisation and resource demand would create a situation where many if not most inhabitants of Planet Earth took their physical environment for granted, appropriating its bounties and neglecting the ecological balances needed to sustain life. Over time, this would spawn a counter-reaction from observers disturbed by the disastrous consequences of such **anthropocentric** paradigms and focusing instead on the need for a **stewardship** of nature. The mindset that this latter constituency would propose came to be known as ecological.

> ■ **Anthropocentrism:** View that humans are the central feature of all existence.

> ■**Stewardship:** Idea that one entity has a practical if not moral obligation to take responsibility for another.

It is important to clarify the diversity of the strands comprising ecological thinking today. Each has its own history and reflects different sensitivities that can best be understood in the context of the historical economic circumstances where it arose.

■ Early strands of ecological thinking

It was in 1869, shortly after Charles Darwin published his text on the scientific principles driving the evolution of species, that German philosopher Ernst Haeckel is said to have coined the term 'ecology', derived from the Greek words for house (οικος or *oikos*) and speech (λόγος or *logos*). Thus, ecology discusses every aspect of a community's ability to inhabit a certain place – an approach that is, intentionally, **holistic**. Unlike other sciences that have more of a singular focus and are therefore less capable of fully accounting for the complex web of physical interdependencies and evolutionary interactions between living beings and their surroundings (Begon *et al.* 2006), ecology is multidisciplinary, always viewing its objects of study in the context of the many different factors enabling survival. Over time, this has enabled the constitution of a whole body of theories, principles and discoveries specific to this new discipline.

> ■ **Holistic:** View that a system is defined by the interactions between its components rather than by their sum total.

Haeckel was not the first to engage in what would be recognised today as ecological thinking. In the late 18th century, for instance, the English demographer Thomas Malthus devised a series of laws showing how population growth will cause a crisis in situations characterised by finite resources, with Malthus himself focusing on the likelihood of war. His paradigm continues to be applied today. Som e analysts focus on the social alienation affecting large segments of a population whenever a narrow constituency acquires a disproportionate share of available resources (Chamberlain 1970). A newer Malthusian approach involves linking globalisation and new solvent demand from emerging economies such as China or India to **resource depletion**, which will be discussed in Chapter 2, or the **degradation of the biosphere**, the focus of Chapter 3 (Friedman 2009). In many cases, ecological distress is best analysed in light of the size of the population concerned.

> ■ **Resource depletion:** Exhaustion of irreplaceable stocks of raw physical commodities consumed as a result of human activity.

> ■ **Degradation of the biosphere:** Where damage, often in the form of pollution caused by human activities, is done to the natural support systems sustaining life.

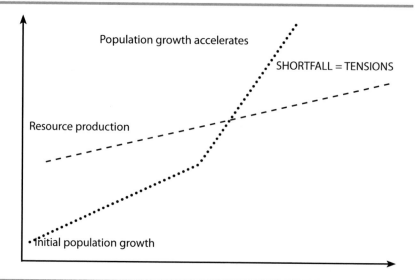

Population growth accelerates

SHORTFALL = TENSIONS

Resource production

•Initial population growth

Figure 1.1: Malthusian tension between population growth and resource supplies

Another notable thinker from the early 19th century was German botanist Alexander von Humboldt, who applied rudimentary ecological principles to forestry projects across Latin America and India. It is significant that the countries where Humboldt conducted his experiments were places of great political and economic interest to England and Spain, the colonial powers of the day – an early example of how material interests ('applied research') are as much a driver of scientific study of the natural world as the pure desire for knowledge ('basic research'). Thus, given the preponderance of agricultural economics during this era, it is no surprise that Humboldt's discoveries disseminated quickly throughout European farms. The link between science and business has a long history.

Key issue	... material interests ('applied research') are as much a driver of scientific study of the natural world as the pure desire for knowledge ('basic research').

At the same, the motivation driving many other 19th century writers with an interest in the environment was not material but spiritual – a strand that also remains present in today's ecological mindset. In 1854, New England essayist Henry David Thoreau wrote a seminal compilation entitled 'Walden' extolling a human civilisation harmonised with its natural surroundings and promoting a recognisably environmentalist agenda. Similar attitudes were advocated 40 years later in California by John Muir, explorer of Yosemite Park and founder of the Sierra Club, and in England by the author Beatrix Potter, who purchased large tracts in the northern Lake District to preserve land from development. Potter's actions were a sign of the concerns felt by some in Europe and North America, following the rapid industrialisation of their economies, at the prospect of an idyllic countryside being destroyed by manufacturing plants that the poet William Blake would denounce as 'satanic mills'. Vestiges of this concern persist in some of the land planning laws that remain in place today, including 'green belt' restrictions limiting growth at the edges of many modern cities (see Chapter 4).

The first half of the 20th century was an industrial era marked by the rise of Fordist mass production and consumption. There were a few notable ecologists, like the American forester Aldo Leopold, an 'aesthetic conservationist', or President Theodore Roosevelt, whose decision to protect millions of acres of wilderness were driven by more practical purposes – a division that continues to characterise the ecological mindset today (Ekirch 1972). By and large, however, the environment was a peripheral issue in most societies at the time, including in countries whose economic trajectories had been very different from the developed West – an international differentiation marking Ecology and Management studies to this day (see Chapter 8). A poignant example was Russia's old Soviet regime, which in its rush to conquer a vast territory undertook, for instance, the astounding step of reversing the direction of major rivers to enhance their economic utility. Similarly, the uncontrolled deforestation of vast swathes of Latin America and Asia – following a pattern set a few centuries before in the older industrialised countries – also wreaked havoc on local (and ultimately, global) environments. A final example from the 1930s was the abandonment of great swathes of farmland in the US state of Oklahoma as a result of 'dust bowls' caused by mismanaged soil practices. All in all, this was an era when economics superseded ecological thinking in societies whose evolution had been deeply scarred by the devastations of the Great Depression, two world wars and, in the developing world, crushing poverty.

■ Rise of a modern mass movement

The more positive global economic circumstances of much of the late 20th century would coincide, on the other hand, with growing acceptance of an **ecological imperative**. Such changes raise questions about the extent to which the ecological mindset derives from a 'social

■ **Ecological imperative:** View that ecosystem protection is a priority for all social, political and economic endeavours.

ecology' reaction to environmental damage – a mindset grounded in science and real social political interactions – or from a 'deep ecology' vision rooted in a quasi-religious attitude towards nature. The debate continues today.

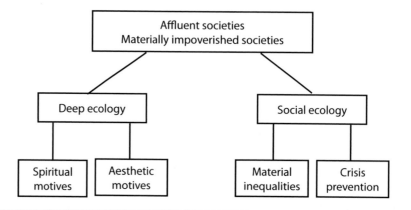

Figure 1.2: Different strands of the ecological mindset

? How much does ecological thinking owe to spiritual tendencies?

Effluents: ■
Outflows, runoffs or sewage from a transformation activity.

The social ecology approach can be witnessed in the chain of events following the mid-20th century 'Green Revolution' that had sought to eliminate starvation by using technology to increase agricultural productivity. A key element of this drive was the widespread introduction of pesticides such as DDT that were causing serious harm to water systems worldwide. The rising volume of industrial **effluents** was also having the same effect, one notorious case being Japan's Minimata Bay disaster, where mercury outflows from a local factory poisoned local fish stocks, increasing cancer rates and the number of children born with deformities. The end result was the 1962 publication of a book that became a seminal work for the global environmental movement: *Silent Spring*, written by the American marine biologist, Rachel Carson. The resonance of this text was such that governments worldwide began to set up quality authorities and enact legislation forcing business interests to modify working practices. One effect is that many chemicals companies started researching new ways of increasing crop yields. Over time, this would contribute to the development of genetically modified (GM) organisms, which in time would become another topic of controversy for environmentalists. The lesson from this chain of events is that, much in the same way as environmentalists highlight the interdependency of natural processes, there is also an ecological relationship between the different business, political and social forces whose actions impact on the environment. Ecology is as much as social science as a natural one.

? To what extent is ecology and management a natural or social science?

... in the same way as environmentalists highlight the interdependency of natural processes, there is also an ecological relationship between the different business, political and social forces whose actions impact on the environment.

It was in the late 1960s and early 1970s that the global environmental movement finally achieved self-awareness. Professors at the University of California at Santa Barbara, having witnessed the devastation wreaked on the local coastline by an oil spill in 1969 (and in the wake of other high profile disasters, such as the oil tanker *Torrey Canyon*'s 1967 crash on the shores of Cornwall), launched one of the world's first environmental studies degree programmes. Texts produced by this vanguard (such as Garrett Hardin's famous 'Tragedy of the Commons', see Chapter 4) lay the economic foundations for the new discipline, in conjunction with other seminal works such as Paul Ehrlich's *The Population Bomb* (1968) and E.F. Schumacher's *Small Is Beautiful: Economics As If People Mattered* (1973). Some observers also trace this sudden rise in environmental awareness to Apollo moon flight images taken of a beautiful but vulnerable Planet Earth – imagery underlying the title of a famous 1972 treatise by British scientist James Lovelock, 'Gaia as seen through the atmosphere'.

> **?** How does the modern green movement split between aesthetic and utilitarian motivations?

The sum total of this intellectual output meant that by the mid-1970s, ecologists had the intellectual means to build a vocal constituency. The activist organisation Greenpeace, founded in Vancouver (Canada) in 1972, launched a number of high-profile campaigns (e.g. against nuclear testing and commercial whaling), operating alongside older groups such as World Wildlife Fund (1961) and Friends of the Earth (1969). At first, however, these movements had little resonance in the general public. Although increasing amounts of scientific evidence about the ecological imperative were already available in the 1970s, few citizens felt the problem deeply enough to change behaviour. Interest in the environment, crystallising in events such as the first 'Earth Day' organised on 22 April 1970, seemed largely confined, in the industrialised world at least, to academic constituencies or the margins of society (often offshoots of early 'hippy' movements). Several governments began to diffuse environmental messages – one example being a huge campaign launched by France's Giscard regime (under pressure from René Dumont, who in 1974 became one the world's first green presidential candidates) calling upon citizens to 'hunt down waste' ('*chasse au gaspi*') and reduce the mountains of litter plaguing the French countryside. Such efforts were few and far between, however.

The same apathy permeated much of 1980s, a decade whose predominant **zeitgeist** is largely deemed to have been the advancement of material and individual welfare, as evidenced by many political and cultural indicators in the United States, the world's hegemonic state at the time. This mindset was famously encapsulated in the dictum from Oliver Stone's emblematic film *Wall Street* that 'greed is good' – a philosophy diametrically opposed to the **green sacrifice** that is a pillar of much ecological thinking. Similarly, many economies like India, China and Brazil that are in the process of emerging today suffered from abject poverty for most of the 1980s, meaning that their main priorities would have been material rather than ecological development (see Chapter 8). In contexts such as these, most citizens would have viewed environmentalism as largely irrelevant and possibly provocative.

By the 1990s, however, there were clear signs in many countries that militant greens were no longer the sole proponents of an ecological mindset. One indicator was the growing numbers of politicians seeking to co-opt green ideas, often for electoral branding purposes but also because a series of disasters over the previous 15 years (see Table 1.1) had convinced many of the need to finally face up to the ecological imperative. In Germany, the world witnessed the first serious attempt by a green movement to gain political power. 'Die Grüne', originally led by Petra Kelly and Joschka Fischer, was born out of anti-nuclear power demonstrations that had gained publicity and admiration worldwide. At a transnational level, 1987 saw both the Brundtland Commission's seminal report enshrining the concept of 'sustainable development' as well as the Montreal Protocol's restrictions on further use of harmful CFC compounds which were creating a hole in the Earth's ozone layer. This one decision had a decisive effect on the industrial activities of refrigerator manufacturers worldwide. It is also one of the first examples of a global policy driven by actors' sense of the ecological imperative both constraining companies' room to manoeuvre and creating opportunities for commercial expansion (in the shape of a new demand for HCFC compounds characterised by a lesser **environmental footprint** than CFCs). It would not be the last.

Zeitgeist:
Dominant paradigm at a particular moment in history.

Green sacrifice:
Actors' willingness to renounce personal material advantage in favour of ecological benefits enjoyed by the wider community.

? Do certain eras lend themselves more to the ecological mindset more than others?

Environmental footprint:
Measurable effects of an activity on the ecosphere.

Year (s)	Country/region	Incident	Description
1960s onwards	Soviet Union	Aral Sea	Destruction of lake due to water diversion
1976	Italy	Seveso	Factory explosion causing cloud of toxic dioxins
1978	France	Amoco Cadiz	Oil tanker spill of ca.1.6m barrels on Brittany shores
1976–78	USA	Love Canal	Chemical dumpsite, health hazard for local residents
1979	USA	Three Mile Island	Nuclear plant leaks
1980s	Global, esp. Australia	Ozone layer	Increased solar radiation causing rise in skin cancer
1984	India	Bhopal	Chemical plant explosion, thousands of deaths
1986	Ukraine	Chernobyl	Nuclear plant explosion
1989	USA	Exxon Valdez	Oil tanker spill of ca.1.2m barrels on Alaska shores
1997	Asia	Smog cloud	Deforestation fires causing 3200 km long air hazard
1990s	Europe	BSE	Mad cow disease, herd slaughters, human deaths

Table 1.1: Late 20th century disasters sparking greater green sensitivity

Another key factor was the advance of globalisation. This had a contradictory effect, with the explosion in world trade increasing demands on planetary resources (see Chapter 8) even as the concomitant rise in information exchanges sparked global environmental consciousness. Such awareness would spread further through the efforts of the 'eco-pedagogy' movement that the Brazilian educator Paolo Freire founded in the wake of the UN's 1992 Rio Earth Summit. The idea being pushed here (by thinkers such as Austrian philosopher Ivan Illich) was that all academic curricula should be based on ecological values insofar as materialistic definitions of happiness are inherently 'counter-productive'. This new value system, diametrically opposed to the one conveyed in most corporate marketing campaigns at the time, would in turn pave the way for the rise of 'social marketing', one category of which 'green marketing' (see Chapter 7).

? In which societies might the ecological mindset still be considered marginal, and why?

Corporate responsibility: ■ The idea that a company should ensure that all of its actions are both legal and ethical.]

By the 2000s, most societies worldwide featured active green lobbies, often led by 'eco-barons' (Humes 2009) or visionaries – politicians, scientists, activists, entrepreneurs and even cultural icons – whose green words and deeds resonated through the international media. Ecology has become a permanent fixture on the social and political agenda: at a governmental level; but also at the personal level, as witnessed by the profusion of personal stories about lifestyle changes ranging from car-free days to household experiments in living without appliances. Today's green sensitivities can be partially analysed within the context of many employees' increasing desire to hold their company accountable for the consequences of its actions (see Chapter 5) – an idea encapsulated in the growing field of **corporate responsibility** (CR). Yet it is important to remember that CR is comprised of many subcategories, with recent studies indicating that even though environmental responsibility is the dominant reference for companies seeking to prove their CR credentials, it is the one that is least important to consumers' estimation of a company's CR image and subsequent purchasing behaviour (Anselmsson and Johansson 2007). For many individuals, the environment remains just one area of concern among many and is not an absolute imperative.

At the same time, there are ample signs that ecology has risen up many companies' agenda in recent years. Explanations for this trend can vary, however. In many industrialised countries, it is headline events – like Hurricane Katrina which devastated New Orleans in 2005, or the red toxic sludge disaster that overwhelmed the Hungarian town of Kolontar in 2010 – that have convinced increasing numbers of citizens to accept the ecological imperative. Some commentators are already predicting that ecological problems will soon replace labour issues as the number one CR concern in the world's industrialised countries, simply because they are more relevant to wealthy societies' direct welfare concerns than other CR variables such as labour standards (Vogel 2006). In larger emerging countries such as China, on the other hand, support for environmentalism might stem from governments' fear of 'ecocide' (see *Chapter 1 online case study*) against a background of over-population and accelerated industrialisation (Zanier 2008). Irrespective of motives, there is little doubt in the 2010s that more and more citizens everywhere want politicians – and managers – to take the ecological imperative seriously. The question then becomes the best way of achieving this goal.

Pre-1970s	Post-war societies stressing material success; environmentalism dominated by aesthetic conservationists	**Table 1.2:** Timeline of post-World War II green sensitivities
1970s	Seminal texts on ecological imperative; fears of over-population; oil crises, economic stagflation and cultural sea changes	
1980s	Culture of materialism but also series of disasters; Brundtland commission, Montreal Protocol; Green Party born in Germany	
1990s	Globalisation strains resources but IT and new global governance mechanisms raise awareness of interdependency; CR spreads	
2000s	**Climate change** fears; economic emergence of LDCs raises spectre of resource competition/depletion scenarios	■ **Climate change:** Lasting variation in temperatures and weather.
2010s??	Effects of recession on consumerism in older industrialised countries vs rising standard of living in LDCs	

■ Basic science for managers

At a deeper conceptual level, the new discipline of Ecology and Management seeks to overcome the centuries-long divorce between economics and science by asserting the interdependency between the two – a linkage famously expressed in the seminal green business concept of 'natural capitalism' (see *Web Resource 1.1*). It remains that this re-connection will only take root if all managers – not just R&D or manufacturing specialists – are intellectually equipped to integrate ecological (thus scientific) principles into their business decisions. The first step towards empowering managers with this capability is to diffuse relevant knowledge about basic science (biology, chemistry and physics) together with earth sciences (water, land, atmosphere).

? Why is it important for managers working in non-industrial functions to have some scientific knowledge?

... overcome the centuries-long divorce between economics and science by asserting the interdependency between the two.

Key issue

■ General principles

Environmental *biology* contains many principles that are relevant to future managers' applied level, the concept of 'bio-utilisation' speaks to new uses of organisms as raw materials, one example being plant-based plastics. This approach also includes concepts such as 'biomimicry' and 'biomorphism' (see Chapter 6) that refer to an enhanced use

Sustainability: ■
Capacity for survival
for unlimited period of
time through repetition
of existing regulation
mechanisms or adoption
of new ones, enabling
adjustment to changing
circumstances.

Ecosystem: ■
Sum total of living 'biotic'
flora or fauna and inanimate
'abiotic' elements whose
interactions enable life on
Earth, often through the
self-sustaining food chains.

of design technology to create goods that will imitate the properties of the natural world (Steffen 2009). More broadly, such efforts are part of a general search for **sustainability** in the original sense of this term, i.e. the capacity of organisms (or **ecosystem**s) to self-perpetuate. Species' ultimate survival depends on their evolutionary ability to defend themselves against external risks. This is a key issue in sectors whose long-term viability is predicated on adaptation to external dangers such as climate change. For companies, this means integrating sustainability mechanisms into their physical operations and organising feedback with the outside world to check that these measures remain suitable. Models for such approaches can be found in the survival processes, reproduction cycles and food chains that organisms and ecosystems develop to survive (see Figure 1.3).

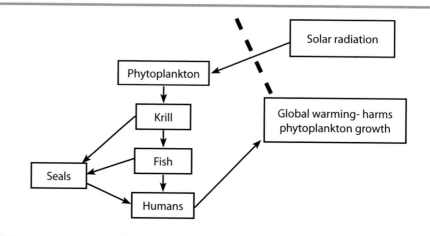

Figure 1.3: Potential disturbance of food chain interdependencies

Key issue

For companies, this means integrating sustainability mechanisms into their physical operations... Models for such approaches can be found in the survival processes, reproduction cycles and food chains that organisms and ecosystems develop to survive.

Sustenance: ■
Factors supporting the
existence of life.

Lastly, environmental biology also helps to identify the mechanisms by means of which nature recycles the death of some organisms into **sustenance** for others – focusing on a 'cradle-to-cradle' cycle as opposed to 'cradle-to-grave' approaches (McDonough and Braungart 2003). As Chapter 6 demonstrates, such processes will in the future become increasingly relevant to companies' materials management, transformation and recycling strategies.

At a broader level, environmental *chemistry* refers to all of the molecular interactions affecting land, sea and atmospheric systems (see 'Earth Sciences' section below) – first and foremost being photosynthesis, the process by means of which the sun's energy is converted into a sugar called ATP that stores chemical energy and underpins the food chains for all of the flora (and thus fauna) found on Earth. Similarly, managers also stand to benefit from familiarising themselves with the effects of chemical weathering processes such as oxidation, carbonation or hydrolysis (Bloom 1969) since these help to determine the durability of the physical assets that a company accumulates. Chemistry is also the main discipline for pollution studies, a key topic in environmental business. This is because some compounds are a health hazard for humankind, fauna and flora (triggering reactions that impede normal sustainability processes); and also because it is useful from a business perspective to ascertain the extent to which contamination resulting from one party's waste affects another party's welfare. As demonstrated in Chapter 3, the damage that a pollutant causes is in part a function of the physical environment's ability to dilute its effects. For instance, the first factory to spill effluents into a river may not have a noticeable effect on the local biosphere, but if many facilities do the same thing, the consequences will be much more severe. In addition, given that very few industrial systems are self-contained – i.e. almost all of them produce waste – it is crucial that managers have basic understanding of chemistry to minimise their outputs' negative impact (e.g. through the use of **biodegradable** materials or 'anaerobic' oxygen-free decomposition methods) and/or to enhance their inputs' quality (i.e. by prioritising organic over synthetic compounds). Such knowledge is all the more useful to managers due to the new green economy's focus on companies auditing and reporting their environmental footprint (Chapter 5).

■ **Biodegradable:** Molecular compounds whose residues merge harmlessly into the environment once they have decomposed.

Environmental *physics* offers managers a powerful analytical framework both at an applied level (ecological engineering including the preservation/restoration of ecosystems or construction of green buildings) and at the broader level of Isaac Newton's basic laws of thermodynamics (Saperstein 1975) and motion. One Newtonian postulate is that energy flowing from one body to another is neither created nor destroyed but at most changes forms. Thus, it is impossible to get more energy out of a physical operation than the amount put in, i.e. all activity necessarily draws upon energy resources and is only worthwhile insofar as the output is economically more useful than the input. This calculation is complicated by Newton's second 'entropy' law postulating that some of the energy transferred during a physical operation will necessarily be wasted, often in the form of heat (see Figure 1.4). Unless this 'heat waste' is re-captured, other energy inputs will have to be found to fuel future operations. Clearly, the more efficient an operation is (i.e. the less heat it wastes or the more heat it re-captures), the less it requires additional energy inputs. Hence the growing interest in **closed loop** systems (buildings, industrial processes, etc.) that maximise recycling and energy conservation. This approach is also being applied to areas like power infrastructure whose efficiency will be increasingly crucial in a future characterised by the depletion of conventional energy resources (see Chapter 2).

Closed loop: ■
System whose existing components suffice for its continued functioning, i.e. which requires no further inputs.

Lastly, note Newton's famous law that in a closed system comprised of two objects, neither can act without forcing the other to react. Originally formulated to describe physical forces in general, one corollary is that in a closed system such as an ecosphere, no physical operation can occur without impacting on its surroundings. Indeed, the bigger an operation, the greater the impact. Thus, insofar as Planet Earth constitutes a closed system, it has limited capacity to accommodate human economic activity in the absence of compensatory regenerative efforts.

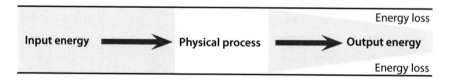

Figure 1.4: No perpetual motion: physical processes lose energy due to entropy

Key issue

... insofar as Planet Earth constitutes a closed system, it has limited capacity to accommodate human economic activity in the absence of compensatory regenerative efforts.

■ Earth sciences

There are several ways in which *water sciences* (including hydrology and oceanography) interest environmentally-minded managers. Because water is essential to all life on Earth, the sustainability of drinking water sources has always been a central focus for ecologists, who have long criticised companies for wasting and (above all) polluting supplies. The protection of clean water captured in underground water tables, rivers, lakes and glaciers has become a growing area of concern for populations worldwide. New conservation techniques such as 'rainwater harvesting' (see Chapter 9) have enormous architectural and infrastructural implications. Similarly, advanced research in wetlands/meadowlands environments has significantly enhanced general understanding of ecosystems' self-regulating mechanisms. There is also great interest in the role that water systems play in shaping land masses via processes such as erosion, subsidence and the transportation of nutrients or sediments. Otherwise, with fertiliser nitrates increasingly running off to create oxygen-deprived 'dead zones' in many coastal waters – and given global warming's negative impact on agricultural productivity – there has been rising economic interest in 'aquaculture', the practice of growing organisms in water environments for food and even as potential power sources (see Chapter 10). Lastly, there is the requirement that more and more companies worldwide produce environmental impact reports detailing the effects of their activities on local and global water systems.

For managers, the main *land science* is geology, or the study of the surface of the Earth, together with its main adjuncts: mineral and rock formations; or crop and soil management. The first category provides knowledge that can be of crucial value in sectors such energy (i.e. petroleum, natural gas and coal); mining (i.e. minerals like bauxite for aluminium, iron for steel, copper for wiring or silicon for conductivity; elements like chlorine provoking chemical reactions; or uranium, driving nuclear power); or construction (buildings safe from subsidence or earthquakes). As for crop/soil management, this is first and foremost of importance to managers in agribusiness, a sector that seems destined to account for a larger percentage of overall economic activity in the years to come as future supply/demand imbalances cause foodstuffs' relative price to rise in comparison with manufactured goods or services (see Chapter 9). Lastly, note increased interest in organic materials such as cellulose or other forms of biomass that have value as alternative fuel sources.

The main *atmospheric science* is climatology and/or its short-term weather-focused variant, meteorology. The starting point for this field is solar radiation. As aforementioned, this energy form is converted through photosynthesis and stored in plants where it becomes the primary fuel source for all life. Note that the energy can either be tapped directly from the plants where it is accumulated or indirectly after they have died and decomposed into fossil fuels.

In addition, solar radiation is a source of heat. Until recently, this heat would dissipate into outer space at a rate enabling moderate temperatures across much of the planet, thus the rise of human civilisation. With greenhouse gas accumulating in the outer atmosphere as a result of human activity (see Chapter 3), however, this dissipation mechanism has weakened. The net effect is that ambient temperatures are trending upwards, with potentially devastating consequences for life on Earth. Given this scenario, it is clear that managers everywhere need to be familiar both with how expected global emission reduction initiatives will affect their operations, and with how a predictably hotter planet (and/or more volatile weather) will influence their long-term prospects. If global warming's effects are as serious as currently feared, it is impossible to imagine a future in which Ecology and Management remain separate concerns.

Table 1.3: Environmental science for managers: main concepts and uses

		Leading concepts	Uses
Biology		Sustainability	Reproduction cycles and food chains; recycling/cradle-to-cradle thinking
		Bio-utilisation/mimicry	Natural inputs; imitation of natural design
Chemistry		Planetary processes	Photosynthesis; weathering
		Contamination studies	Dilution/decomposition of pollutants/waste; biodegradability
Physics		Eco-engineering	Green buildings and design
		Energy conservation	Minimising of entropy-related (heat) waste; efficient production/distribution of energy
Water sciences		Drinking water	Husbandry methods (rainwater harvesting); auditing and reporting of usage/pollution
		Aquaculture	Foodstuffs; power sources
Earth sciences		Geology	Fossil or other fuels as energy resources; minerals as primary industrial resources
		Crop/soil management	Agriculture; biomass for non-food purposes
Atmospheric Sciences		Climatology	Climate change/global warming
		Solar radiation	Sourcing 'current' sunlight (photosynthesis) or 'ancient' (**finite** fossil fuels)

Finite: ■
Quantity characterised by limited total supply.

Key issue   If global warming's effects are as serious as currently feared, it is impossible to imagine a future in which Ecology and Management remain separate concerns.

1

■ The estrangement of management and ecology

It is one thing to use scientific principles to explain the usefulness of managers developing an ecological mindset. It is another to determine why this approach has not spread earlier and more widely within the business community. As aforementioned, the principles underlying environmental science have been widely known for many years now. Moreover, newspapers abound with stories of the bottom line benefits for companies of going green – one case from summer 2010 being the discovery by 51 EDF Climate Corps fellows working at US Fortune 1000 companies of the potential for $350 million in net lifetime operational savings (Mills 2010). Given economists' presumption that people will make rational decisions in most circumstances (Becker 1976), one would have expected managers paid for their forward thinking to have organised the ecological imperative into a core corporate function a long time ago, imbuing it with as much legitimacy as more traditional areas such as production, marketing or finance (Bresciani and Oliveira 2007). Just as surprising is how few students are enrolled nowadays in the kind of engineering, technology or energy studies that would position them favourably in green business, despite this sector being widely expected to become one of the world's main growth drivers in the years to come (Peacock 2010). Discovering why current and future managers have not been rushing headlong into this new field of activity is a good starting point for determining under what conditions this could happen in the future.

Until recently, many members of the international business community tended to mock environmental activists as irrelevant and/or utopian (Monbiot 2007; Hofstra 2007) – even going as far, in some cases, as to ignore and/or undermine scientific evidence of impending catastrophes such as climate change (Revkin 2009), often because they preferred to promote a hostile political ideology (Jacques 2009). To varying degrees, apathy towards environmental concerns remains widespread in a number of countries (see Chapter 8) and indeed companies. Examples of the latter include the astounding quote attributed to ex-Chrysler CEO Lee Iacocca, 'How much clean air do we need?' (Grossi 2009); scathing attacks by European discount airline Ryanair's controversial CEO Michael O'Leary on so-called 'eco-nuts' and 'environmental headbangers' (Harrison 2006); or documented efforts by leading businessmen in the United States to sabotage some of the

Obama Administration's environmental policies. Rejectionist attitudes of this kind stem from a variety of motivations.

■   Managerial incentives

One of the key premises underlying this book is that any global shift to a green economy will be time-consuming and, above all, expensive, especially for companies forced to replace current unsustainable sunk investments prematurely with costly and relatively untested new green assets and technologies. Since it may not always be possible for all costs to be passed onto consumers immediately, accepting the ecological imperative may very well reduce profits for companies, at least in the short run – raising questions about how different managers might wish to arbitrage their immediate versus their long-term interests. Above all, as Chapter 4 details, most companies have not had to bear the full cost of their activities until now, with the rest of society carrying the burden of the pollution they produce or the resources they deplete. Companies would lose this advantage if their environmental footprint were fully 'internalised' (incorporated into their cost structure). Similarly, the willingness of environmentally-oriented managers to adopt green practices might also diminish if they expect the benefits of this shift to accrue to society as a whole and not to their companies alone. By definition, the ecological imperative is partially rooted in group-interest but this requires, in turn, that individual managers be willing and/or able to sublimate their material self-interest (see *Web Resource 1.2*).

? Do what extent does some managers' short-term orientation impede their companies' greening?

The stereotypical accusation that managers are more prone to **venality** than other social constituencies draws some theoretical substantiation, oddly enough, from Milton Friedman and other opponents of 'corporate social responsibility' for whom companies' sole responsibility is to maximise profits. Just as oddly, the opposing caricature that managers are no more motivated by gain than anyone else in society receives some support from none other than Karl Marx, whose theory of 'economic determinism' states that everyone – not just the capitalist class – is driven by material self-interest. A compromise view would be that greediness is no more prevalent among the managerial class than it is in the whole of society (D'Amico 2008). This position has the merit of enabling some differentiation, if not within national cultures, then at least between them – a fundamental precondition for analysing the ecological mindset in comparative terms.

Venality: ■
Willingness to sell one's services for a material reward.

? How much altruism is required to adopt the ecological mindset?

Tracing the historical evolution in managers' corporate role also helps to create a framework for assessing their sensitivity to issues (such as the environment) that affect the community as a whole as opposed to one company alone. Note along these lines the existence of a large body of management literature focused on the relationships and obligations linking owners, managers and wider society. Part of this corpus discusses how the growth of huge, multidivisional corporations during the early 20th century gave birth to a whole class of professional managers who did not necessarily have the same concern for a local community's welfare as owner-managers of smaller family-run enterprises might have had (Vogel 2006).

A different argument would be that enlightened shareholders – viewing the ecological imperative as an inevitability with respect to which their company had to position itself sooner rather than later – could become the driving force behind a company's greening process. Conversely, 'agency theory' states that in huge multidivisional entities where ownership is separated from corporate control, it is unclear that owners' 'principal' interest – assumed in this case to be profit maximisation – will align with managers' 'agent' interests. One reason for this may be because managers may feel deeper roots in their social (and physical) environment than distant institutional investor shareholders with little stake in the local community's welfare. This latter analysis appears particularly relevant to the modern world of globalised financial markets. The fear here is that remote shareholders, seeking only to maximise returns, will pressure local managers into actions that could have dire consequences for stakeholders but not for the shareholders themselves. In turn, this creates a kind of **moral hazard** – an example of 'market failure' and a reason why new theories of environmental economics have had to be developed (see Chapter 4).

■ **Moral hazard:** Where incentives are skewed so that a party is motivated to take a risk because it does not suffer the consequences if things go wrong.

■ International business effects

In a similar vein, the theory of financialisation (Froud *et al.* 2006) differentiates between the traditional vision of companies' role as social institutions with obligations to all kinds of stakeholders from the newer, 'neo-liberal' market-oriented view that their sole purpose is to maximise owners' returns. According to economist Milton Friedman, for instance, it is acceptable for companies to focus on so-called 'shareholder value' to the exclusion of other considerations as long as they respect the law. The problem with this concept in an international business context is that legalities can vary greatly from one country to another (see Chapter

Carbon emission trading schemes: ■————
Mechanisms whereby participants receive (or buy) initial permits enabling maximum carbon emissions over a specific period. These can only be exceeded by buying fellow participants' unused permits. Conversely, unused permits can be resold for a profit, providing an incentive to emit less carbon.

8). This occurs because governments implement entirely different policies, reflecting factors such as their countries' cultural attitudes or stage of socio-economic development. When deciding where to locate new investments, multinational enterprises (MNEs) often focus on variations in national regulations, playing one government against another and forcing each to lower its standards, especially when a poor country desperate for inwards investment is involved (Sitkin and Bowen 2010). It will, for instance, be tempting for MNEs to take advantage of international variations in the implementation of **carbon emission trading schemes** by directing business towards countries characterised by lower carbon prices, higher emission allocations and generally laxer environmental regulations. Thus, it is the inconsistency in different regimes' sense of the ecological imperative that explains, in part, the slow implementation of green business practices worldwide.

Key issue

... tempting for MNEs to take advantage of international variations ...by directing business towards countries characterised by ...laxer environmental regulations.

A second specifically international factor in the dissemination of green business practices derives from the dismantling of protectionist trade barriers over the past 30 years. The net effect has been an expansion in cross-border trade: between firms; but also within them (with an estimated 60 per cent of all international business today comprised of intra-firm trade). Applying classical theories of national specialisation and comparative advantage at a corporate level (see Chapter 8), many MNEs have sought to maximise plant-level economies of scale by splitting global production between distant specialist factories, with each focused on a particular stage of the manufacturing process (components, assembly, etc.). This fragmentation makes sense at a corporate level as long as the costs associated with the ensuing intra-plant flows, i.e. logistics costs largely driven by energy bills, remain modest. At some point, however, skyrocketing fuel prices will mean that today's 'de-materialised' MNE configurations are no longer economic, forcing managers to reintegrate the geographic constraint of distance into their thinking. Whether they make this adjustment in a timely fashion depends on their ability to look beyond the current fashion for a 'shrinking world' paradigm to an ecologically more realistic vision of a 'world that is shrinking'.

All in all, it is companies' ability to internalise sustainable thinking – both domestically and internationally – that will determine the
future of Ecology and Management (see Box 1.1). One obstacle to the
adoption of the new mindset is the difficulty inherent to any change
situation, explained in part by the way in which most managers' innate
inertia or conservatism prevents them from welcoming new routines
(Doppelt 2008) in the absence of strong leadership (see Chapter 5). This
would intimate that the impetus for widespread corporate transition
to sustainability comes from enlightened leaders. There are famous
examples of CEOs who have almost single-handedly driven their
companies' green conversion: Jeffrey Immelt from General Electric,
with the eco-efficiency focus of its new Ecomagination product line;
Ray Anderson from carpet company Interface Inc., which has made
more than 50 per cent progress towards the goal of eliminating 'any
negative impact it has on the environment by the year 2020' (Mazur
and Miles 2009); Jeffrey Swartz from clothing company Timberland,
which has committed to be carbon neutral by the year 2010; and many
others – most of whom can be found among the membership of the
World Business Council for Sustainable Development (http://www.
wbcsd.org/).

- Diversify across generations
- Adopt to change
- Celebrate transparency
- Avoid compartmentalization
- Form groups and protect young
- Integrate measurements
- Improve with each cycle
- Rightsize regularly
- Foster longevity not immediate gratification
- Waste nothing
- Recycle everything
- Borrow little

Box 1.1: Principles of
sustainable business
(adapted from Werbach
2009)

Alongside this, other observers hold the belief that corporate
sustainability necessarily relies on staff-level initiatives, exemplified
by eBay's Green Team units, where employees convene at their own
behest to discuss and implement green actions such as solar incentive

schemes or carbon offset programmes (Nguyen 2008). Managers are also citizens, meaning that they bring values developed in their private lives into the workplace (Hertz 2002). They construct green values after reading media reports rife with predictions of a **dystopian** future; or because the curriculum taught at the business school from which they graduated increasingly features a number of sustainability elements (Finn 2008). Professional environmentalists are not the only members of society to acknowledge the ecological imperative.

Dystopia: ■——————
Disturbing/nightmarish future – opposite of 'utopia'.

Key issue

Managers are also citizens, meaning that they bring values developed in their private lives into the workplace.

Exaggerating the overall benefits of existing environmental actions would be quite misleading, however. Getting employees to bring their own cups to work instead of using Styrofoam cups may be laudable but the impact pales in comparison with the total **ecological deficit** accumulating at present in the business sector and, of course, society as a whole. When a 2008 World Wildlife Fund report announces that planetary resources are being consumed about 30 per cent faster than they can be replenished – so that two Earths will be needed by the mid-2030s to sustain modern civilisation if it continues to grow as it is doing at present (WWF 2008) – it is hard to argue that the corporate sustainability drives witnessed until now (whether bottom-up or top-down) suffice to address the problem. Indeed, it is crucial to avoid the 'cheerleading' approach to environmentalism characterising many if not most business books in this field. Giving students – future managers and executives – the wrong impression of how much progress has actually been achieved so far does people a disservice by lulling them into a false sense of security. The reality is that the vast majority of companies are already very aware of how hard it would be to fully embrace the ecological imperative. Clearly they find this very daunting. Understanding the reasons for their apprehension is a key step towards overcoming it.

Ecological deficit: ■——————
Excess of human consumption of planetary resources over their natural regeneration.

Key issue

... companies are already very aware of how hard it would be to fully embrace the ecological imperative. Clearly they find this very daunting. Understanding such apprehension is a key step towards overcoming it.

■ Obstacles and pathways

1 Some national cultures traditionally tend towards the attitude that humankind has dominion over nature.

Executives can use their status as a platform for disseminating a sense of the ecological imperative (publications, education, advertising).

2 The environment is just one corporate responsibility (CR) priority among other worthy issues.

Corporate responsibility efforts should delineate clearly between different strands to enhance general empathy with each.

3 Managers often ignore Planet Earth's physical limitations.

They can learn basic scientific principles through lifelong learning programmes.

4 Employee incentives focus on short-term financial performance to the detriment of other considerations (such as environmental consequences of behaviour).

Performance assessment can be redesigned to include sustainability.

Case study: Detroit focuses on SUVs not survival

American consumers have traditionally enjoyed lower fuel prices than their counterparts across the industrial world. This may have been explained at first by the fact that the country had its own petroleum sources, but prices remained low even after reserves began to fall in the 1960s. The persistence of this low price policy must therefore be attributed to other factors, first and foremost being US households and businesses' expectations that fuel must remain cheap to perpetuate a longstanding travel culture in which individual car or truck drivers regularly cover great distances: because the USA is so big; but also because its urban (and suburban) growth has been organised along extensive lines with little focus on public transportation solutions.

The basis for many of the long-term design decision taken by America's 'Big 3' automakers in Detroit was the assumption that politicians in Washington would always cater to these public expectations and keep fuel prices low (i.e. by eschewing the heavy fuel taxes found in most other industrialised countries). GM, Ford and Chrysler specialised in large, fuel-inefficient vehicles that satisfied US consumer preferences but would become both uneconomic in a context of higher oil prices, and unsustainable when greenhouse gas emission reductions later became a priority.

The first ecological constraint – the risk of higher fuel prices due to the depletion of global petroleum reserves – had been known to Detroit since the twin oil crises of 1970s, when the Big 3 had lost significant market share to smaller, more efficient models offered by Japanese rivals Toyota, Honda and Datsun. After lobbying Washington to restrict imports, the US companies gained some time but instead of putting it to good use by investing in more efficient models, they took the cheaper option of continuing to turn out the big gas-guzzlers that American consumers had traditionally favoured. Indeed, a documentary entitled, 'Who killed the electric car' has revealed the underhand methods used by different government and industry parties to undermine an EV1 battery-run vehicle launched in California in the early 1990s. This was an era when US resistance to the ecological imperative was very strong at all levels.

The counter-oil shock of 1986, leading to a dramatic fall in fuel prices, seemed to justify the Big 3's overall strategy. Indeed, with energy inflation seemingly under control, the American carmakers decided to invest massively in the light truck segment, promoting household purchases of minivans, 4x4, pick-ups and sport utility vehicles. These vehicles were anything but efficient and despite a modicum of technological progress, fuel consumption averages actually fell in the USA between the 1980s and the 2000s. At the same time, strong sales of light trucks, which accounted for 54 per cent of all new vehicle purchases in the US in 2008 versus 22 per cent in the 1980s, helped to restore the Big 3's profitability for a while. This domestic success would come with a heavy cost, however, since it lulled US auto executives into thinking that they did not have to take account of certain long-term global trends – first and foremost being higher fuel prices.

The energy crisis of 2006–07 caused oil prices to more than double to $140/barrel, heightening US consumers' interest in the kind of fuel-efficient cars that the Big 3 had never developed to any great extent. By this time, Toyota had come out with its Prius hybrid model, which not only uses less fuel but also emits less carbon dioxide, a key contributor to global warming – the second ecological constraint that Detroit used to ignore. In most if not all other countries worldwide, automakers have accepted that governments will impose measures requiring vehicles producing lower CO_2 emissions, and have adjusted to this by making the appropriate R&D and design investments. Examples include BYD from China, which leveraged its battery capabilities to produce a full line of competitive electric cars; Dacia from Romania or Tata from India, specialising in inexpensive low horsepower models aimed at emerging economies where households can only afford modest vehicles; and older European and Japanese carmakers' efforts to improve their models' ecological performance.

In contrast, US automakers continued to suffer from the self-imposed restriction that consumers and industrialists should only be 'prepared to integrate the environment in their economic decisions as long as this causes no hardship' (Bust 2002). This unwillingness to face up to the ecological imperative was partially shaped by the political climate of the early 2000s, when the Bush Administration (with its close links to the oil industry) actively sought to 'challenge the science' of climate change (Burkeman 2003). In the end, however, Detroit's refusal to adjust to environmental realities was fatal. By winter 2010, Chrysler and GM had gone bankrupt and Ford's prospects largely depended on the success of its new Fusion Hybrid. The lesson of this precautionary tale is that managers might always find reasons to ignore the ecological imperative, but they do so at their own peril.

Case study questions

1   What are the causes and consequences of traditionally low fuel prices in the USA?

2   How has the ecological imperative changed the status quo in the US auto market?

3   How might the US and global automobile markets adjust to a more environmentally constrained future?

■ References

Anselmsson, J. and Johansson, U. (2007), 'Corporate social responsibility and the positioning of grocery brands: An exploratory study of retailer and manufacturer brands at point of purchase', *International Journal of Retail & Distribution Management*, **35** (10).

Bauman, Z. (1998), *Globalization: The Human Consequences*, New York: Columbia University Press.

Becker, G. (1976), *The Economic Approach to Human Behavior*, Chicago: University of Chicago Press.

Begon, M., Townsend, C. and Harper, J. (2006), *Ecology: From Individuals to Eco-Systems*, Wiley-Blackwell.

Bloom, A. (1969), *The Surface of the Earth*, Englewood Cliffs, NJ: Prentice-Hall.

Bresciani, S. and Oliveira, N. (2007), 'Corporate environmental str ategy: a must in the new millennium', *International Journal of Business Environment*, 1 (4).

Burkeman, O. (2003), 'Memo exposes Bush's new green strategy', 4 March, available at www.guardian.co.uk, accessed 30 December 2009.

Bust, T. (2002) 'Ford takes revamp back to its roots', *Financial Times*, 4 February.

Carson, R. (1999) *Silent Spring*, Houghton Mifflin.

Chamberlain, N. (1970), *Beyond Malthus: Population and Power*, Englewood Cliffs, NJ: Prentice-Hall.

D'Amico, D. (2008), 'Who's to blame for all the heartache? A response to anti-capitalistic mentalities after Katrina', *International Journal of Social Economics*, 35 (8).

Doppelt, B. (2008), *The Power of Sustainable Thinking*, London: Earthscan

Ekirch, A. (1972), 'The utilitarian emphasis', in R. Nash (ed.), *Environment and Americans: The Problem of Priorities*, Holt Rinehart and Winston.

Erlich, P. (1971) *The Population Bomb*, MacMillan.

Finn, W. (2008), 'Thinking beyond grey pinstripes', 23 January, available at http://business.timesonline.co.uk, accessed 20 October 2008.

Friedman, T. (2009), *Hot, Flat and Crowded*, Harmondsworth: Penguin.

Froud, J., Johal, S., Leaver, A. and Williams, K. (2006), *Financialization and Strategy*, Routledge.

Grossi, M. (2009), 'News blog', 12 February, available at fresnobeehive.com, accessed on 26 December 2009.

Harrison, M. (2006), 'Ryanair boss labels flight critics "econuts, idiots and headbangers"', 7 November, available on www.independent.co.uk, accessed 26 December 2009.

Hertz, N. (2002), *The Silent Takeover: Global Capitalism and the Death of Democracy*, Free Press.

Hofstra, N. (2007), 'Sustainable entrepreneurship in dialogue', *Progress in Industrial Ecology, An International Journal*, **4** (6).

Hume, E. (2009), *Eco Barons: The Dreamers, Schemers, and Millionaires Who Are Saving Our Planet*, Ecco.

Jacques, P. (2009), *Environmental Skepticism: Ecology, Power and Public Life*, Farnham: Ashgate.

Lovelock, J. (2001), *Homage to Gaia: The Life of an Independent Scientist*, Oxford University Press.

Mazur, L. and Miles, L. (2009), *Conversations with Green Gurus: The Collective Wisdom of Environmental Movers and Shakers*, John Wiley and Sons.

McDonough, W. and Braungart, G. (2003), *Cradle to Cradle: Remaking the Way We Make Things*, Rodale Press.

Mills, V. (2010), 'Energy efficiency sleuths uncover $350m in savings', 14 September, available at www.greenbiz.com/, accessed 29 September 2010.

Monbiot, G. (2007), *Heat: How to Stop the Planet Burning*, Harmondsworth: Penguin.

Nguyen, Q. (2008), 'Corporate green teams: sustainable business from the bottom up', 7 June, available at www.greenbiz.com, accessed 29 December 2009.

Peacock, L. (2010), 'Young people switch off to careers in energy', *Sunday Telegraph*, 15 August, p. 2.

Revkin, A. (2009), 'Industry ignored its scientists on climate', 23 April, available at www.nytimes.com, accessed 26 December 2009.

Saperstein, A. (1975), *Physics: Energy in the Environment*, Boston, MA: Little, Brown.

Schumacher, E. (2010) *Small is Beautiful, Economics as if People Mattered*, Harper Perennial

Sitkin, A. and Bowen, N. (2010), *International Business: Challenges and Choices*, Oxford: Oxford University Press.

Steffen, A. (ed.) (2009), *World Changing: A User's Guide to the 21st Century*, New York: Abrams.

Thoreau, H. (2004) Walden, Beacon Press.

Vogel, D. (2006), *The Market for Virtue: The Potential and Limits of Corporate Social Responsibility*, Brookings Institution Press.

Werbach, A. (2009), *Strategy for Sustainability: A Business Manifesto*, Boston, MA: Harvard Business Press.

WWF (World Wildlife Fund) (2008), *Living Planet Report*, available at www.panda.org, accessed 29 December 2009.

Zanier, V. (2008),' The environment: once a problem for the rich, now part of the marketing strategy? A case study on China's environmental communication', *International Journal of Chinese Culture and Management*, **1** (2).

2 Resource Depletion

Learning objectives

After reading this chapter, you will be able to:

- Identify supply and demand pressures affecting conventional energy sources
- Compare the outlook for different energy sources
- Chart scenarios for other manufacturing inputs (mineral and biological)

■ Introduction

The industrial economic model has traditionally been a linear scheme in which material resources undergo transformation processes that then produce products and services – along with unwanted waste. This architecture relies on two conditions: the availability of inputs at an economic price; and the imperative that pollutant by-products appearing at the **end-of-pipeline** do not accumulate to the extent that they endanger the ecosphere within which the activity occurs. These two constraints, the subject of the next two chapters of this book, embody the ecological imperative as most managers experience it.

End-of-pipeline:
Total output following the completion of all transformation processes.]

In the absence of a 'closed loop' production system that has been ecologically optimised so that companies' outputs become inputs to use in subsequent manufacturing cycles (Chapter 6), the acquisition of physical resources is the first step for all material economic activity. Whether inputs are acquired from external sources or produced by a corporate entity specialising in the early, **upstream** stages of a good's value chain is irrelevant to analysis at this point (albeit important in determining the length of a company's overall supply chain, hence its environmental footprint). What counts is whether a company's competitive position allows it to access resources cheaply enough to be able to transform them into sellable products at a profitable price. In turn, this depends on the company's ability to pass on its own inflationary pressures on to **end users**. In some markets, this can be a difficult proposition due to customers' own solvency constraints or because such behaviour leaves the producer open to accusations of profiteering (Hutton 2008). In other markets, price pressures are alleviated through government aid that will often materialise upstream in the form of tax credits or subsidies paid to companies to ensure the viability of a minimum, strategic level of production. The purpose of such measures is to help companies to lower costs so that they can drop their prices to consumers. Even more dramatically, interventions of this kind occasionally seek to stave off the kind of social unrest that will occur when prices skyrocket on staples such as energy or food (as witnessed most recently in summer 2010 when devastating fires in Russia wrecked this country's grain harvest, which usually make an important contribution to global supplies). However, subsidies of this kind are often subject to a number of criticisms. On one hand, market-friendly, **neo-liberal** economists tend to disapprove of the way they distort 'normal' price

Upstream:
Early value chain activities undertaken when processing or transforming a product or service.

End users:
Ultimate customers of a product that is not destined for further enhancement.

Neo-liberal:
Belief in a minimal interference of government in the economy.

mechanisms. On the other, many environmentalists also disapprove of such expenditures, regretting the way that the enormous sums distributed year in year out to typical recipients (farmers, energy companies, etc.) diminish their incentive to migrate towards more energy-thrifty behaviour, while reducing the amount of money available to fund new green activities such as renewables production (Monbiot 2007; Thomas and Chomitz 2009). Yet it remains highly unlikely that a market as significant as energy might ever operate without some degree of government supervision. Certainly, in historical terms this has never been the case.

Key issue

In the absence of a 'closed loop' production system... the acquisition of physical resources is the first step for all material economic activity.

In classical economic theory, where a company struggles to pass higher costs on to customers, this should motivate it to innovate, enhance inputs' productivity (Barbiroli 2009) or adopt substitutes, if any exist. The problem is that certain resources have become indispensable to current transformation processes, with such enormous sums being sunk into input-specific industrial apparatuses (internal combustion engines, gas-fired power plants, etc.) that it would be prohibitively expensive for the company involved to re-engineer its systems. This is one reason why so many managers have been so slow to acknowledge the ecological imperative – adaptation is expensive, and they hope to avoid this cost during their own careers, leaving it to future generations. In a world facing a risk of environmental destruction, such calculations are morally dubious. Given the pressing nature of the ecological imperative, they also appear unsustainable and even irrational. Supply and demand trends for many if not all of the world's natural resources are already signalling the demise of the classic industrial economic model. All indications are that resource depletion is occurring sooner rather than later and constitutes a clear and present danger for companies today.

? Why have companies been slow in weaning themselves off oil?

Key issue

... one reason why so many managers have been so slow to acknowledge the ecological imperative – adaptation is expensive, and they hope to avoid this cost during their own careers.

It would be impossible to list all the factors affecting the availability of all the different natural resources that companies use for their operations. The categorisation used here will distinguish between energy resources that power corporate operations and/or that consumers need to run products; minerals that are moulded into product components themselves; and biological resources dependent on the Earth's ecosystems. Another possibility would be to distinguish between biodegradable resources that can be returned directly to the ecosphere after economic transformation and non-decomposable 'technical' goods that remain in an industrial state and cannot be returned seamlessly into the natural environment (Braungart and McDonough 2009). This latter approach is more relevant, however, to analysis focused on how human activity degrades the very biosphere that is needed sustain life on earth – the environmental deterioration and pollution topic covered in Chapter 3.

■ Energy inputs

There is a good argument that the main interface between economy and ecology resides in the power that humankind derives from natural resources (Monbiot 2007). Two crucial factors in this relationship are technology and above all population size. In older agricultural economies, most energy involved 'current sunlight', with people either eating plants nourished via photosynthesis (see Chapter 1) using them for building materials, or feeding them to animals that could be used for food or clothing (Hartmann 2004). As technological know-how advanced to allow humankind to access 'ancient sunlight' stored in the form of fossil fuels derived from the accumulation of dead plants, people were able to source much greater quantities of energy. This led to **demographic** growth, however the larger populations that ensued could only be sustained by tapping into energy resources above and beyond those provided by current sunlight, i.e. by drawing upon fossil fuel reserves that are by definition finite in nature and will therefore be necessarily exhausted after x years of extraction and consumption. When this occurs, only the very few 'Earth ships' that are self-sufficient in power generation (Freney 2009) will be unaffected. Conversely, the vast majority of actors who rely on external sources of power will have to adapt. Of course, the scenario should also mean greater demand for the services of those companies that specialise in the supply of energy

Demography: ■
Study of population patterns (birth rates, mortality, migration, etc.)

? Are there too many people on Earth?

– something that students currently considering their career prospects may wish to bear in mind.

■ Global supply/demand scenarios

Some factors affecting the future of global energy are specific to this one field. Others relate to long-term societal trends that take the availability of power for granted – an assumption that is likely to evaporate as the effects of resource depletion hit home.

The best way to describe managers' options when faced with resource depletion is the race to adapt. This applies not only to people working for energy companies but also (and maybe above all) to their customers whose current operational modes will no longer be viable once resource scarcity becomes the rule. For the moment, companies (and economies in general) seem to be losing the battle against depletion, with global energy demand having risen by something like 1.6 per cent per annum over the past decade, a figure expected to jump to 2.2 per cent through the year 2020 (Farrell *et al.* 2007). Looking ahead, consultants at the US consulting group McKinsey have tried to calculate future demand based on factors such as the severity of the post-credit crunch crisis downturn in GDP; the implementation of light vehicle fuel efficiency standards; electric vehicles' market share by the year 2020; and above, **energy productivity** (MGI 2009). What they have discovered is quite discouraging. A continuation of current trajectories is likely to mean a 27.3 per cent increase in global energy consumption to 610 quadrillion British Thermal Units (BTUs) by the year 2020. Moreover, even if actors (largely companies) maximise efficiency gains by implementing green technologies and adapted modes of organisation, a 10.2 per cent rise to 513.5 quadrillion BTUs can still be expected, largely as a result of new demand from emerging economies. Thus, without a radical change in perceptions and behaviour, energy consumption is expected to expand even as global resources continue to deplete.

■ **Energy productivity:** Quantity of outputs produced with fixed level of inputs.

Moreover, it appears highly unlikely that further energy price increases will alter this uptrend. Prices have risen more or less constantly since 1998 (see Figure 2.1) without any marked impact on consumption. In other words, movements in primary energy prices do not seem to be an effective way of getting actors to reallocate resources (Jiao *et al.* 2009). At a corporate level, such **inelasticity** translates many

■ **Elasticity:** Correlation between the movement of one variable, like price, and another, like supply or demand. 'Inelasticity' signifies that no such correlation exists.

managers' inability or unwillingness to process available information about resource depletion, intimating in turn that thinking in this area is guided more by psychological or institutional influences (Steininger 2009) than by rational strategising. If so, it is likely that internal corporate awareness raising exercises (Chapter 5) and/or external constraints such as regulations and rationing or quotas (Chapter 4) would be more effective at changing managerial attitudes than pure market mechanisms have been up until now. Clearly, most companies have failed to prepare themselves sufficiently for resource depletion. The first step towards resolving this shortcoming is to become aware of it.

> ? How effective are price signals in the energy market?

Key issue

... inelasticity [to energy price increases] translates many managers' inability or unwillingness to process available information about resource depletion, intimating in turn that much thinking in this area is guided more by psychological or institutional influences...than by rational strategising.

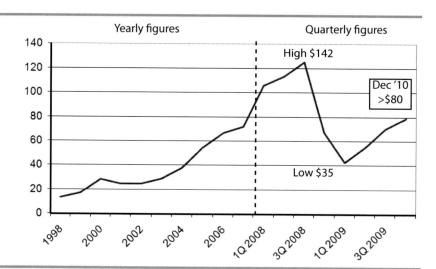

Figure 2.1: Annual averages of first trading day of month spot prices for Brent crude oil in US$ per barrel (http://www.eia.doe.gov/emeu/international/crude1.html)

Energy elasticity: Relationship between changes in a country's economic expansion and its energy use.

A major factor in the ongoing over-consumption of energy is skyrocketing demand from emerging industrial powerhouses such as India and above all China (Bozon *et al.* 2007). Because **energy elasticity** remains high in these countries, their rapid marginal GDP and population growth has had a disproportionate effect on global demand. Despite some commendable sustainability ambitions, the general state of corporate technology in many developing countries has meant comparatively **energy-intensive** manufacturing processes, especially in low-margin firms lacking the financial resources to acquire energy productivity-enhancing technology (King and Slesser 2009). Thus, as

Energy-intensive: Description of activities requiring a higher than average injection of energy resources.

globalisation forces shifts manufacturing away from the Global North, overall energy usage will tend to rise for a given volume of global output. This is especially true due to the internationalisation of many multinational companies' supply chains, with growing volumes of intermediary materials, components and modules being manufactured in distant specialist locations before shipment to their final assembly or sales locations (see Chapter 8). Multinational configurations of this sort are very logistics-intensive and add to total fuel usage. Given that they often involve a prime contractor wilfully abandoning the capability to build the basic components used in its products, they can also be very difficult to change.

Similarly, the sheer number of formerly insolvent developing country consumers who can now afford consumer goods means that global manufacturing (thus energy use) is also on the rise, driven in large part by Chinese and Indian growth rates that are often three times higher than anywhere else in the world. Advances in these countries' power generation and distribution capacities – reflecting the demographic shift from a predominantly rural to a more energy-intensive urban society (see *Web Resource 2.1*) – has added to this dynamic. With all these demand-side trends, it is easy to see why the natural resource sector is rapidly turning into a seller's market. It is also hard to see what might be done about this.

> **?** Is energy price inflation unavoidable today?

Some analysts have outlined an optimistic scenario in which rising global demand for energy starts to abate because enough actors (especially industrialists, who are the biggest energy consumers) feel that it is in their interest to take unilateral steps to reduce consumption. Hence the often-heard argument that the most effective way of overcoming resource depletion is by maximising conservation, a measure that is often estimated to be capable of generating a 20 per cent reduction in overall energy consumption within a reasonably short period of time (Monbiot 2007). This ambition is eminently desirable, however its mathematics are dubious for at least two reasons. The first is a historical phenomenon called Jevon's Paradox, based on the observation that societies whose technological progress enables greater energy efficiency tend in actual fact to increase their total consumption of energy, if only because actors become less worried about resource availability as previous constraints start to fade. One example is the way in which energy consumption has risen more than twice as quickly in UK households over the past 20 years as total energy use, despite significant improvements in key technologies such as heating boilers (Monbiot

2007). Reassured by their improved infrastructure, residents are simply heating their homes more than before. Similarly, there is the increased availability of lower quality, energy-inefficient appliances (refrigerators, lighting) and the lazy misuse of standby switches. Otherwise, the second obstacle to a general reduction in energy consumptions lies in the irrational and/or resentful nature of the human psyche. Many if not most managers are less motivated to engage in a costly transition to sustainability if they sense that competitors will be the ones taking advantage of their sacrifices. As discussed in Chapter 1, the decision to go green is tempered, like many business calculations, by individual calculations of the relative benefits of co-operation versus self-interest.

> **?** Why go green if rivals are not doing the same?

Of course, such t-for-tat calculations are ultimately self-defeating, given that managers everywhere will be affected by the draconian energy shortages that are sure to arise if global demand does not adjust to supply. As ex-BP CEO Tony Hayward said in a well-publicised speech from October 2009, the 'harsh realities of energy' are simple: demand is growing much more quickly than supply; none of the new technologies suffices in and of itself to make up for this shortfall; new supply expansion projects have long lead times; the most energy rich fuel source (coal) is the dirtiest; and the price of carbon is far too low to motivate managers to restructure their companies' resource consumption models. On the face of things, there is no justification for inaction.

Key issue

... tit-for-tat calculations are ultimately self-defeating, given that managers everywhere will be affected by the draconian energy shortages that are sure to arise if global demand does not adjust to supply.

At the same time, many managers find the scale of the energy challenge too daunting to even contemplate addressing it. The IEA has predicted that up to $26 trillion dollars of new investment are needed just to meet projected growth in energy demand by the year 2030 – with a further $10.5 trillion needed to combat the effects of climate change (IEA 2009b). Faced with sums as gigantic as these, some managers prefer to adopt an ostrich approach – often encapsulated in the remark that 'they' (unknown scientists?) will find a solution. Such attitudes lack any basis in tangible reality. This does not prevent them from being widespread.

However, a dilemma as serious as this at least has the merit of attracting a great deal of attention. Leading Ecology and Management thinkers have developed a number of proposals to address it, many of which are recapitulated in the micro-corporate strategies discussed in this book's later chapters. What should be noted at this point is that all of these ideas share the basic premise that resource depletion can only be overcome by adopting of a variety of adapted solutions. This means that everyone – not just specialists working for utility firms – should acquire basic understanding of the reality in the global energy markets. When the challenge that a company faces is as fundamental as keeping its lights on, managers lacking rudimentary knowledge in this area (and/or who take their energy sources for granted) will struggle to match their more attuned colleagues' career prospects.

> **?** Should energy knowledge become a universal management skill?

Table 2.1 breaks global primary energy supplies down by fuel category. These data refer solely to organised energy markets and therefore exclude biomass and waste, crucial power sources for many poorer agricultural communities in regions such as Africa and India (and estimated to account for anywhere between 4 and 10 per cent of global primary energy supplies). The table also excludes leading non-hydro renewable sources such as solar, wind, tidal/wave (see Chapter 10) and geothermal, which altogether account for less than 1 per cent of total supplies. Given the highly publicised target in many EU and other countries that renewables account for 20 per cent of total energy consumption by the year 2020, however, a bright future is clearly on the cards for this particular category of fuel sources.

Oil	Natural gas	Coal	Nuclear energy	Hydro	Total
3,930	2,726	3,304	620	718	11,295
34.8%	24.1%	29.6%	5.5%	6.4%	100%

Table 2.1: 2008 consumption by fuel type in MTOE (million tonnes of oil equivalent) (BP 2009)

Among conventional sources, fossil fuels currently account altogether for more than three-quarters of total energy consumption. At the same time, two of these fuels are destined for depletion in fewer than 100 years' time: oil, whose 1,258 billion barrels of proven global reserves are equivalent to just 42 years of production at current consumption rates; and natural gas, whose 185 trillion cubic metres of reserves are calculated to last 63 years at current consumption rates. Note that proven global reserves of coal are somewhat more abundant, totalling 826 billion tonnes or 122 years of consumption at current rates. As for uranium, the fuel used in almost all nuclear reactions, in 2004 the International Atomic Energy Agency (www. iaea.org) calculated global stocks of about 4.7 million tonnes, good for about another 85 years of consumption.

Along these lines, it is worth recalling that energy is also spent to build the generation infrastructure required to produce fuel in the first place. In addition, transporting energy from its original production location – oil platform, gas field, coalmine, nuclear power plant – to the innumerable locations worldwide where it is consumed also requires a great deal of energy. Depending on the mode of transportation (tanker, pipeline, liquefaction and above all electric lines), up to 30 per cent of all primary energy is typically lost on distribution alone. This number should fall over time as improved technology increases distribution efficiency – one example being the way in which future electric power lines will be able to function over longer distances using high voltage direct current. However, it is just as evident that much energy could be saved – and **energy security** fears allayed – if users were to rede-

Energy security: ■

Confidence that a country (or company) can source the energy it needs to achieve its ambitions.

sign infrastructure to maximise the consumption of locally produced fuels. Thus, as the era of energy abundance comes to an end and actors intensify their conservation efforts – an enormous reorientation drive that will itself produce new growth opportunities for companies – there will probably also be some dismantling of today's long-distance energy distribution networks that were originally built on the premise that distant suppliers' lower energy production costs would outweigh the cost of transporting the fuel in question. This adjustment is easier said than done, however. On one hand, as represented in Table 2.2, there is currently a significant disconnect between the main regions where energy is produced and those where it consumed. Unless this shifts, distribution efficiency is bound to remain a constant concern.

? Is energy provision destined to become a more localised business?

On the other hand, localising energy production to diminish the need for localisation means that some communities will have to develop a power generation infrastructure that is adapted in terms of size to their lesser local needs. The smaller installations required for this kind of **micro-generation** approach will by definition be unable to capture the

Micro-generation: ■

Production of power from small, local sources.

same economies of scale as larger, centralised sources, adding to the overall costs of the shift towards energy localisation.

	Oil		Natural gas		Coal		Nuclear	Hydro
	Cons	Prod	Cons	Prod	Cons	Prod	Cons	Cons
NAFTA	1077	619	751	740	607	638	215	149
S/Central America	270	336	128	143	23	56	5	153
Europe/ Eurasia	956	851	1030	979	528	456	277	180
Middle East	307	1254	295	343	9.4	1	NA	3
Africa	135	488	85	193	110	143	3	22
Asia/ Pacific	1183	381	437	370	2031	2031	120	211

Table 2.2: 2008 energy consumption vs production in MTOE (BP 2009)

2

Note that energy transportation also becomes an issue when a region's consumption of a particular kind of fuel differs greatly from its production of the source in question (nuclear and hydro power can be excluded from the equation since, by definition, they serve users with electricity – which for the moment cannot travel long distances without expending, thus losing, a disproportionate amount of its original power). In macro-economic terms, for any one fuel category, the excess of regional consumption over production will translate into large import needs, with the opposite situation creating an export flow. The most striking energy flows today are clearly Asian-Pacific or NAFTA imports of oil from the Middle East (and, increasingly, Africa). Note as well in Table 2.2 that the small production deficit in European natural gas actually hides large intra-regional imbalances, with Russia and its former satellites being surplus producers and energy-poor Western Europe very reliant on these sources. Indeed, long-term energy security is a constant concern for many European companies – which may explain why executives in this part of the world regularly lobby their national governments to take an active approach in the development of alternative energy sources.

Lastly, it is also worth noting the breakdown of global primary energy consumption by user type (see Table 2.3). This is important because user categories can vary markedly in both consumption and energy intensity terms. One example is the expected rapid rise over the coming decades in transportation-related energy consumption (led by the ongoing expansion in aviation). This differs from the outlook for residential and commercial lighting, which should benefit greatly from the advent of new LED technologies (see *Web Resource 9.2*). Similarly, the main modes of energy of consumption also vary globally, reflecting factors such as regional climate specificities (thus heating needs), agricultural patterns or industrial specialisation. Many consumers tend to view supplies in light of their electricity provision – the most common form of energy today, and one that is destined to rise given the predicted demise in fossil fuels and introduction of electrical automobiles. However, the big picture is that the global energy market constitutes a patchwork of fuel sources and uses.

Table 2.3: Percentage breakdown of energy use by end user category (US EIA 2009)

Industrial	36.6
Electricity generation/distribution	28.7
Transportation	18.9
Residential	10.4
Commercial	5.5

■ Fossil fuels

Before exploring the specificities of the three leading hydrocarbons that are oil, natural gas and coal, readers should be reminded of the price correlation between them, particularly the first two. Thus, on the production side, natural gas is often a by-product of oil exploration. On the demand side, a visible substitution effect exists between these two resources, with higher oil prices tending to spark increased demand for natural gas, thus higher prices for this latter commodity. The two markets are not completely parallel, since oil prices are fixed on a more or less global basis, whereas the gas trade tends to be more regional due to this fuel's particular transportation constraints (somewhat alleviated by the recent expansion in liquefied natural gas). Along these lines, note the much more localised nature of the market for coal, whose pricing structure is closely linked to local factors such as seam depth, extraction methods and logistics. As oil and gas prices rise over time, the costs of liquefying coal will also become increasingly justifiable. Facilitating a fuel's transportation turns it into a more viable direct substitute for its rivals.

Oil

In December 2009, the International Energy Agency (IEA) issued an Oil Market Report providing a concise overview of this cornerstone of the global energy sector. Key findings included the stability of demand, quantified at 84.9 mb (million barrels)/day at the time of the report but expected to rise to 86.3 mb/day within the year – reaching 29.6mb in the Americas, 26.4mb in Asia Pacific and 15.4mb in Europe. The expected global total for 2014 was 91 mb/day. All this demand growth was expected to come from the developing world, with the global oil intensity (i.e. consumption of oil/rate of economic growth) predicted to continue falling in the older OECD industrialised countries. This is due to slow GDP growth in this part of the world following the 2008 credit crunch, increasingly stringent fuel economy standards, industrial restructuring and ongoing gas-for-oil substitution trends. On the supply side, efforts to increase global capacities are expected to partially alleviate medium-term pressures, as a result of greater contributions from Russia and above all from OPEC countries, mainly Saudi Arabia but also Nigeria and Iraq. Calculations in the oil market are complicated, however, by issues such as national storage policies (usually calculated in number of days of average consumption), the differential speeds with which natural gas is being liquefied into oil equivalent products, spare drilling capacities in leading producer nations (reflecting policy decisions about how quickly oil should be extracted from existing fields at a given moment in time) and global refining capacities, determining the amount of crude that can be actually distilled into usable oil-based products. The IEA's way of representing the overall balance in the oil market is to compare demand with global supply (excluding OPEC crude capacities), before assessing the extent to which this covers potential needs. Thus, the increased 'call on OPEC crude and stock change' represented in Table 2.4 could be analysed as a reduction in the OPEC's 'effective' spare capacities (i.e. its ability to meet demand).

? Should higher oil prices be welcomed as a fillip for greater corporate sustainability?

	2010	2014
Global demand	86.33	90.86
Global supply ex OPEC crude	57.33	58.70
OPEC crude capacity	35.66	36.90
Call on OPEC crude and stock change	29.00	32.16
Effective OPEC spare capacities	5.67	3.74

Table 2.4: Medium-term scenarios for the global oil market (million barrels/day)(IEA 2009a)

The IEA did not appear overly concerned about this trend since it assumed that sluggish economic growth following the 2008 credit crunch, along with accelerated improvements in the global economy's oil intensity, would give current capacity projects enough time to catch up with demand growth. This short-term hiatus should enable oil prices to remain reasonably calm. Whether this is a good thing remains to be seen, however. By masking the signals that managers need to justify an accelerated shift away from an oil-based economy, a calming in oil prices reduces the incentive to prepare companies for the upheavals associated with the upcoming move to a post-oil economy.

Natural gas

Recent discoveries of large new natural gas fields in North America and Russia have increased global supplies of an energy source that, at its current production-to-reserve ratio, should take about 20 years longer to deplete than oil. Moreover, a new technique for tapping natural gas from shale rock, which is very rich in organic material, has raised the possibility of anywhere from a 50 to a 160 per cent increase in many regions' gas reserves over the next few decades – including Western Europe, which has become highly dependent in recent years on gas imports from Russia (Krauss 2009). The main problem is that shale processing generates enormous greenhouse gas emissions. Natural gas itself may be 'cleaner' than oil but it aggravates climate change dynamics when derived from shale (or for example, from underwater frozen methane hydrate gas deposits, as which Japan is looking to exploit).

It remains that exploratory drilling for shale has already started in energy-hungry but resource-poor countries such as Poland or Germany, where gas prices are high and rising. Indeed, all Europe has recently experienced a rush towards gas, partially because the EU's climate change commitments reduces the attractiveness of 'dirty coal' but also because it take so long to build nuclear power plants or develop a functional renewables sector. Of course, as gas starts to account for a growing proportion of the European (and US) energy mix, its depletion calculations will also shorten.

Coal

Although coal, as aforementioned, has a longer production-to-reserves ratio than other fossil fuels, its market has recently been subjected to severe price pressures due to skyrocketing demand in China, where the energy generation sector tends to be dominated by this one source.

In late 2007, for instance, China became for the first time ever a net importer of coal, despite its substantial domestic reserves (currently estimated at about 50 years of production). This had the effect of sending global prices sharply higher (Oster and Davis 2008), up from a long-term price of around $40/metric tonne (mt) to a peak of nearly $150/mt. Coal prices then fell back to around $55/mt as the effects of the credit crunch hit but, like oil, soon resumed their uptrend to trade as high as $100/mt in May 2010. Note the great volatility of coal prices over time. These rapid moves translate the adjustment of extraction quantities to inventory and sales as well as different logistics performances and policies worldwide (port infrastructure, tariffs, etc.). This makes it difficult to generalise about demand behaviour, hence depletion scenarios, for coal. Clearly, coal's relative cheapness and abundance has made it the energy of choice for many emerging industrial nations. The degre of any one country's affinity for this fuel source will depend, however, on attitudes towards the ecological imperative. Because burning coal produces so much CO_2, countries where pollution considerations outweigh economic concerns will try as far as possible to avoid coal – at least until real progress is achieved through carbon capture and storage technology (see *Web Resource 3.2*).

Nuclear

Until a few short years ago, devoted environmentalists were united in their opposition to atomic fission as an energy source, given justifiable fears about the dangers of radioactivity (the so-called 'zero or infinity' arbitrage between the low risk of an accident occurring and its devastating effects were it to happen). Nuclear power has also been widely criticised due to the cost of building safe reactors, with official statistics often neglecting nuclear plants' end-of-life decommissioning charges. Such criticisms remain well-founded yet there has been a sea change in attitudes towards the nuclear industry: because general energy depletion concerns have sparked fears of impending fuel shortages; because the climate change crisis puts a premium on fuels such as nuclear that do not emit greenhouse gases; and because safer and more energy-efficient reactors are constantly being developed. As a result, many governments that had hesitated to increase the role of nuclear in their energy mix have changed policy. This includes the United Kingdom, which in early 2010 announced a massive programme to build ten new reactors within ten years' time.

Nuclear power's role in future global energy supplies is bound to be patchy, however. On one hand, the technology is not distributed evenly across the world, with attempts by non-nuclear nations (such as Iran) to build reactors often being opposed for geopolitical reasons. Secondly, green sensitivities continue to vary enormously, as witnessed most poignantly by Germany's official policy of abandoning all nuclear power even as its neighbour, France, remains world champion for this fuel source (which accounts for something like 80 per cent of all French electricity generation). Of course, the outlook for nuclear could change dramatically if scientists ever developed waste-free 'fusion' processes using a variety of fuels such as deuterium, lithium or magnesium, whose reserves are almost infinite. The problem is that generating energy generation in this way (imitating the processes that power the sun) remains more science fiction than fact.

■ Non-energy inputs

Whereas some natural resources are used as energy sources and some as foodstuffs, others become physical inputs for manufactured goods (with a few commodities like oil serving several purposes). One way of categorising the non-energy resources feeding directly into companies' industrial cycles is to distinguish between minerals and biological substances. The former constitute a category worth studying less because of specific depletion concerns and more because most mineral commodities lend themselves to the kinds of conservation and recycling activities that would have the effect, when generalised throughout a company's physical operations (see Chapter 6), of reducing overall resource consumption. As for biological resources, this is a topic that can be discussed both in the present chapter covering resource depletion and in the following one covering pollution, given the connection between these two problems where living organisms are concerned.

■ Industrial mineral resources

With the exception of encrypted files found on the US Geological Service's www.usgs.gov/ website, information about global mineral deposits is generally less comprehensive than data on global energy reserves. This is probably because the depletion scenarios associated with many of the minerals used in modern industrial processes run into several hundreds of years instead of a few short decades. At some abstract level, it is true that minerals are also finite, non-renewable commodities that are just as vulnerable to over-consumption as energy resources are. This is less of a problem with minerals, however, since most can be recycled and reused relatively easily. The main question here is the economics of these operations, which depend on factors such as the qualities of a particular mineral (its weight or propensity to corrode after industrial processing) and its ease of transportation. With gold, for instance, almost all of the ore that has ever been mined remains in circulation. As for copper, this mineral is often smelted together with other substances but usually retains enough value to be worth recovering as scrap. Chromium, on the other hand, can lose some of its structural integrity when used in an industrial process and therefore trades at a discount when it comes in recycled form. In other words, one of the key determinants of mineral resources' availability is the arbitrage between the cost of sourcing new ore and the cost of organising **reverse logistics** and reprocessing the products that have been returned via such channels. If products have been designed in a way that facilitates the separation of biological or chemical elements from inert mineral ones when they get to the end of their useful lives (see Chapter 6), recycling can become a plentiful source of minerals (Braungart and McDonough 2009). Unfortunately this is rarely the case, given that many products are designed with **planned obsolescence** in mind, thereby adding to a company's ultimate sourcing needs. Industrial mineral resources are as much of a financial and organisational challenge as an ecological one.

■ **Reverse logistics:** Where a company organises shipment channels enabling the return of its used goods for recycling purposes.

■ **Planned obsolescence:** Where companies design products to wear out so that consumers are forced to buy replacements.

Industrial mineral resources are as much of a financial and organisational challenge as an ecological one.

Key issue

Minerals can be divided into metals and non-metallic resources. The latter category is the more abundant and includes all kinds of minerals commonly used in agricultural or chemical industries, including calcium, potassium, sulphur and nitrates, as well as clay and sand resources used for building materials. There is one metallic mineral that enjoys similar abundance – iron, the leading metal in industrial processes such as steel-making and an element that can be used by itself or else in an alloy together with metals such as manganese, cobalt and nickel.

Aside from iron, the other geo-chemically 'abundant' metals – i.e. that account for more than 0.1 per cent of the weight of the Earth's crust

– are aluminium, manganese, titanium and magnesium (with many experimental scientists hoping to use the latter to spark nuclear fusion-based power generation processes). Geo-chemically scarce metals, on the other hand, include well-known names like copper, lead, zinc, gold, silver and platinum. Some analysts are concerned that supplies from this latter group will be unable to match rising demand, especially copper or platinum, which are prime inputs in growth sectors such as construction and transportation (used, respectively, for wiring or catalytic converters and hydrogen fuel cells). Similarly, some worries have been expressed about depletion scenarios if developing countries start to consume scarce metals as intensively as older industrialised countries have done.

All in all, however, this remains a marginal concern. For instance, most observers do not attribute the price inflation that hit the mineral markets in 2007 to the spectre of depletion but to a poor adjustment between mining output and total demand. In a market that has been as internationalised as the metals market – which is often characterised by great distances between production and consumption locations (i.e. between mines and markets) – adjusting production to inventory or demand levels can be very difficult. Thus, a company's direct access to mineral resources is largely a reflection of its position in a particular supply chain. This depends in turn on two factors. Firstly, companies with sufficient financial capabilities may seek to secure their mineral inputs by engaging in upstream ('backwards') **vertical integration**, i.e. purchasing their own suppliers – in this case, mining companies – to avoid having to source inputs externally. A prime example is the recent flood of Chinese industrialists acquiring mines in Africa. Secondly, some metals can only be mined in very few locations, meaning that their producers will enjoy a quasi-monopoly. One example here is the new market for so-called 'rare earth' minerals such as dysprosium, terbium and neodymium, key substances that can be used as magnets in military applications but also in green products like generators for wind turbines or engines for hybrid cars like the Toyota Prius (Bradsher 2009). Another rare earth is lanthanum, a useful substance for electric batteries that are destined to become an increasingly important fuel source for vehicles as the world's petroleum reserves deplete. Indeed, a technological battle has broken out over which mineral should set the standard for the new generations of batteries expected to hit the markets over the next few years (see Chapter 9). Current interest in lithium-ion solutions benefits the few countries (mainly Bolivia and

Vertical integration: ■
Where a firm controls, and/or moves towards controlling, both the upstream and downstream sides of its value chain.

Chile) that have this one ore in abundance. How their governments manage national supplies will go a long way towards determining the future for such goods. It is safe to assume that lobbyists from across the world have been making their way to La Paz and Santiago de Chile, hoping to influence this process.

More than 95 per cent of proven global rare earth reserves are in China, giving the country almost complete control over what is becoming a key strategic sector. In light of certain longstanding Chinese political traditions, it is doubtful that Beijing will agree to flood the global market with these and other cheap mineral supplies. This means that non-Chinese companies will soon be scrambling to satisfy their mineral input needs, with several major mining companies unsurprisingly having already started a global hunt for new rare earth deposits. Of course, this chain of events is entirely predictable in international business theory – resource scarcity has always been a leading driver of overseas expansion.

■ Biological resources

As Chapter 1 discussed, analysing natural resources in ecological terms means viewing elements in light of the processes sustaining their life cycles. For many resources, an approach of this kind will centre on very long-term evolutions (formation of fossil fuel, mineral ores deposits, etc.) that may seem of little immediate interest to managers. On the other hand, where companies are directly dependent on resources shaped by immediate biological processes, the health of the ecosystem in question becomes an issue of prime importance.

One leading biological resource is water, which companies use in many different ways: as a fluid to cool machinery; as a vessel to carry off unwanted by-products and dilute noxious effluents; as a cleaning agent; as a foodstuff, etc. Water management can of course be analysed from a resource perspective, insofar as human economic activity is often at fault for the depletion of water sources. This can be a consequence of indirect actions (i.e. climate change shrinking glaciers or causing drought) or direct ones (i.e. overuse of finite sources). Otherwise, water is a very broad topic that can also be dealt with from a pollution perspective, or else in terms of the effects on agriculture and urban living. These two angles will be covered, respectively, in Chapters 4 and 9.

Other leading biological resources play a role in different species' food chains. A prime example is the stock of fish in the sea, which has

Habitat: ■
Where a population
normally lives.

been dwindling rapidly following long years of overfishing and the pollution of marine **habitats** (see *Chapter 2 online case study*). Efforts to improve the situation – for instance, by replacing wild species such as tuna with farmed fish – can create ancillary problems, such as the new farmed stocks' over-consumption of 'forage fish' that underpin other species' food chain (Greenberg 2010). The lesson at this level is that once an ecological balance has been disturbed, solutions must address the root cause of the problem (here, over-consumption) rather than its manifestation (shortage of forage fish). The difficulty resides in the fact that to many managers, the latter will seem easier to address than the former.

Finally, it is worth studying a major biological resource – forestry products (i.e. wood) – that has value for companies both in and of itself and also due to its effects on surrounding ecospheres. Forests are an ecosystem unto themselves, embodying **biodiversity** principles by

Biodiversity: ■
Extent to which genuses
of living organisms vary
within a given ecosystem.

providing a habitat and nutrients for other flora (and usually fauna, including pollinating bees) that in turn help trees to sustain their own regeneration cycles. Removing any one participant from this overall process raises a serious risk of undermining an equilibrium that will often have taken thousands of years to evolve – one example being the way that accelerated deforestation in Haiti, resulting from intensive demand for wood as a fuel source in this poor country, has caused massive mudslides culminating in floods and a critical loss of agricultural topsoil (Helmore 2008). It is no surprise that many leading environmentalists have looked to forestry for first order principles, nor that one of the main sustainability NGOs to cooperate with managers worldwide is the Forest Stewardship Council (www.fsc.org).

Biomass: ■
Raw materials derived from
recently harvested plants
and used for energy or
heating purposes..

Humans have used wood for millennia for a variety of purposes: as **biomass** (see *Web Resource 2.2*) to be burned for heating or power purposes; as construction material; to make products like paper, etc. Most temperate regions (in Western Europe and the USA, for instance) used to be almost entirely covered with trees. Forest destruction goes back many centuries and has been a major contributor to climate change. In and of itself, burning trees would be carbon neutral if new specimens were planted to replace older ones (with the CO_2 emitted by the former being sucked in by the latter). Due to the historical absence of sustainable forest stewardship, however, many more trees have been cut down over the years than the numbers replaced. This imbalance has accelerated in recent decades as industrialised logging companies attack dense tropical forests located in equatorial regions like the

Brazilian Amazon or Indonesia. The scale of this activity is so great that many scientists fear it will send climate change past the 'tipping point' threshold where global warming becomes irreversible – as exemplified most poignantly by the desertification of parts of the Amazon basin.

This explains the increasing number of international policy initiatives (see http://www.un-redd.org/) aimed at slowing and even reversing the trend towards forest depletion, often by creating incentives for companies to stop the destruction of the world's tropical rainforests. Governments are very aware of the ecological danger of continuing the current trajectory and have established a series of mechanisms that either compensate developing countries where logging is most prevalent or encourage the replanting of trees in the Global North. For many communities, trees are becoming big business.

For many communities, trees are becoming big business.   **Key issue**

At a more practical level, companies (and consumers) are complicit in the depletion of wood resources when they purchase products associated with unsustainable forestry practices. The current consensus is that it is ecologically healthier to only use wood from fast growing trees planted in 'nursery forests' specifically designed for regular logging and re-growth – the idea being that older forests, which are usually accompanied by dense undergrowth, are carbon-rich and should be left untouched. To promote this policy, the FSC has devised a certification system (see Chapter 5) attesting to the origin of different wood supplies. The system is imperfect and, indeed, there have been many stories of companies misusing FSC labelling and/or misrepresenting their adherence to its stewardship principles. Nevertheless, the FSC system has succeeded in drawing managers' attention to the risks associated with the depletion of this particular resource.

What remains to be seen is whether an initiative of this kind can suffice to save ecosystems that continue to be coveted for their industrial value in a world characterised by a growing population of citizens hungry for material well-being. It seems doubtful that the FSC alone will save tropical forests in the absence of massive government intervention. The economic forces stacked against the resource conservation agenda seem overwhelming, especially in countries already suffering from severe poverty – yet which are responsible for few of the economic actions that have put humankind in this tenuous position .

■ **Obstacles and pathways**

1 Resource depletion will raise the price of raw materials.

Companies need to analyse their productive apparatus to determine where changes can be made to achieve greater resource productivity.

2 Utility rates will rise disproportionately to compensate for the cost of energy lost during the electrical distribution process.

Managers should study potential 'off-grid' solutions (i.e. micro-generation).

3 Security concerns will hamper international trade in energy products.

Multinational enterprises can engage in backwards vertical integration.

4 Demand for mineral resources sparks price hikes.

This justifies the further implementation of reverse logistics arrangements.

Case study: Peak oil

Energy rich and relatively cheap to drill or transport, crude oil ('petroleum') is the blood flowing through the veins of international business. Oil fuel derivatives are the benchmark for all primary energy supplies – to the extent that other resources' energy content is usually analysed in 'million tonnes of oil equivalent (MTOE)'. Oil is also a generic component for a vast array of products, including hard and soft plastics (petro-chemical mixes) pharmaceuticals, fertilisers and foodstuffs. The fact that it might run out one day is clearly a prime environmental constraint for business. Calculating when the 'post-oil economy' will arrive is crucial to all companies' scenario planning.

One tool in this area is the 'peak oil' concept in use since the 1950s, when American geologist King Hubbert devised a method for predicting when half of all reserves of oil (and by extension, half of all non-renewable resources) will deplete. Hubbert's concept started with the observation that even as US domestic oil production was expanding in the mid-20th century, the rate of growth was falling (Strahan 2007). He deduced that this could only be attributed to natural conditions, meaning that the production curve would reverse its uptrend one day and then plummet until oil was completely exhausted. Based on his assessment of US 'ultimate reserves' at the time (i.e. total amount of oil that the industry can ever extract), Hubbert predicted that domestic supplies would run out within about 15 years. He proved to be correct. Half a century later, similar calculations were applied to predict the depletion of Britain's North Sea oil (and gas) reserves. They too appear to be correct.

Hubbert's concept revolves around the observation that the porous rocks comprising an underground oil field are subject to pressures facilitating the upwards flow of crude. This means that extraction is easy when companies first drill but also that the useful pressure will abate once the most accessible crude has been extracted. This generally occurs after some 35 to 40 per cent of the total reservoir is gone. Companies' subsequent decision – namely how much to invest in extracting the remaining reserves – is an economic question that depends on extraction technology (which improves over time) and above all on market prices. In resource supply terms, however, geologists can use 'peak oil' to get a good idea of the total quantity of oil contained in any one field. Moreover, given the immense exploration efforts in this sector over the years (and generally good knowledge about the kinds of geological structures where oil is likely to be found), few if any major fields remain unknown. In other words, with a relatively small margin of error, reliable knowledge exists on how much – or more importantly, how little – oil is left in the world. The same applies to natural gas, another widely used fossil fuel often found in and around oil fields. It then suffices to extrapolate current demand curves for the two resources to calculate time to depletion.

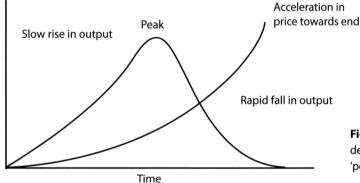

Figure 2.2: Graphic depiction of Hubbert's 'peak oil' construct

For both oil and gas, almost all experts agree that reserves amount to much less than 100 years of consumption. Indeed, there is every chance that this timeframe will shorten due to skyrocketing demand from newly industrialised countries like China and India. As oil giant Chevron said in a 2008 advertisement, whereas it took 125 years for humankind to use the first trillion barrels of oil, the next trillion are likely to be used within 30 years. In fact, many scientists now predict that within 50 years, planet Earth will no longer contain a single drop of oil. In 50 years, some of the students reading this book will still be working.

Clearly, predictions in this area are subject to events. New seabed oil fields near Mexico and Brazil have recently been made accessible using ultra deepwater drilling rigs (Mouawad 2009) that, despite BP's 2010 Gulf of Mexico disaster, are likely to remain in operation. Attention is also being paid to the possibility of replicating this technique in the harsh environments of the North and South Pole. Such approaches may be very expensive but they are economically justifiable if oil prices rise enough. It remains that big discoveries of this kind are few and far between and do not alter the general scenario. The same can be said of the huge stock of 'tar sands' found at the base of the Rocky Mountains in the Canadian province of Alberta. The quantities involved may be significant but separating the oil from other elements would require more energy than the amount derived from mining the fields. This undermines the tar sands' usefulness, as does the fact that their combustion exudes enormous quantities of CO_2. Indeed, this may be one silver lining of oil depletion – many of the dangerous greenhouse gases that past and present human activity has released into the atmosphere come from this one hydrocarbon.

The likely scenario of supply shortages and price hikes is bound to spark a variety of corporate substitution policies revolving around efficiency measures (see Chapter 6) and alternative fuel sources (see Chapter 10). The main strategic question for companies, however, is whether they be able to wean themselves of oil before it runs out. Indeed, there are some indications that oil field production is already starting to drop off at an accelerated rate, with – the International Energy Agency calculating that just to replace the current decline in output, 45 million barrels of daily capacity – equivalent to about four times Saudi Arabia's current capacity – must be found by the year 2030 (Chazan 2008). This is highly unlikely to occur. For tomorrow's managers, resource depletion (one of the two pillars of the ecological imperative) is truly a race against time.

Case study questions

1   Why is oil such a crucial energy source?

2   What is the outlook for future oil production?

3   What are the implications for (international) business strategy?

■ References

Barbiroli, G. (2009), 'The limitedness of natural and environmental resources as an opportunity for sustainable yet competitive solutions', *International Journal of Business Environment*, **2** (3).

Bozon, I., Campbell, W. and Lindstrand, M. (2007), 'Global trends in energy', February, available at www.mckinseyquarterly.com, accessed on 8 August 2009.

BP (2009), *Statistical Review of World Energy*, available at www.bp.com, accessed 15 January 2010.

Bradsher, K. (2009), 'China tightens grip on rare minerals'. *The Observer*, 13 September, *New York Times* insert, p. 5.

Braungart, M. and McDonough, W. (2009), *Cradle to Cradle: Re-Making The Way We Make Things*, London: Vintage Books.

Chazan, G. (2008), 'Oil-field production drops are accelerating', *Wall Street Journal-Europe*, 13 November, p. 10.

Farrell, D., Nyquist, S. and Rogers, M. (2007), 'Making the most of the world's energy resources', February, available at www.mckinseyquarterly.com, accessed on 8 August 2009.

Freney, M. (2009), 'Earthships: sustainable housing alternative', *International Journal of Sustainable Design*, **1** (2).

Greenberg, P. (2010) *Four Fish: The Future of the Last Wild Food*, Penguin Press.

Hartmann, T. (2004), *The Last Hours of Ancient Sunlight*, Three Rivers Press.

Hayward, T. (2009), 'The harsh realities of energy', available at www.bp.com, accessed 15 January 2010.

Helmore, E. (2008), 'How Haiti hopes to break the cycle of disaster: restoring its lost forests', *The Observer*, 23 November, p. 44.

Holy, N. (2009), *Deserted Ocean: A Social History of Depletion*, Milton Keynes: Authorhouse.

Hutton, W. (2008), 'Don't make the consumer pay for these inflated fuel prices', *The Observer*, 3 August, p. 35.

IEA (International Energy Agency) (2009a), *Oil Market Report*, available at http://omrpublic.iea.org/currentissues/full.pdf, accessed 16 January 2010.

IEA (International Energy Agency) (2009b), *World Energy Outlook Fact Sheet*, available at www.iea.org, accessed 19 January 2010.

Jiao, J, Fan, Y. and Wei, Y. (August 2009), 'The structural break and elasticity of coal demand in China: empirical findings from 1980–2006', *International Journal of Global Energy Issues*, **31** (3–4).

King, J., and Slesser, M. (2009), 'Can the world make the transition to a sustainable economy driven by solar energy', *International Journal of Environment and Pollution*, **5** (1).

Krauss, C. (2009), 'In shale, new way to tap gas', *The Observer*, 24 May, *New York Times* insert

MGI (McKinsey Global Institute) (2009), 'Exploring global energy demand', available at www.mckinseyquarterly.com, June, accessed 15 January 2009.

Monbiot, G. (2007), *Heat: How We Can Stop the Planet Burning*, London: Penguin.

Mouawad, J. (2009), 'Oil industry sets a brisk pace of new discoveries', 23 September, available at www.nytimes.com, accessed 14 January 2010.

Oster, S. and Davis, A. (2008), 'China's demand for coal reverberates around the globe', 12 February, *Wall Street Journal-Europe*, p. 1.

Steininger, Karl (2009), 'Environmental illusion in the depletion of common property resources', *International Journal of Environment and Pollution*, **4** (3–4).

Strahan, D. (2007), *The Last Oil Shock: A Survival Guide to the Imminent Extinction of Petroleum Man*, London: John Murray.

Thomas, V. and Chomitz, K. (2009), 'From crisis to opportunity', *The Guardian*, 16 February.

US EIA (Energy Information Administration) (2009), *Total World Delivered Energy Consumption by End-Use Sector and Fuel*, available at www.eia.doe.gov/, accessed 20 January 2010.

3 Pollution

Learning objectives

After reading this chapter, you will be able to:

- Identify a range of pollution sources generated by business activities
- Detect the effects of pollution on companies' physical environment
- Set pollution within a sectoral context.

◼ Introduction

It is difficult to say who has greater responsibility for the damage being done to the ecosystems that sustain life on Earth: the companies manufacturing the goods that consumers use; or the households purchasing such items. At a certain level, however, this is a moot question – to the extent that companies pollute and suffer from pollution, they clearly bear at least some responsibility for the deterioration of the natural environment.

Chapter 1 detailed the basic principles of Newtonian thermodynamics, to wit, the idea that matter is never destroyed, and that all action provokes a reaction. The former concept is the basis of the **throughput** logic that states how all inputs found at the beginning of a physical process are also present at its end, albeit in a changed form. Thus, if a company begins a transformation activity with inputs that are damaging the environment, these will still be present afterwards and require safe disposal. The latter concept is key to **toxicity** studies, based on the self-evident scientific principle that foreign substances cannot be repeatedly injected into a biosphere without ultimately provoking disturbance. The implication here is that companies' treatment of their natural environment as a waste bin is at best an example of **ecological myopia** and at worst a case of criminal neglect. As such, the subject of pollution raises questions pertaining not only to ecological sciences but also to managerial value systems (see Chapter 5). Since the dawn of time, societies have looked the other way while polluters have polluted. After millennia of environmental deterioration, such apathy is no longer feasible.

Throughput: ◼
Holistic overview of elements in all of their different stages as they transit through a transformation process.

Toxicity: ◼
Extent to which a substance causes harm to different living organisms.

Ecological myopia: ◼
Unwillingness or inability to envision the long-term environmental consequences of one's own behaviour.

? How difficult is it to attribute responsibility for line pollution?

◼ Pollution sources

Analyses of corporate pollution often start by comparing point, line and surface sources of pollution (Sen 2009). The former category refers to emissions, effluents and other outflows with a single identifiable origin that can be either movable or stationary. This differs from non-point source pollution, such as when water tables are polluted by the runoff of nitrogen-based fertilisers used throughout the whole of a farming district – or in the case of an urban runoff, when contaminated discharges from a variety of industrial or household sources find their way into the sewers. As for line pollution, this refers to all waste coming from a particular sector, one example of which is smog from automobile traffic. Whereas emissions from one vehicle might be classified as point source pollution, the overall problem is so enormous that solutions need to be sought at a broader macro level encompassing all road vehicles. Analysts will therefore focus on traffic in general as a line source of pollution, with some referring to an 'area source' when multiple pollutants are involved, or to a 'volume source' when emissions' geometric aspects also enter the equation. Further distinctions can be made between pollutants' area of impact (upper atmosphere, at the Earth's surface, deep underground or some combination thereof) and whether they occur constantly or intermittently. Lastly, 'surface source' pollution is a commonly used term in water pollution studies and refers to water running off urban or rural surfaces and carrying contaminants such as organic or inorganic chemical substances, as well as hazardous bacterial or viral **pathogens**.

■ **Pathogen:** Biological agent causing disease in living organisms.

The reason why it is so important to identify pollution categories is because each requires a different set of responses. Depending on whether a particular kind of pollution has a single origin or not (and whether it affects one or many actors), there will be a marked variation in the level of political outrage that is caused and in companies' legal liability. A mainstream activity with a small negative impact on one small actor will receive a very different response than a single source pollution event that devastates an entire community – one disastrous example being an incident from 1986 at Bhopal in India when a Union Carbide chemical plant exploded, causing the death of thousands. Pollution is a very general word encompassing a variety of situations.

■ Toxicity studies

Scientists have several ways of apprehending the pollution caused by companies and its effects. Usually, the main focus will involve examining the damage caused when pollutants interact with their surroundings, i.e. the level of toxicity. In turn, this will depend on a host of factors, first and foremost being the possibility of 'dilution', or the principle that the lower the concentration of a pollutant in proportion to the agents (water, solvents) capable of dissipating its effects, the greater the chance of containing any negative side effects. Thus, an element that is non-toxic in small doses will often become toxic in larger quantities. Of course, the notion of concentration must be understand not only in volume and quantity terms but even more importantly in terms of the pollutant's capacity for causing harm, and to what extent it might be broken down into something less noxious. Clearly, radioactive waste from a hospital or nuclear power station causes greater harm and dilutes less effectively (or indeed, not at all) than de-greased sludge taken from factory machines. Note that this latter instance raises a second issue, namely whether the product used to eliminate an unwanted substance should also be classified as a pollutant, as is often the case when companies use chemical additives for their cleaning properties. Problems of this nature have sparked enormous interest in the field of **green chemistry**.

Green chemistry: ■
Where companies develop and apply natural compounds producing certain performance attributes while avoiding the bio-hazards associated with traditional industrial compounds.

Other kinds of analysis will focus on how pollutants disperse from their point(s) of origin. Liquids, solids and gases spread throughout the environment at varying speeds. In turn, this affects surrounding ecosystems' ability to withstand their presence. In general, the safest waste disposal involves solids, since it is relatively easier to contain their seepage into their surroundings. Indeed, some companies' pollution strategies start with the transformation of liquids or gases into solids – a prime example being when industrialists insert scrubbers inside their factory chimneys to capture particles that would otherwise be spewed out as gas. Of course, such 'end-of-pipeline' systems are expensive, raising questions as to the company's willingness (or obligation) to assume the costs of pollution control.

At a physical level, there is an additional problem with the way that solids will – over time and depending on their storage condition – often mutate into gases or liquids that, respectively, are emitted or leech into the surrounding environment. One example is the way in which some of the refuse normally stored in purpose-built landfills degrades into methane, a potent greenhouse gas. Companies' waste disposal schemes are always enhanced when their creators possess a modicum of scientific knowledge.

Key issue

Companies' waste disposal schemes will always be enhanced when their creators possess a modicum of scientific knowledge.

A further series of questions relates to the control of airborne pollutants stemming from a whole range of sources: industrial smokestacks; motor vehicles; mass deforestation; and even the incineration processes undertaken by companies trying to dispose of waste accumulated in other forms. On one hand, what this means is that the science of climate change (see later in this chapter) is quickly becoming a key focus for the corporate sector – and, indeed, for society as a whole, with national governments devoting increasing resources nowadays to identifying the linkages between human activity and climate change. Despite the inexactness of this construct, according to Newtonian principles it is unassailably logical that emitting unnatural quantities of carbon dioxide into the atmosphere will have a major effect on planetary meteorology (see Figure 3.1). Yet there is a widespread tendency to neglect the fact that the sky is also a finite ecosystem – despite the countless individuals over the centuries who have suffered serious health problems from breathing in industrial particulates. A whole corpus of studies analyses the speed and direction with which gas particles disperse (Pospisil and Jicha 2010) depending on variables such as temperature or wind speed. Micro-environments everywhere are prone to variable pollution patterns, meaning that the same gas emission can have different effects in different locations. This has direct implications for the kind of immediate pressures that companies responsible for such emissions are likely to face.

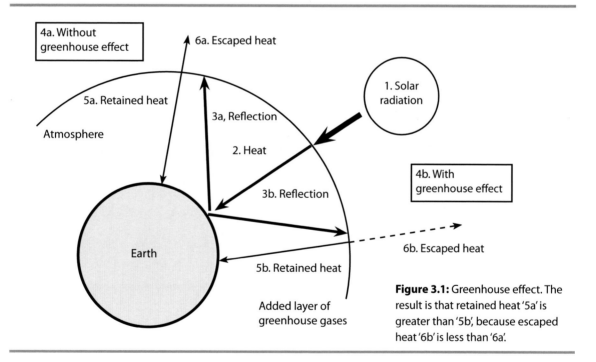

Figure 3.1: Greenhouse effect. The result is that retained heat '5a' is greater than '5b', because escaped heat '6b' is less than '6a'.

The same can be said about pollutants in liquid form, although such releases, insofar as they are more localised, can be easier to quantify – thus to identify and sanction – than gas. A large corpus of research exists on the effects of liquid effluents, often materialising in the concentration of contaminants such as heavy metals found in human

Biota: ■
Living organisms in a
particular biosphere at a
given period of time.

bodies or other **biota** found in the more or less immediate vicinity of the pollution (Garcia-Sanchez *et al.* 2008). The main questions at this level are the effluent's mobility – partially a function of its thickness ('viscosity') – and whether the substances leeching from the source activity in the form of runoffs or sediments are accumulating in the tissues of surrounding life forms at levels exceeding recommended safety thresholds. Such determinations highlight the key role that scientists play in debates about acceptable levels of pollution. In October 2009, for instance, a hazardous waste disposal company called Red Industries was responsible for a cyanide leak that interrupted bacterial sewage treatment processes and caused untreated substances to spill into England's Trent River, killing thousands of fish along a 20-mile stretch (Meikle 2009). The UK Environment Agency announced after subsequent analyses that the effects of this food chain disaster were short-term and 'not a concern for health' but only once the river had been re-oxygenated with hydrogen peroxide. This decision was based on scientists' assessment of the local environment's capacity to overcome what had been a serious assault on its regenerative processes – the type of judgement that will often meet with scepticism when it condones further use of an already fragilised ecosystem as a receptacle for industrial waste. At a broader level, what is at stake is the total pollution exposure that humans or the planet can endure safely.

? What level of pollution is safe and/or acceptable?

■ Pollutant inventories

If all companies worldwide were to design their industrial systems from the very start in such a way as to produce zero pollution (see Chapter 6), by definition there would be no need to inventory toxic releases (see *Web Resource 3.1*). Indeed, a small number of companies have announced their intention to work towards this goal. A leading example is the clothing manufacturer Timberland, which in 2005 gave itself the aim of becoming carbon neutral. Another is Dupont Chemicals, whose toxic releases, landfill waste and cancer-causing chemical emissions have fallen by up to 75 per cent since it first began to take concerted sustainability actions in the late 1980s. However, producing less pollution is not the same as producing none at all. Only a handful of companies actually seek zero footprint. The vast majority pollute and will continue to do so for the foreseeable future.

There are different ways of analysing pollutants as a business phenomenon. One is by the duration of substances' toxicity. Some forms of radioactive waste, for instance, have a half-life of 10,000 years, an unfathomable span that raises questions about the cost of safe **sequestering** (i.e. the debate over the Yucca Mountain repository in the US state of Nevada). Carbon dioxide emitted into the atmosphere, on the other hand, takes 100 to 200 years to dissipate, while another greenhouse gas, methane, only lasts about 20 years (but has a stronger effect during that time than CO_2). Then there is the question of the impetus driving an inventory of corporate pollutants, since this could theoretically affect the types of substances that will be identified. There are long lists of pollutants discovered in studies commissioned by regulatory agencies; by companies seeking to prove their compliance with national regulatory requirements (i.e. in the USA, the 2010 Toxic Chemicals Safety Act); or by scientists trying to advance the boundaries of knowledge. Such investigations do not provide a reliable picture of corporate pollution, however, since the information that each conveys is necessarily incomplete and even biased towards whatever ecological concern preoccupies the interests commissioning the survey. Indeed, the only way to ensure a complete inventory of corporate pollutants – thus to achieve an accurate assessment of the stresses that business puts on the biosphere – would be for all companies worldwide to engage in a full and honest accounting of their total physical inputs and outputs. This kind of reporting is starting to take root (Chapter 5) but remains very patchy, with different countries, sectors and/or companies displaying varying degrees of willingness to assume the costs associated with full-blown environmental accounting.

■ **Sequestering:** Containing an unwanted substance so that it does not permeate into and damage the surrounding environment.

? How reliable is current knowledge about corporate pollution?

Until such practices become universal, however, observers must necessarily rely on whatever information is made available.

... the only way to ensure a complete inventory of corporate pollutants...would be for all companies worldwide to engage in a full and honest accounting of their total physical inputs and outputs.

Key issue

Many of the largest pollution studies seem to focus on atmospheric issues nowadays. This is no surprise given the increasing prioritisation of climate change nowadays (see Table 3.1). To varying degrees, the same substances can be expected to appear on most pollutant lists, depending on whether they materialise in gaseous form following an incineration process, in sediment form after transportation in a liquid effluent or in an unadulterated form as a solid.

Table 3.1: List of main atmospheric pollutants (www.citepa.org)

Type	Sources include:
Solid particles	
Asbestos fibres, dust	Mineral extraction, cement works, steel works, glassworks, quarries
Gases	
SO_2 Sulphur dioxide	Power stations, refineries, combustion plants
NO_x Nitrogen oxides	International combustion engines, forest fires
CO Carbon monoxide	Motor vehicle exhaust fumes
CO_2 Carbon dioxide	Fossil fuels
VOC Volatile organic compounds	Chemical solvents, paints, printing, glues
CH_4 Methane	Coal mine, landfill sites, livestock
CFC Chlorofluorocarbons	Aerosol propellants, foams, fire extinguishers, refrigerators
HF Hydrofluoric acid	Aluminium fusion, glass fibre makers, brickworks
Heavy metals	
As Arsenic	Glass-making, metal working
Cd Cadmium	Burning solid mineral fuels, heavy fuel oil
Cr Chromium	Production of glass, cement, ferrous metals
Hg Mercury	Chlorine production, waste incineration
Pb Lead	Fusion of lead, manufacture of batteries
Se Selenium	Glass production, use of heavy fuel oil
Zi Zinc	Combustion coal/fuel oil, industrial metals processes, waste incineration
Other pollutants	
NH_3 Ammonia	Agriculture activities
PCDD-F Dioxins	Incineration, fuel combusion

Synthetic: ■—————
Human-made. The opposite of natural.

Many of the substances featured on this list are natural elements that become pollutants once their unnatural concentration in a local environment creates a toxic effect. Selenium, for instance, is used in low doses by humans as a vitamin supplement yet causes poisoning in birds and fish when it bioaccumulates in their food chain. Other substances are classified as synthetic compounds. This latter category is impossible to inventory in its entirety, if only because of industry's ongoing invention of new variants. Moreover, the pollutant effect of a **synthetic** compound can vary widely depending on how well it is contained. For instance, some plastics are innocuous to touch but become lethal to marine life as they dissolve over time. Otherwise, common flame retardants such as polybrominated diphenyl ether (PBDE) can be stored safely in fire extinguishers but have the toxic effect of decreasing female fertility when found in furniture cushions, carpet padding and other household items (e360 digest 2010). In short, the pollution characteristics of some substances will be determined as much by their business use as by their innate physical properties.

... the pollutant effect of a [substance] can vary widely depending on how well it is contained.

Key issue

■ Environmental impacts

After this overview of the sources of pollution, it is worth understanding their effects. Knowledge is important to companies for several reasons. At an ethical level, it would be a complete denial of corporate responsibility for managers to prioritise financial returns with no regard for the ecological (or social) consequences of their actions. Indeed, to preclude such ecological myopia, consulting firms such as Trucost (www.trucost.com/) have quantified corporate footprints in monetary terms (see Table 3.2). This is a serious initiative that might also herald the formal integration of pollution into managers' financial calculations – especially given Trucost's astounding discovery in 2010 that the **externalities** produced by the world's leading 3000 companies (calculated on a market capitalisation basis) amount to nearly 7 per cent of the firms' combined revenues. This is a legal and financial anomaly that may well be redressed – in a way that is potentially very detrimental to business – if the economic theories driving most modern policy prescriptions start to incorporate environmental considerations that have been neglected so far (see Chapter 4).

■ **Externality:** Impact of a transaction on a third party.

? Are there any circumstances in which managers can afford to ignore pollution?

Sector	Cost of environmental damage, in billion US$
Utilities	420
Basic materials	312
Consumer goods	281
Industrials	201
Oil and gas	175
Consumer services	74

Table 3.2: Cost of damage to the environment by business sector (see Trucost chart in *The Guardian*, 20 February 2010).

Table 3.3: Annual environmental costs for the global economy (see Trucost 2010)

Source	External costs in 2008 (billion US$)	in % GDP 2008	External costs in 2008 (billion US$)	in % GDP 2050
Greenhouse gases	4,530	7.54	20,809	12.93
Water abstraction	1,226	2.04	4,702	2.92
Pollution (SOx, NOx, PM, VOCs, mercury)	546	0.91	1,926	1.20
General waste	197	0.33	635	0.39
Natural resources (fish, timber)	96	0.16	543	0.34
Other ecosystem services, waste...	NA	NA	NA	NA
Total	6,596	10.97	28,615	17.78

At a more personal level, sustainability is not only of paramount importance to local residents directly exposed to the pollutants that a company produces but also to its own staff members. After all, it would be highly irrational for anyone to prefer money over personal health. Otherwise, in more practical terms, corporate footprints are increasingly important in determining brand reputation, employee motivation and innovativeness – not to forget legal liability (e.g. the £20 billion bill awaiting BP as a result of the 2010 Gulf of Mexico Deepwater Horizon oil disaster). All in all, it is clear that managers who ignore pollution impacts are likely to experience lesser career development as the ecological imperative, in all of its dimensions, gradually enters the international business psyche.

■ Air quality and climate change

Air quality was the focal point for environmental critics of the industrial age. As far back as Victorian times, observers would lament the damage done to forests surrounding the mill towns spread across England's Midlands. This inauspicious beginning was followed a century later by several episodes of killer smog. One was in 1948 in Donora Valley in the US state of Pennsylvania, where a thick fog trapped carbon monoxide and sulphuric acid emissions from local steel mills to create a lethal concoction. Four years later, something similar happened in London when a mixture of fog and coal smoke brought visibility to almost zero and killed thousands. Since then, it has been illegal to light a coal fire within the confines of Greater London. Entrepreneurs have reacted by creating companies selling smokeless fires.

By the 1970s, things were so bad that high school athletes in the suburbs of Los Angeles, an automobile-mad city prone to smog resulting from thermal inversion effects, were occasionally obliged to abandon daytime sporting activities. Within a few short years, however, local and national governments were reacting to this situation by enacting vehicle emission standards, culminating in headline events such as the stringent fuel consumption regulations that Japan adopted in 1999, or the European Union's ban on all leaded gasoline from 1 January 2000. Automakers were induced and/or forced by tighter controls to lower emissions, leading to platinum-based catalytic converters being widely fitted to cars from the 1970s onwards, and ultimately to today's wave of fuel-efficient vehicles and electric cars. Similar air quality efforts have been witnessed in sectors other than transportation, one example being steel-making, where increasingly stringent Environmental Protection Agency requirements meant that by the 1990s, US companies were spending the equivalent of 20 to 30 per cent of their new plants' capital costs on compliance technology (ISTC 2009). By the dawn of the new millennium, the developed world had achieved a great deal of progress in the battle against localised air pollution.

The same cannot be said about many cities in emerging economies such as Mexico or China, where development often seems more pressing priority than the ecological imperative (see Chapter 8). The hope here has mainly been that in the absence of stringent air quality standards, improvements will come from the diffusion of **best practice** anti-pollution technology. Still, given the emerging economies' growing share of global manufacturing and passenger vehicle use, it is questionable whether market-based solutions are effective enough. The sight of thousands of Beijing pedestrians wearing smog masks bodes poorly for the future. The same applies to the thousand-mile-long clouds of smoke that accumulate over South East Asia due to the massive forest fires that are set intentionally in these regions and because countless local households cook using inflammable materials such as biomass. Of course, as happened in the OECD countries during the 1970s, some entrepreneurs will view the developing world's pollution problems as business opportunities, one example being the invention of 'biolite' stoves that can reduce black carbon emissions by 90 per cent (Siegle 2010). It is very troubling, however, that the ecosphere must deteriorate to this extent before the causes of its demise are addressed. The question must be asked whether business solutions to ecological catastrophes are a case of too little too late.

Best practice: Optimal performance becoming a benchmark for actors pursuing a similar line of activity.

? Is air quality worse in LDC megalopolises than in the wealthy world, and why?

Key issue

... as happened in the OECD countries in the 1970s, some entrepreneurs will view the developing world's pollution problems as business opportunities.

Heat

A related but much bigger and more frightening challenge has arisen in recent years, namely climate change, an issue that is universal by its very nature. A clear overlap exists between traditional air pollution and this new problem. Whereas some of the particulates spewed into the air since the beginning of the industrial age may have reached the lower strata of the atmosphere before falling back to the Earth's surface in the form of acid rain, other industrial emissions have released carbon dioxide and other gases into the upper atmosphere, creating what has come to be known as a **greenhouse effect**. The ensuing risk of potentially uncontrollable global warming is so daunting that no society (or company) in the world can afford to ignore it.

Greenhouse effect: ■
Condition where heat (often in light form) entering a partially hermetic environment is prevented from dissipating.

Calculations of CO_2 are a good starting point for apprehending this phenomenon. Before the Industrial Revolution, CO_2 levels varied from 180 parts per million (ppm) at times when Earth was cold to 280 ppm during hot periods. After 250 years of industrialisation, it is estimated that CO_2 levels are at 380 ppm and rising. The accounting is as follows: human activity currently adds 3.5 ppm annually; natural carbon sinks (oceans and trees) absorb 1.4 ppm at most; so a minimum extra 2.1 ppm of CO_2 are being added to the air every year (Monbiot 2007).

The problem is that to have any real chance of limiting global warming to an average two-degree rise by the year 2010, scientific consensus is that total emissions must be capped at 450 ppm. Unfortunately, forecasts in a seminal 2006 study called the Stern Report (Table 3.4) predict much higher levels.

Table 3.4: Stern Report CO_2 levels scenarios (2006)

	2020	2030	2040	2050
At current rate of annual emission, number of gigatonnes (GGT) of CO2 equivalent gas is	55	61	72	85
To keep concentrations down to 550 ppm, annual GGT of CO2 equivalent emissions must be	47	40	38	32
To keep concentrations down to 450 ppm, annual GGT of CO2 equivalent emissions must be	31	18	15	14

Moreover, even the current observed rise in average global temperatures – calculated as ca. 0.7 degrees over the past century – is known to cause problems of enormous severity. Firstly, the yields of many crop genuses (like rice, soybeans and maize) suffer when temperatures exceed certain levels. Then there is the rise in sea levels resulting from the accelerated melting of polar icecaps. Indeed, a few island states already face a clear and present danger of being entirely submerged, with the same fate subsequently feared for sediment-rich agricultural lands located along coastal deltas in countries such as Bangladesh. Similarly, fresh drinking water sources in many poorer coastal metropolises – Shanghai, Manila, Jakarta, Bangkok, Kolkata, Mumbai, Karachi, Lagos, Buenos Aires and Lima – run a risk of contamination due to saltwater flooding (Monbiot 2007). All of these trends have consequences for business. The erection of protective barriers is rapidly turning into a growth activity for construction companies capable of handling such enormous projects, in the aforementioned locations but also in more affluent cities such as New York, London, Tokyo and Amsterdam The insurance and offshore drilling industries, on the other hand, will be devastated by the predicted rise in hurricanes' intensity and frequency – one example being Katrina, which famously battered New Orleans in 2005. In all probability, even at current levels, climate change is destined to make meteorological events more erratic – an example of how environmental uncertainty weighs upon business by destabilising managers' investment horizons.

> **?** Which sectors will suffer from climate change? Which if any will benefit?

... environmental uncertainty weighs upon business by destabilising managers' investment horizons.

Key issue

Moreover, there is a strong possibility that things will get markedly worse. As evoked above, planet Earth already has two natural sinks that take CO_2 out of the air. One is comprised of all the trees and plants that use carbon dioxide to make carbohydrates, the basic nutrients used by vegetation. Unfortunately, whereas CO_2 makes plants grow, the amounts that they can consume are also limited by other constraints, such as a lack of water or sunlight. The plant sink effect is therefore expected to abate, all the more so because uncontrolled deforestation (see Chapter 2) has reduced the total number of trees on Earth. There is great concern about a feedback mechanism where ever-rising temperatures make it harder for vegetation to grow, reducing the overall carbon sink, leaving more CO_2 in the air and sparking further temperature rises. In addition, as temperatures rise this vicious circle will be compounded by the growing acidification of the oceans, the world's second main carbon sink. In acidic water, marine organisms that consume CO_2 (and deposit it on the ocean floor when they die) will find it harder to make shells and will absorb less CO_2, leading in turn to higher temperatures. If these feedback mechanisms are not countered by some as yet unspecified natural offset, the deep fear is that the temperature rise could exceed a tipping point where it becomes self-fulfilling and uncontrollable. Human health is bound to deteriorate in this hotter world, not only because of the stresses placed on food sources but also due to direct health risks, since heat is also predicted to increase the transmission of disease from animals and insects to humans (Shah 2009). Note also that dust clouds such as the one that overwhelmed drought-stricken Australia's urban centres in September 2009 carry viruses that penetrate deeply into the human body (Vidal 2009). Given outcomes such as these, the topicality of companies' air emissions profile is self-evident.

■ Terrestrial and aquatic damage

Land and water pollution are separate concerns that should be studied as such. Still, it is also worth mentioning the links between the two. On one hand, water is the main agent transporting pollutants whose sediments often leave toxic deposits in the surrounding soil systems even after the liquid has evaporated. On the other, pollutants stored non-hermetically on land can seep underground and infiltrate aquifers or other water systems. Indeed, the atmospheric pollutants discussed in the previous section also interact continuously with the Earth's terrestrial and aquatic systems. The basic ecological principle of interdependency applies not only at the micro level of chemical reactions but also at the more macro level of the biosphere.

On-land waste storage

Pollutants infiltrate terrestrial environments in different ways. Section III below analyses this phenomenon from a sectoral perspective, focusing on the soil damage caused by the misuse of agricultural pesticides and fertilisers, the negative externalities associated with many mining practices and the pollution from countless manufacturing, transportation and power generation activities. On the other hand, the focus here is on waste storage, an area of activity for which few global statistics exist. The United Nations Statistics Division is currently trying to address this problem to ensure the adequacy of national and international waste management efforts. As Chapter 5 will discuss, one of the first steps towards achieving sustainability is to increase understanding of the ecological imperative, in part to compensate for the myopia that has dominated for so long.

The first observation in this area is that the largest and most hazardous pollution flows are rarely perceived by the public (see Table 3.5). Industry produces by far the greatest tonnage of waste, with recent studies indicating that consumer goods account for only 6 per cent of total physical output in the US, versus the 94 per cent comprised of upstream 'non-products' such as perfluorocarbons, dioxins or PCBs (Friend 2009). Indeed, one of the main green industrialisation drives involves raising the ratio of products to non-products in a given value chain, redressing a senseless situation where 'for every pound of trash that ends up in municipal landfills, at least 65 more pounds are created upstream by industrial processes' (Makower 2009). At the same time, it is politically difficult, in a free market economy, for the authorities to impose on companies a particular breakdown between intermediary goods and end products, with managers tending to make decisions in this domain based solely on business arguments such as costs or technology. At the same time, there are many occasions where municipal dumps or landfills overflowing with environmentally unfriendly products such as synthetic nappies (diapers) or bin liners have focussed public dissatisfaction with companies. The bad publicity associated with this outcry (see Chapter 7) will often be the spark causing the company in question to react.

? Why is there so little knowledge about the accumulation of pollutants?

Type of waste	%
Industrial solid waste from manufacturing processes	57
RCRA waste including medical waste, septic tank pumpings, industrial process waste, slaughterhouse waste, pesticide containers, incinerator ash	39
Industrial hazardous waste – toxic ingredients found in paints, pesticides, printing ink and other chemicals	2
Municipal solid waste	1

Table 3.5: Estimated breakdown of US 'gross national trash' (Makower 2009)

Note: RCRA waste is that covered by the US Resource Conservation and Recovery Act, 1976.

The area where the public and private spheres collaborate most closely is municipal solid waste (MSW), amounting to an estimated 2.02 billion tonnes globally in 2006 and predicted to rise by 37 per cent by 2011 (KNP 2008). MSW can be studied from different perspectives, one being the trade in waste products, a growing international business activity that only seems to capture the headlines when dangerous materials such as bio-hazards or nuclear waste are involved (see *Web Resource 6.2* discussion on international recyclate markets). A second perspective relates to the possibility of companies' separating different waste streams (see Table 3.6) to facilitate future recycling. Municipal authorities worldwide are starting to view waste management as a profit rather than a cost centre. At some point, companies may start to do the same.

Table 3.6: 2008 breakdown of US municipal solid waste (www.epa.gov)

	%
Paper	31.0
Yard trimmings	13.2
Food scraps	12.7
Plastics	12.0
Metals	8.4
Rubber, leather, textiles	7.9
Wood	6.6
Glass	4.9
Other	3.3

One hurdle to the mass recycling of municipal waste derives from the old business strategy of planned obsolescence, one of whose effects has been the replacement of higher quality natural inputs by cheaper industrial components that generate more hazardous forms of waste when the product in question comes to the end of its working life. An example from the shoe sector would be the way that leather soles have steadily given way to cheap and non-biodegradable synthetic soles that are made of lead and plastics and therefore emit noxious particles upon decomposition. In more conceptual terms, recycling becomes difficult when companies mix non-reusable synthetic 'technical' components indiscriminately with organic 'biological' flows (Braungart and McDonough 2009). The end result is that neither product stream can be salvaged and both end up adding to the overflowing landfills that municipalities worldwide are struggling to manage.

Lastly, on-land waste storage problem cannot be fully analysed without reference to population growth. When mass manufacturers of fast moving consumer goods first marketed easily disposable products in the mid to late 20th century, the world had 3 billion inhabitants. With a global population that has more than doubled to ca. 6.7 billion in 2010, this 'throwaway' culture appears entirely unsustainable. In other words, business strategies that seemed ecologically feasible in one era were no longer possible in another. The lesson here is that sustainability is never a constant but instead requires ongoing adaptation: not only in managers' actions; but also in their thinking.

Key issue

... business strategies that seemed ecologically feasible in one era were no longer possible in another.

Water pollution

At best, societies' responsibility for the havoc that pollution (and over-fishing) has wreaked upon the world's aquatic systems results from the myopic assumption that oceanic and other major water bodies are big enough to dilute any volume of pollutants (see *Chapter 3 online case study*). At worst, people have not even cared.

Inconsistent support for water quality testing attests to some companies' widespread (some would say criminal) negligence in this area. On one hand, modern science is fully capable of plotting the multiple interactions between bodies of water and their environs, as well as the extent to which a given system can withstand one or several of the factors that might damage water quality and/or disrupt the food webs upon which local flora and fauna rely (Fausch *et al.* 2010). Such factors, called **stressors**, include dams and diversions; channelisation (the creation of artificially straight waterways); deforestation; chemical spills; biological invasions; and climate change itself. If a company responsible for point source pollution is prepared to pay for an in-depth analysis of the consequences of its actions on local water systems – or if it is politically and legally obliged to do so – the technology already exists to do so.

■ **Stressor:** Any agent disturbing the biological processes of another.

Yet according to some observers, evidence exists that this kind of know-how is wielded more often to analyse accidents attributable to public sector actors – such as the accidental release of organic effluents from wastewater treatment plants – than to analyse chemical effluents more closely associated with private commercial activities (Phillips and Chalmers 2009). This curious tendency on the part of many social partners not to scrutinise corporate water pollution with the same rigour as public effluents may reflect an overriding sense that water is a common resource, hence an asset for which the state alone is responsible. Yet this makes no sense in economic (much less ecological) terms, since it is tantamount to asking the

3

? Why are corporate
water pollution
regulations generally
so lenient?

wider community to pay the price for benefits accruing to smaller constituencies (see Chapter 4). It also exemplifies the need for a legal framework in which corporate environmental liabilities are spelt out more clearly than they are in most countries today.

Confusion in this area might be explained by the fact that pollution sources are not always readily identifiable. For instance, the predatory fish that are a part of the diet of many households worldwide have consistently shown levels of toxic methylmercury surpassing what most authorities would consider safe. Yet many government agencies (such as the US Food and Drug Administration) refuse to require the publication of health warnings, in part because of pressure from fishing industry lobbyists such as the National Fisheries Institutes and the US Tuna Foundation (Hightower 2009). Insofar as specific sources of mercury pollution remain unknown, the argument is that restricting all fish sales would unfairly penalise producers bearing no responsibility for this problem. Of course, this position does not help the diner unknowingly consuming poisonous fish.

On other occasions, even when a company is clearly guilty of egregious water pollution, the state may not always prosecute. Recent tests in the US state of West Virginia, for instance, have shown that drinking water from the tap 'contains arsenic, barium, lead, manganese and other chemicals at concentrations that federal regulators say could contribute to cancer and damage the kidneys and nervous system' (Duhigg 2009). The sources of these pollutants were well-known, with neighbouring coal companies having been quite open about the illegal concentrations of chemical by-products that they were pumping into the water tables around their mines. Yet in this instance like many others, the authorities declined to intervene. Such inaction can often be attributed to uncertainty about the precise link between water pollution and human disease, or more procedurally, to an administration's lacking the resources to bring cases of misconduct to court. In reality, the crux here is the arbitrage that a society makes between citizens' private concerns and companies' financial interests. In turn, this bears some relation to that a society running sectors of activity that are more or less prone to pollute.

Key issue   ... the crux here is the arbitrage that a society makes between citizens' private concerns and companies' financial interests.

■ Sectoral factors

The physicality of primary and secondary sector activities means that they are the direct cause of most corporate pollution (Levinson 2009). Note that this book does not share some analysts' conception that the tertiary sector is de-materialised. After all, people continue to operate and travel in a real, tangible world. It is simply easier to analyse the tools used to conduct tertiary sector missions (i.e. information technology) within the confines of the relevant primary and secondary sector activities.

There is a lack of data about the precise sectoral breakdown of corporate pollution except in the one area that seems to monopolise analysts' attention today – greenhouse gases (Table 3.7). The general understanding is that, on average, something like 37 per cent of global CO_2 emissions come from industrial sources (led by a few main sectors such as cement, petroleum refining and iron and steel); 32 per cent from homes and commercial buildings; 23 per cent from transportation (with almost half from automobiles); and the remainder from agriculture and other small users (Neale 2008). This varies markedly from one country to another, however, reflecting factors such as climate; the prevalence of passenger cars; levels of anti-pollution technology in factories; or national endowments in natural resources such as timber. The 2006 data for the UK, for instance, showed a breakdown of 37 per cent for buildings, 34 per cent for transportation and 29 per cent for industry. But even this categorisation is too broad, with some end user categories emitting more CO_2 than others. For instance, heating in buildings accounted for something like 10 per cent of all UK emissions (the same as car travel); lighting and appliances in buildings 8 per cent (the same as cement-making); and petroleum refineries, iron and steel making and truck freight 6 per cent apiece. Thus, these seven end-user categories alone accounted for 54 per cent of the country's total CO_2 emissions.

The implication here is that concentrating green business investments in a few key sectors should produce disproportionate environmental benefits (see Chapter 9). This is especially true given that a number of activities that emit enormous quantities of CO_2 (i.e. logging and deforestation, sectors whose combined global emissions exceed those of the USA or China) already have cost-effect technological solutions at their disposal (CI 2009). Conversely, it may be less efficient for a society, at a macro level, to disperse its sustainability investments. The problem, of course, is that societies rarely take macro decisions of this kind – companies operating at a micro level do.

Table 3.7: 2005 percentage of global CO2 emissions by end users (CI 2009)

Sector	Billion tons CO_2 equivalent	Percentage
Energy	28.4	61.4
- Electricity and heat	12.3	26.6
- Manufacturing and construction	5.2	11.2
- Transportation	5.4	11.6
- Other fuel combustion	3.8	8.2
- Fugitive emissions	1.8	3.8
Industrial processes	1.9	4.0
Waste	1.4	3.1
International bunkers	1.0	2.1
Land-use change (inc. peatland drainage) and deforestation	7.5	16.3
Agriculture	6.1	13.1
Total	46.3	100

■   Primary activities

The most important primary sector is agriculture (see Chapter 9), for whom the main pollution problem is the soil quality constraint with which countless farmers have had to contend since the dawn of history. In simple terms, the soil covering the face of the Earth is itself a biotic organism comprised not only of 'dead' rocks but also living nutrients sustained by organic matter. These nutrients are also the agents providing plants with the sustenance that they need to grow. Once plants die, they decompose into further nutrients (sometimes called 'humus') that will feed later generations, thereby creating a sustainable fertility cycle. Problems arise if something perturbs this process. This might include depleting agricultural lands by over-working them and making it hard for a sufficient nutrient base to develop.

? Who decides which sectors are most apt to reduce pollution most quickly?

As for the main pollutants damaging the quality of the world's agricultural lands, ironically enough they are usually pesticides and fertilisers, the very agents that farmers use to maximise crop yields. Pesticides have long been criticised for the toxic residues that they leave behind, which can ultimately accumulate in human tissue. As for nitrogen-based fertilisers, they have become very inefficient, with as little as 30 per cent of the quantities being disseminated actually

interacting with plant life. The rest tends to run off from fields and accumulate in global water systems (onshore and subsequently offshore),
where it 'over-fertilizes the water, producing such large volumes of
algae and other biomass that it consumes all the oxygen in the water,
causing the ecosystem to crash' (Pearce 2009). Note additionally the
long-term impoverishment of soil when too much fertiliser has been
used – a prime example being the problems experienced in the once
fertile southern reaches of California's Central Valley.

The other primary activity with serious pollution problems is
mining. As Jared Diamond explained in his bestseller *Collapse* (see
Chapter 1 online case study), unscrupulous mine owners have long used
the legal concept of limited liability as a buffer to avoid prosecution for
environmentally disastrous practices that maximise their short-term
profits while forcing the rest of society to shoulder the clean-up costs.
One common practice involves using toxic chemicals such as arsenic
to separate minerals from dirt, without proper disposal of the ensuing **slurry** (Duhigg 2009). Another 'enviro-crime' is the habit of using
explosives to scalp off entire mountaintops simply because this makes
it easier for mining companies to access underground ore – with the
subsequent debris being dumped randomly and killing off entire
ecosystems. Lastly, the leakage of heavy metals from decommissioned
mines is often a major source of groundwater pollution (Zuquette *et al.*
2009). What is interesting here is that these effects only become visible
years after a mine has been abandoned. In other words, to assess a
company's footprint more accurately, the residual consequences of its
actions must also be brought into the equation.

■ **Slurry:** Liquid thickened
by the solid particles that it
has accumulated, often after
use as a cleansing agent.

■ Secondary activities

It is impossible to list all of the ways in which manufacturing activities
cause pollution. Nevertheless, there is value in noting three seminal
principles in this area.

- ■ Industrial products are the summation of a multitude of processes
  and value chains, each of which has its own footprint. A good
  example here is one developed by Braungart and McDonough (2009,
  p. 81) to describe textile factories. The water used to clean fabrics will
  accumulate and run off carrying a series of toxins and heavy metals
  (i.e. cobalt or zirconium) as well as any finishing chemicals used
  to shape the fabric. Note that such chemicals often exude slowly
  over the life of the good and are inhaled by consumers. In addition,

textile operations will produce solid waste (trimmings and loom clippings) that often contain petrochemicals. The effluents and sludge produced by a textile plant's machinery contain further pollutants that may be hazardous. All of these elements need to be disposed of (whether incinerated or sent to landfills), raising the possibility that further toxins will be released at this juncture – not to mention the pollution secreted when the fabrics are transported between their place of production, assembly, retail and consumption.

■ Modern industry's relatively infrequent use of biodegradable inputs means that increasing amounts of semi-processed or complete goods are made out of materials such as plastic whose life spans are much longer than the functional purposes for which they were created. Goods ranging from diapers to water bottles to cell phones (Wargo 2009) or old computer hardware (see Chapter 6) accumulate as landfill waste long past their useful lives. As they degrade, they often release uncontrolled toxic substances into the environment.

■ Industrial negligence remains widespread, despite growing pressure from stakeholders. A multitude of online reviews and specialist websites have sprouted up in recent years to denounce wanton corporate pollution, with examples ranging from accusations levied at Coca Cola in India that its products contain excessive amounts of pesticides (and that it indiscriminately discharges waste water into the fields surrounding its plants, see www.indiaresource.org/), to anger with the runoffs from Shell's oil drilling rigs in Nigeria's Ogoni delta. As discussed further in Chapter 5, pollution control is as much a question of corporate values as of science.

Note that the power generation sector is often considered the world's biggest polluter, although there is an ethical debate whether utility companies or their customers are ultimately responsible for this state of affairs. The amount of pollution generated during the production and distribution of electricity depends on a host of factors, including the particular primary fuel consumed to produce the current and the technology used to reduce the activity's overall footprint. Along these lines, see *Web Resource 3.2* for a discussion of the carbon capture and storage techniques being developed to offset CO_2 from burning coal, the world's most abundant but also dirtiest fuel source.

The transportation sector is also a major source of secondary sector pollution. This is due, on one hand, to the huge size of the global market for passenger vehicles, almost all of which have been powered until now by smog-producing, petrol-based internal combustion engines.

Secondly, there is the more structural problem of multinational companies (MNEs) subcontracting logistics activities, which as afore-mentioned have proliferated in recent years due to the globalisation of supply chains (see Chapter 8). The problem is that some MNEs act as if their reliance on third party logistics providers obviates their responsi-bility for the transportation services that they hire – creating a grey area that can often lead to non-quality and subsequently to environmental disaster. Examples include recurrent oil spills caused by transport-ers' hiring of sub-standard tankers – and more specifically, a terrible instance in 2006 when Dutch trading company Trafigura chartered a vessel called the *Probo Koala* that subsequently dumped two tonnes of toxic hydrogen sulphide in and around the Ivory Coast's capital city of Abidjan, killing 15 persons and injuring up to 30,000 others. Allegations were made that it took Trafigura an unseemly amount of time to admit indirect responsibility for this lethal act of pollution. Cases of this kind provide further evidence that the battle against corporate pollution is as much a question of managers' mindsets as an issue of scientific knowledge.

■ Obstacles and pathways

1 The source of a particular flow of pollutants is not always clear.

It is in companies' interest to develop emission/effluent monitoring systems.

2 As understanding of pollution effects grows, companies will increas-ingly be held liable for their behaviour in this area.

They need to develop knowledge in areas such as green chemistry as a prelude to industrial reorganisation.

3 Global warming seems unstoppable.

There is an urgent need for companies to develop climate change risk scenarios.

4 Too much waste is being sent to landfill.

Products should be designed with a view towards their ultimate recyclability.

Case study: Steeling South Africans against pollution

As a firm that has itself emerged from an impoverished home country (India) to become world leader in the steel sector, the multinational Mittal is a figurehead of globalisation. With its preferred internationalisation mode being the acquisition of longstanding rivals, Mittal pursues a volume strategy based on maximum geographic coverage. Economies of scale, often calculated in capacity utilisation terms, are crucial in a sector such as steel that is highly vulnerable to variations in global economic activity. Stated simply, Mittal possesses significant fixed assets and needs them to be up and running.

In 2002, for instance, Mittal acquired a 67-year-old, 5683-acre plant at Vanderbijlpark, located in South Africa's industrial heartland about 70 kilometres south of Johannesburg (SAPA 2009). For as long as local residents could remember, the plant had polluted the area, belching heavy smoke from its chimneys and letting poisonous black dust waft over its dumpsites. Steel is a fundamentally dirty industry but the hope was that the new owners, with their ostensible commitment to social and environmental responsibility, would have the means and desire to reduce the pollution that Vanderbijlpark produces.

Years later, serious questions remain as to whether Mittal has done enough. On one hand, residents complain of a plague of serious health disorders; livestock is often born deformed; and metal surfaces such as food tins or window frames rust uncontrollably. On the other, Mittal has been trying to rehabilitate the site's old slurry storage dams, along with other waste disposal sites, for a total cost of about $57 million. It also has plans to place a soil covering over the slagheap of spent materials. The question is whether these efforts are enough. It is true that some residents' health problems result from years of toxins in the air and water table – pollutants that accumulated before Mittal took over and for which it cannot be held responsible. This argument is difficult to sustain, however, given the continued pollution that took place even after the group was in charge.

The debate came to a head in January 2010 when Mittal South Africa was shortlisted with five other candidates for the Public Eye Global Award that the Davos World Economic Forum gives to the firm viewed as having demonstrated the most noteworthy lack of corporate responsibility over the previous year (GAAM 2010). Vanderbijlpark, Mittal's biggest and most profitable operation in South Africa, was nominated due to its dumping of toxic waste; failure to clean up past and present contamination in the plant's vicinity; opposition to stringent air quality controls; and lack of transparency. A local environmental activist denounced the company for the way it uses political connections to 'protect [its] polluting industry'. He also asserted that the group is guilty of similar misconduct elsewhere, citing a similar pattern at its facilities in Kazakhstan and Ohio (USA) and evoking its 'appalling safety record', exemplified by the high number of fatalities among miners. All in all, the picture painted is one of a firm that has the resources to further combat environmental deterioration – Mittal's main shareholder being one of the wealthiest men in the world – but does not always choose to do so.

The company's website (www.arcelormittal.com/) contains an environmental responsibility section where it represents sustainability as one of its core values, exemplifed by the fact that its steel products can be recycled time and again. In a similar vein, another insert refers to the estimation that 80 per cent of the company's waste was recycled in 2006. Critics might point out that recycling products after they have already generated enormous pollution is tantamount to closing the barn door only after the horses have bolted. Mittal's website recognises that steel making is carbon-intensive, but then goes on to state that 'real progress will mean substantial expenditure on new technologies, and we will be looking to governments and regulators to ensure that this level of investment is supported by government backing'. An interesting question is whether the company will undertake such investments if the public sector does not provide financial assistance.

Case study questions

- *Why might South African residents have had cause for celebration when Mittal acquired the Vanderbijlpark steelworks?*

- *To what extent can South Africans be satisfied with Mittal's environmental performance since taking over?*

- *From Mittal's perspective, what is the value of pollution reduction?*

■ References

Braungart, M. and McDonough, W. (2009), *Cradle to Cradle: Re-Making The Way We Make Things*, London: Vintage Books.

CI (Conservation International) (2009), 'Deforestation, logging and ghg emissions: current facts', December, available at www.conservation.org, accessed 26 January 2010.

Diamond, J. (2006) *Collapse: How Societies Choose to Fail or Succeed*, Penguin

Duhigg, C. (2009), 'Clean water laws are neglected, at a cost in suffering', 12 September, available www.nytimes.com, accessed 28 January 2010..

e360 digest (2010), 'Exposure to flame retardant decreases female fertility', 27 January, available at http://e360.yale.edu/, accessed 29 January 2010.

Fausch, K, Baxter, C. and Murakami, M. (2010), 'Multiple stressors in north temperate streams: lessons from linked forest-stream ecosystems in northern Japan', *Freshwater Biology*, **55**, Supplement 1.

Friend, G. (2009), *The Truth About Green Business*, Upper Saddle River, NJ: FT Press.

GAAM (2010), 'ArcelorMittal's polluting South African plant shortlisted for Public Eye Global Award…', 19 January, available at www.globalaction-arcelormittal.org/, accessed 2 February 2010.

Garcia-Sanchez, A., Anawar, H.M., Moyano, A., Alvarez-Ayuso, E, Munez, C. (2008), 'Concentrations of heavy metals in plants grown on polluted mining soils', *International Journal of Environment and Pollution*, **33** (2–3).

Hightower, J. (2009), 'A call for tougher standards on mercury in fish', available at http://e360.yale.edu, 26 January, accessed 2 February 2010.

ISTC (Illinois Sustainable Technology Center) (2009), *Primary Metals Pollution Prevention Notebook*, available at www.istc.illinois.edu, accessed 29 January 2010.

KNP (Key Note Publications) (2008), *Global Waste Management Market Assessment 2007*, July, available at www.researchandmarkets.com/, accessed 1 February 2010.

Levinson, A. (2009), 'Pollution and international trade in services', April, available at www.nber.org, accessed 1 February 2009.

Makower, J. (2009), *Strategies for the Green Economy*, McGraw-Hill.

Meikle, J. (2009), 'Waste firm banned after deadly cyanide leak in Trent river', *The Guardian*, 9 October, p. 21.

Monbiot, G. (2007), *Heat: How We Can Stop the Planet Burning*, London: Penguin.

Neale, J. (2008), *Stop Global Warming: Change the World*, London: Bookmarks Publications.

Pearce, F. (2009), 'The nitrogen fix: breaking a costly addiction', 5 November, available at http://e360.yale.edu/, accessed 28 January 2010.

Phillips, P. and Chalmers, A. (2009), 'Wastewater effluent, combined sewer overflows, and other sources of organic compounds to Lake Champlain', *JAWRA Journal of the American Water Resources Association*, **45** (1).

Pospisil, J. and Miroslav, M. (January 2010), 'Particulate matter dispersion modelling along urban traffic paths', *International Journal of Environment and Pollution*, **40** (1–2).

Sapa-AP (2009), 'Arcelor Mittal South Africa dismisses pollution claims', 25 September, available at www.corpwatch.org, accessed 2 February 2010.

Sen, O. (2009), 'The effect of aircraft engine exhaust gases on the environment', *International Journal of Environment and Pollution*, **8** (1–2).

Shah, S. (2009), 'The spread of new diseases: the climate connection', 15 October, available at http://e360.yale.edu/, accessed 31 January 2010.

Siegle, L. (2010), 'Ethical living', *Observer Magazine*, 12 September.

Stern, D.(2006), *Stern Report*, available at www.hm-treasury.gov.uk/, accessed 16 April 2009.

Trucost (2010), *Universal Ownership: Why Environmental Externalities Matter to Institutional Investors*, UNEP Finance Initiative – PRI .

Vidal, J. (2009), 'Dust clouds take deadly viruses across the world', *The Observer*, 27 September, p.14.

Wargo, J. (2009), 'Pervasive plastics: why the U.S needs new and tighter control', 12 November, available at http://e360.yale.edu, accessed 2 February 2010.

4 Environmental Economics and Politics

Contents

Environmental economics

Environmental politics

Learning objectives

After reading this chapter, you will be able to:

- Adapt concepts of value to include the ecological imperative
- Adapt market theory to include environmental externalities and public goods
- Determine the shape of the international political environmental agenda
- Identify different influences on environmental policy-making.

■ Introduction

> The ideas of economists and political philosophers, both when they are right and when they are wrong, are more powerful than is commonly understood. Indeed, the world is ruled by little else. Practical men, who believe themselves to be quite exempt from intellectual influences, are usually the slaves of some defunct economist.
>
> John Maynard Keynes (1936)
> *The General Theory of Employment, Interest and Money*

> **?** Can an ecological perspective fit into existing social and economic paradigms?

One of the premises underlying this book is that the only accurate way of analysing business is within the economic and political contexts of the societies where it operates – frameworks that the business world itself will have helped to shape. Assessing the current and future prospects of Ecology and Management therefore means looking at relevant economic and political theories and practices. As Keynes indicates in his famous quotation above, today's **paradigms** derive from particular

Paradigm: ■
Worldview, general philosophy.

philosophical stances – many of which ignored the ecological imperative, which as Chapter 1 discussed, has only recently been viewed as a priority concern in most societies. Hence the value of incorporating environmental considerations into economic theory, before examining their political implementation.

■ Environmental economics

There is little doubt that a market-oriented 'classical' economic philosophy has characterised the international business environment since the early 1980s, taking over from a previous paradigm that was more accepting of government 'interventionism'. The current mindset will not necessarily last – economic history is characterised by recurring cycles, with shifts from one paradigm to another usually occurring after people become disenchanted with the status quo due to a deep crisis (e.g. the Great Depression of the 1930s, stagflation in the 1970s). As such, there is a possibility that the 2008 credit crunch and the international recession that followed will spark yet another paradigm shift. For the moment, however, classic economics (or their modern variant, 'neo-liberalism') continue to dominate most political discourses. The problem is that in certain key respects, this paradigm may be incapable of fully attending to the ecological imperative (Speth 2008).

■ Incompatibilities of classical theory

> It is not from the benevolence of the butcher, the brewer, or the baker, that we can expect our dinner, but from their regard to their own interest.

Adam Smith (1776), *The Wealth of Nations*

Smith's seminal treatise, which laid the foundations for modern capitalism, asserted that individuals should have the freedom to conduct their economic affairs as they see fit. This is because of his prediction that in the absence of the kind of distortions that governmental action injects into the market, people will necessarily seek to maximise their material self-interest, with the sum total of these individual behaviours combining to create an outcome maximising overall welfare. The process would be driven by price mechanisms, with prices signalling to buyers or sellers how they should modify their demand or supply behaviour until the overall market eventually reaches an equilibrium ensuring optimal allocation of resources.

This paradigm has been subject to deep scrutiny throughout history, perhaps most cogently in the writings of the British economist John Maynard Keynes. Noting that 'in the long term, we are all dead', Keynes demonstrated the dangers of building economic theory solely on the basis of markets' internal logic, while ignoring the social pain of the adjustments needed to achieve any long-term equilibrium. This is not to say that classical economics lack any merit. Notwithstanding a long tradition of idealistic calls for a form of economics transcending the venal notion of 'money for money's sake' (NEF 2006), Smith's vision of self-interested actors is hard to contest. Moreover, ample historical evidence exists to suggest that market mechanisms can be a relatively efficient way of organising economic interactions. However, like all philosophies, they are imperfect. Without going as far as eco-socialists do in castigating resource-hungry, growth-oriented capitalism itself as bearing full responsibility for Planet Earth's ecological distress (Foster *et al.* 2009; Kovel 2007), it is clear that classical economics run foul of the ecological imperative on at least two levels: the assumption that amalgamated self-interest translates into optimal group outcomes; and the reliance on prices as accurate signals of value.

> **?** Is capitalism fundamentally at odds with an ecological mindset?

Self-interest vs. group interest

In 1968, Professor Garrett Hardin wrote what would become the seminal text in modern environmental economics. Hardin postulated a 'tragedy of the commons' situation (see Figure 4.1) in which individual shepherds come across open meadows where their herds can graze for free, an advantage that each will understandably try to maximise, in line with Smith's self-interest principle. The problem lies in the finite nature of the commodity in question. If two herds graze in the meadow and consume the grass more slowly than the local ecosystem's natural rate of replenishment, then the pursuit of self-interest by each is sustainable and there is no reason not to continue thusly. However, once the total number of sheep using the meadow rises so that total consumption exceeds the replenishment rate, amalgamated self-interest is no longer sustainable. Competing for a limited resource, the sheep will end up grazing the grass all the way down to its roots so that its natural renewal processes cannot function, meaning that the meadow will die. It is at this point of resource depletion that short-term self-interest is harmful to long-term group-interest – and in a sense, to long-term self-interest as well.

Key issue

... (once) total consumption exceeds the replenishment rate, amalgamated self-interest is no longer sustainable.

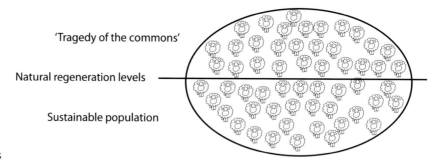

'Tragedy of the commons'

Natural regeneration levels

Sustainable population

Figure 4.1: Maximum consumption threshold for common (natural) resources

The implication of Hardin's theory is that competing economic actors will necessarily dilapidate **public goods** in the absence of an authority regulating access to such goods. The issue here is whether public or private sector interests should assume this regulatory role. As noted by Diamond (2006), government quotas can be impractical at times (i.e. it would be impossible to restrict access to the open oceans) and often involve high policing costs. On the other hand, privatisation (which in Hardin's example would mean dividing the common property into individual allotments) is also problematic due to the difficulty

Public goods: ■
Goods that are 'rivalrous' but 'non-excludable', meaning that (1) their consumption by one party will prevent others from enjoying them, yet (2) no one can be excluded from their use.

in subdividing many resources (i.e. migratory species). Even worse, depending on private owners' personal arbitrage between short and long-term returns, each may calculate that it is in their interest to over-exploit a resource in the present instead of ensuring its sustainability over time. Having said that, economist Elinor Ostrom was specifically awarded the Nobel Prize for demonstrating that individuals in a commons situation will sometimes band together to form collectives capable of protecting public resources (Wearden and Pilkington 2009). This discovery may need to be adjusted for Diamond's insight that self-policing is only likely to work if the groups involved are homogeneous and comprised of people who trust one another and 'expect to share a common future and pass the resource on to their heirs' (2006) – one example being when neighbouring farmers share water resources for irrigation purposes and delegate the power to arbitrate over distribution matters to an elected country water district (c.f. www.lindencwd.com). All in all, the tragedy of the commons is a strong construct highlighting some of classical economics' limitations in conditions defined by real ecological constraints.

> **?** Should people be expected to police their own resource consumption?

Mispricing and disincentives

The construct of 'natural capitalism' (see *Web Resource 1.1*) evokes another area where classical economics do not account for ecological realities, to wit, the endemic under-pricing of natural resources – a situation that Hawken and other leading proponents of the ecological mindset equate to a subsidy paid by the natural world (and/or by future generations) to enable today's civilisation to live beyond its means. In classical theory, if supply of a commodity falls behind demand, its price will rise, in which case demand will either fall or else supply will rise until a new equilibrium is reached. The problem is that this basic mechanism does not work very well with finite resources, whose **relative pricing** is – according to new theory – far too low. An example is provided by global petroleum reserves, whose prices have started to rise as reserves deplete (Chapter 2). According to classical theory, this should lead quite normally to lower demand. Indeed, this is exactly what happened in 2007 when oil hit a record high of $140 per barrel: interest heightened in carpooling solutions; farmers diverted crops to biofuel; and investment rose in alternative fuel research. The problem is the relative lack of elasticity to price characterising the demand for oil. In volume terms, the aforementioned changes were actually quite marginal, with the vast majority of oil consumers having no other

> ■ **Relative price:** Value attributed to one category of asset compared to another.

choice than to continue buying the commodity regardless of its price. It is one thing for theory to postulate that higher prices will displace demand – it is another to have the substitute products allowing this to happen.

Key issue	... another area where classical economics do not account for ecological realities...[is] the endemic under-pricing of natural resources.

A secondary demand-side problem relates to companies' ability to pass on to customers the true price of the natural resources they use. When prices rose in April 2008 for iron ore and other raw materials used as steel production inputs, multinational enterprises (MNEs) such as ArcelorMittal tried to restore their profit margins by adding a surcharge on products. The MNE had problems implementing this decision, however, due to the poor financial health of many of its customers, including US automakers Ford and General Motors (Mathews 2008). Expressed in terms of global value chains, higher costs at an early upstream stage will have to be subtracted from intermediary producers' profits if customers further **downstream** cannot afford the inflation that will occur once the 'subsidy' comprised of today's artificially low natural resource prices is withdrawn.

Downstream: Later value chain activities relating to the interface between a company and its customers.

Just as daunting is the problem raised by supply-side adjustments to resource depletion. Again according to classical theory, as prices rise, producers should be motivated to increase output (see Figure 4.2). Indeed, this is exactly what has occurred to some small degree, one example being oil companies' decision to re-open fields whose exploitation would be uneconomic at lower prices (Strahan 2007). It remains that only a limited amount of extra oil is being pumped: because the largest, most accessible reserves have already been extracted; and due to the simple yet often forgotten reality that there is a finite supply of oil on Earth. As for the economics of substitution, it is true that higher oil prices tend to spark greater research into alternative fuel sources. The problem, however, is that technological progress is always very slow, expensive and ultimately uncertain. Moreover, investors' willingness to invest in alternative sources of fuel is undermined by the erratic price signals coming out of an oil market that is dominated by volatile speculators (Piranfar 2009). This is yet another level at which classical economic theory does not fully account for the difficulties of adjusting to an ecologically constrained future.

? Is the ecological imperative being priced correctly?

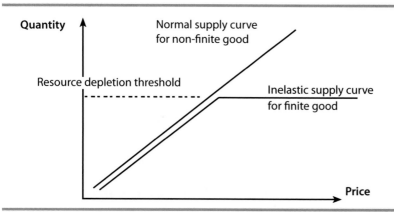

Figure 4.2: Inelasticity of supply to price in case of a finite good

Yet if these adjustments are not completed by the time resources deplete and/or resource prices become prohibitive, the world will be condemned to a terrible 'dystopian interlude' during which time the 'old economy' will have crumbled even before the 'new economy' has had a chance to take root (see Figure 4.3). To avoid this scenario, the **precautionary principle** argues that it is in everyone's interest to accelerate the shift to more ecological practices through greater resource husbandry and technological investment. For several reasons, however, this is easier said than done. Many managers are clearly aware that resources are running out but hold a blind and unreasoned faith that some unnamed party will come up with a substitute technology. Others calculate, quite cynically, that the impending upheaval will occur after they have maximised their personal gain from the status quo: because 'financialisation' focuses companies on short-term aims such as maximised return from **sunk costs** instead of on the longer-term **lifecycle assessment** that is an integral part of the ecological mindset; and because the daunting costs inherent to any paradigm shift can easily lead organisations into a kind of **ecological inertia**.

■ **Precautionary principle:** Philosophy that when faced with an indeterminate choice, the best option is the one that minimises potential risks.

■ **Sunk costs:** Sums already invested in assets that cannot be sold off.

■ **Lifecycle assessment:** Analysis of an asset's total value including acquisition price, performance and residual value.

■ **Ecological inertia:** Slower adaptation to environmental problems than would be expected using rational analysis.

Yet if these adjustments are not completed by the time resources deplete and/or resource prices become prohibitive, the world will be condemned to a terrible 'dystopian interlude'.

Key issue

To complicate matters, actors who have the foresight to accommodate the ecological imperative often pay a penalty. This is because most environmental technologies and products are at an infant stage (see Chapter 10) or else have not attained the critical mass that will allow them to achieve economies of scale and attract new buyers, thereby triggering the kind of virtuous circle that helps a new business to take

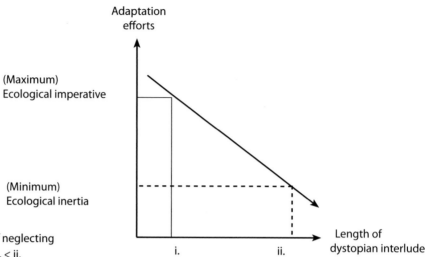

Figure 4.3: Consequences of neglecting the precautionary principle: i. < ii.

off. One example comes from the field of renewable energy, where the average kilowatt-hour of electricity produced from conventional fuel sources is somewhere between 10 and 18 cents in the USA, versus 36 cents for solar panel-generated electricity (Pernick and Wilder 2007). Until this price differential shrinks and even reverses, market forces will dissuade participants from investing in renewable energy – even though this is arguably the only rational behaviour over the long run. A free market advocate might respond that market prices, if left to their own devices, would ultimately lead to behaviour modification. Yet by the time this rectification occurs, Planet Earth may be close to running entirely out of oil or hitting a tipping point in terms of global warming. The real problem is that current economic systems lack accurate information about the cost of environmental inertia: very few people on Earth have taken the trouble to calculate how soon oil reserves will deplete (see Chapter 2); and not many have tried to assess the real cost of climate change. Another way to express this is to say that the ecological imperative is currently underpriced – but humankind does not have enough time for more accurate pricing signals to work their way through the marketplace. Classical economics argues that markets should be allowed to achieve their own equilibrium. Environmental economics, on the other hand, argues that after years of burdening Earth's ecosystems, such patience is an unaffordable luxury. The two disciplines work to entirely different timescales.

? Are market mechanisms an effective mechanism for driving the shift to renewable technology?

Key issue

... the ecological imperative is currently underpriced – but humankind does not have enough time for more accurate pricing signals work their way through the marketplace.

■ Difficulties formulating a new discipline

A cogent body of theory cannot be based solely on criticisms of its predecessors but must also contain its own internal logic. Some good work has therefore been achieved developing theories specific to 'ecological economics', which is somewhat more narrowly focused than 'environmental economics'. The key construct in this sub-discipline is that economic development (which should be understood in qualitative rather than quantitative terms) must become achievable under 'stationary state' conditions of zero growth (Meadows *et al.* 1972; McKibben 2008). It is noteworthy that the original green critique of growth for growth's sake has spread in recent years beyond the environmentalist movement. In 2009, for instance, Nobel Prize winners Amartya Sen and Joseph Stiglitz co-published a report commissioned by French president Nicolas Sarkozy questioning the suitability of GDP growth as a measure of economic health – an anomaly exemplified by the way in which increased driving (reflected in expanding car and fuel sales) will normally be categorised as output growth, thus something good, whereas in reality it means that people squander time in traffic jams and suffer from bad air quality (Goodman 2009). As noted by German social scientist Meinhard Miegel, 'What is the point of seeking growth when it leads to depression, family break-ups and the collapse of society?' (author's translation, from Kunz and Sattler, 2009).

4

? Is zero growth a realistic (or even desirable) goal?

A second seminal principle sets ecological economics in a context defined by natural science (see Chapter 1). Here, leading figures such as Romanian mathematician Nicholas Georgescu-Roegen have built first order theories around Newton's thermodynamic laws of physics, postulating that the dispersion of energy witnessed in nature (so-called 'entropy') is a reality also found in the field of economics. The premise is that true efficiency means maximising the amount of energy (derived directly or indirectly from the sun) that can be kept in a useful form as a natural resource, human-produced service or even waste – which can hopefully be recycled to become a new input resource (see Figure 4.4). Conversely, to the extent that resource depletion (the over-exploitation of 'natural capital') and/or pollution undermine the Earth's 'carrying capacity' or ability to sustain economic cycles, all human activity is bound to suffer from diminishing returns unless there is some techno-logical progress.

Furthermore, ecological economics maintains that it is wrong to assert, as classical economics does, that assets' future value should nec-essarily be discounted to reflect their present value. Quite the contrary, capitalising an asset's present value into the future by extending its useful lifespan through resource and energy conservation measures is deemed a superior measure of economic efficiency. This is a very constructive proposal but its application encounters a major hurdle, namely the prevalence in today's society of monetary profitability as a criterion of success. For many if not most companies, shareholders' profit objectives constitute the chief priority. Ecological economics does not speak to this reality.

> **?** Is economic efficiency necessarily defined in monetary terms?

Key issue

[In ecological economics], capitalising an asset's present value into the future by extending its useful lifespan through resource and energy conservation measures is deemed a superior measure of economic efficiency.

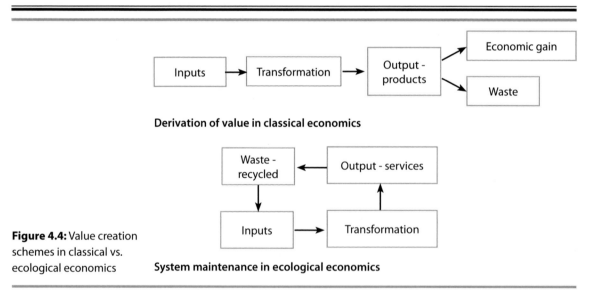

Derivation of value in classical economics

System maintenance in ecological economics

Figure 4.4: Value creation schemes in classical vs. ecological economics

Because environmental economics do incorporate monetary per-spectives, it is more renowned than its ecological sibling. Yet neither of these sub-disciplines enjoys as serious a reputation as many other branches of economics. This may be because neither has fully resolved two fundamental questions in this area: how to assess exchange value; and how to attribute responsibility. Once theorisation advances along these lines, they are bound to be considered more mainstream.

Variable assessments of exchange value

In line with the environmentalist premise that physical (and social) interactions can only be assessed accurately in light of the interdependencies that sustain them, it must be assumed that absolute ecological value does not exist. Instead, for any one country, social segment, individual or company, ecological value will necessarily depend on a number of parameters, including culture-based views of the natural world (collective consciousness conveyed through folklore and other narratives); attitudes towards materialism in general; or experiences of habitat stewardship and resource husbandry. In turn, these factors can vary depending on the resources available at a given moment in time. A well-known construct called 'Maslow's hierarchy' (see Figure 4.5) argues cogently, for instance, that actors will only prioritise certain goals if other basic material needs such as food and shelter have been satisfied. Hence the ongoing international business debate about the extent to which the ecological imperative constitutes a priority in poor countries (see Chapter 8).

? Is ecological value relative or absolute?

4

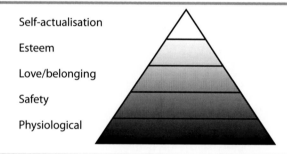

Self-actualisation

Esteem

Love/belonging

Safety

Physiological

Figure 4.5: Maslow's hierarchy – where does environmentalism fit in?

The assessment of ecological value is further complicated by other factors as well. At one level, it is extremely difficult to calculate what resources should be spent on biodiversity to enable the survival of species that produce no direct economic value per se but contribute to the health of an overall ecosystem. At another, it is almost impossible to ascertain the monetary value of investing today to ensure that unborn future generations will enjoy an ecosphere that is healthy and diverse. Environmental stewardship may be justified for aesthetic-moral reasons (Davidson 2008) but there is also a case to make that the wanton destruction of species is reprehensible because it deprives future generations of an opportunity to put their necessarily more advanced technological cultures to good use. Assessing value in terms of this latter point, which refers to the arbitrage between present and future that is a constant in all economic debate, is particularly hard to do, given variations in the value attributed to time in different cultures worldwide.

Similar difficulties arise when ascertaining the respective value of competing demands for resources. This can be exemplified by the arbitrage between human material wealth and the rights of flora and fauna. In the past, only very marginal and/or utopian movements would advocate giving rights to non-humans. However, recent bodies of law that restrict cruelty to animals have set a more mainstream precedent for this approach. At the same time, allocating a precise figure to different flora, fauna and human populations' relative claims to the bounties found on Planet Earth necessarily involves some arbitrary attribution of value.

The same can be said about efforts to value competing constituencies' right to well-being. An example is the yew tree, which has been shown to possess anti-cancer properties and therefore forms the basis of well-known treatments such as Taxol (Hartzell and Rust 1990). The problem is that current demand for yew-based drugs outstrips the tree's natural regenerative powers. Sustainability principles dictate that yew logging be restricted to ensure the survival of the species but this would translate into higher prices and cause a dearth of life-saving drugs for patients. Under such conditions, it is almost impossible to ascertain the 'right price' for saving the yew tree.

Lastly, ecological problems do not have the same effect on all constituencies within a given society at a given point in time. For instance, some segments of society will have greater or lesser proximity to landfills or waste disposal sites, whereas others may have better access to pristine waterways or parklands. Otherwise, air pollution may concentrate in urban centres where commuters work but do not live – in many agglomerations, it is the underprivileged classes that live in the worst affected zones. The concept of **ecological justice** means that different situations should be valued according to the extent to which each affects and/or is caused by a narrow or broad cross-section of society. Fairness and community solidarity are issues in environmental economics, much as they are in neighbouring branches.

Ecological justice: ∎
Extent to which different segments within a society enjoy equal access to a sustainable environment.

The problem of responsibility

Market failure: ∎
Inability of a market system to achieve an optimal outcome (allocation of resources, accurate pricing, etc.).

Pollution – which as aforementioned constitutes one of the two pillars of the ecological imperative as envisioned in this book – is the leading form of **market failure** in the field of environmental economics (see *Web Resource 4.1.*). It constitutes the classic case of an externality that, it should be remembered, can have either positive or negative effects on third parties. An example of a positive externality would be a re-forestation contract between a timber company and a local government, where the restoration of the local biosphere intensifies general pollination processes – thereby helping neighbouring farmers, who will enjoy benefits that they did not earn. Conversely, the pollution generated by one party's economic activity (e.g. car drivers) constitutes a negative externality since it imposes harm (i.e. smog) on innocent bystanders who did not deserve this disadvantage. Both instances are economically inefficient insofar as they enable 'free riding', with actors either benefiting from outcomes for which they are not responsible or else not paying for damages for which they are responsible. The incentive to free ride necessarily raises doubts about the solidity of the economic theories structuring the situations in which such behaviour can occur.

With a negative externality such as pollution, it is almost impossible for the market alone to devise an appropriate price structure, due to the absence of any direct relationship between the party causing the benefit or damage and the party enjoying or suffering it. Ensuring a compensatory redistribution of value will require intermediation, usually involving the state (via the tax system) or else a competent body that has been delegated authority towards this end, increasingly nowadays on a cross-border level (see Chapter 8).

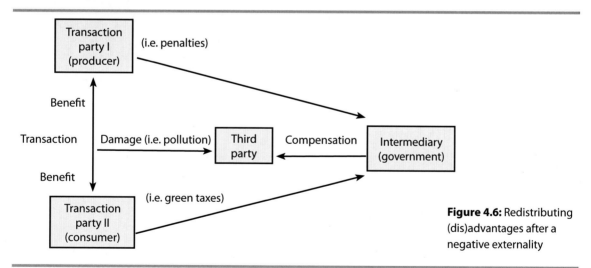

Figure 4.6: Redistributing (dis)advantages after a negative externality

The traditional approach followed in environmental economics has been based on the 'polluter pays' principle, where penalties are assessed to induce the party responsible for the pollution to pay its cost ('internalising the externality'). The hope here is that this party will be dissuaded from repeating its reprehensible behaviour and invest in new systems generating less pollution. The economic difficulty lies in calculating what level of penalties might achieve this behavioural change. Clearly, the higher the levy, the greater the probability that the polluter will shift gears. Historically, however, business lobbies have been very successful at convincing governments not to impose 'punitive' levies – the net effect being that it is often more economic for perpetrators to pay a fine while continuing to pollute (Goodin 1999). Moreover, few if any state authorities actually expect a pristine environment in areas affected by industrial pollution. Indeed, governments vary greatly in terms of the levels of pollution they consider acceptable, as witnessed by the former Bush Administration's repeated efforts to relax environmental standards in the United States. Lower expectations of this kind are particularly fraught because they encourage companies to implement cheaper de-pollution technologies (Freeman *et al.* 1973). Note along these lines the difference between the cost of 'mitigating' pollution (not producing any in the first place) and 'abating' it (cleaning it up afterwards). The former strategy is superior from an environmental perspective but it can also be more expensive: due to the higher costs of designing and implementing pollution-free industrial systems; but also because polluters often escape having to pay for the damage they cause. Such financial considerations reduce companies' incentive to adopt mitigation strategies – a failing of modern economics in value assessment terms but also at a moral level (Hale and Grundy 2009). It explains why pollution control constitutes one of the areas where environmental economics and politics interlink the most.

> **?** Should MNEs be regulated to cut carbon emissions or merely given incentives?

Key issue

... financial considerations reduce companies' incentive to adopt mitigation strategies – a failing of modern economics in value assessment terms but also at a moral level.

At the same time, given the levels of pollutants that have already accumulated in the ecosphere, mere 'abatement' is rarely enough nowadays to address the ecological imperative. It is, however, very prevalent, if only because it lets actors claim that they are facing up to their environmental responsibilities without having to undertake costly major adjustments. An example of this is carbon offsetting, exemplified by the Clean Development Mechanism (CDM) that came out of the 1997 Kyoto Protocol. CDM lets wealthy countries fulfil their emission reduction goals by funding cheap **clean energy** projects in

Clean energy: ■
Energy captured, distributed and used in a way characterised by a minimal environmental footprint (mostly involving renewable sources).

the developing world. It does not ask them to cut their own emissions. Similarly, a criticism of the 'cap and trade' carbon emission trading schemes (see *Web Resource 4.2*) currently being rolled out to address the climate change crisis is that permit allocations are too high to motivate rapid behavioural change – especially since polluters exceeding their allocations can simply buy other participants' unused allowances. Ecologically, the schemes' effects would be greater if governments did not allow anyone to exceed their assigned limits. In a democratic market economy, however, such authoritarianism seems fairly inconceivable.

Finally, note that many companies cannot even afford to implement full-blown mitigation programmes. Thus, in the aftermath of the 2008 credit crunch, there was great concern that companies recovering from the crisis would use their diminished financial strength as a pretext for returning to bad old unsustainable practices instead of viewing the crisis as an opportunity to prepare for an ecologically constrained future (Klein 2009). Chants of 'drill baby drill' at McCain rallies during the presidential elections held that year symbolise the vulnerability of ecological thinking to commercial fortune. They also symbolise the indelible link – in the environmental arena like many others – between economics and politics.

■ Environmental politics

Whereas some observers trust companies to come up with carbon reduction and energy efficiency solutions even before their governments do (Hirschland *et al.* 2008), others doubt that market mechanisms are capable in and of themselves of provoking the requisite level or speed of restructuring (Farrell *et al.* 2007). Many environmentalists have expressed disappointment with the general lack of progress towards environmental sustainability in the new century. The take-up of energy-efficient appliances has been disappointing; utilities still seem to prefer conventional fuels to green alternatives; and despite the automobile wreckage schemes that many governments offered in the wake of the 2008 credit crunch, consumers have been slow to swap their older models for new fuel-efficient ones. The net effect in countries such as the UK is that greenhouse gas emissions have fallen by less than 1 per cent per annum, as opposed to the 2–3 per cent annual drop required to meet the targeted lowering of emissions by 80 per cent before 2050 (The Economist 2009). Note as well a growing fear that the draconian

? To what extent should the state be the driver behind companies' shift towards greater sustainability?

Feed-in tariffs: ■
Sums that a utility (often supported by the state) pays to private parties producing their own renewable energy.

Grid: ■
Interconnected power supply infrastructure bringing energy from where it is generated to the sites where it is consumed.

deficit reduction strategies advocated by certain political parties will undermine the main mechanisms that governments use to green their economies: **feed-in tariffs** benefiting households or companies that sell excess self-produced energy to the national **grid**; subsidies enabling utilities to expand their renewable capabilities, etc. This is particularly worrying given the private sector's general reluctance to engage further capital in new industries during a time of recession. In the absence of private funding, the state necessarily assumes a more crucial role in ensuring investment growth.

Key issue

... given the private sector's general reluctance to engage further capital in a new industries during a time of recession...the state necessarily assumes a more crucial role in ensuring investment growth.

Several factors complicate analysis of public environmental action. On one hand, individual states –equated in economic terms to public non-market institutions (Greenwood 2008) – often struggle to implement policy due to interference from neighbouring countries. The competition for natural resources, for instance, is global in nature. Nor does pollution respect national borders. At the same time, many environmental policy decisions are specific to a particular time and place, insofar as their relevance depends on variable national circumstances. One example is the way that different governments reacted to the 2008 credit crunch and the ensuing recession. In some countries, economic hardship slowed the transition to sustainability. In others, the crisis was viewed as an opportunity to accelerate (Jones 2009). The end result is a very uneven application of green policy tools worldwide.

■ National and global policy frameworks

The environmental policy framework is based on the twin pillars of legislation and political action. In terms of the former, the sum total of laws, regulations, conventions and treaties affecting companies' environmental rights and obligations is much too diverse to summarise here (Bell and McGillivray 2005). Managers should have some familiarity with seminal concepts in this field, such as the conditions under which a company's **licence to operate** can be awarded or revoked; the 'public interest' criteria used to determine a state's right to intervene in private sector transactions to protect the environment; the extent of a company's liability for the environmental externalities associated with its activities; and the redress available to any victims of

Licence to operate: ■
Permission to engage in a productive activity.

such actions. Given the considerable international variation in the way such concepts are treated, it is almost impossible for any one MNE to possess all of the knowledge that it needs in this area – which explains why commercial environmental law has in recent years become one of the world's fastest growing service sectors. Initiatives such as international environmental lawyer Polly Higgins' widely publicised petition to the United Nations that 'environmental transgressions be classified and tried as international crimes of ecocide' (Siegle 2010) are laying the foundations for a whole new field of business law – one that is likely to shape a new corporate environment for many years to come.

On the other hand, a well-defined model already exists for a number of environmentally-oriented political actions. The decentralisation ethos embedded in most ecological initiatives means that many green policies are organised at the local level, even if certain advanced regions tend to set the pace for the rest of the world. One such trailblazer is Germany, where generous state-subsidised feed-in tariffs have encouraged many households to engage in renewables-based micro-generation – the best example being the fully sustainable community of Vauban, a suburb of Freiburg, the world's leading centre for solar panel manufacturing. Another pioneer is California, whose stringent energy efficiency programmes in sectors as diverse as building standards or public lighting (see Chapter 9) mean that per capita electricity consumption has stayed flat in the state over the past 30 years, even as it grew by 60 per cent in the rest of the USA (Romm 2008). Note that the California state government in Sacramento has also been working on legislation that would impose zero carbon emission caps on cars but also, potentially, on companies (Calcars 2006). If enacted, managers working here would no longer have the option of adapting their companies to the ecological imperative but instead be forced to do so. Of course, when this sort of authoritarian approach is applied in one location alone, it is likely to spark legal battles and/or cause an exodus of firms unwilling to adapt to it.

This explains the widespread notion that political action in this area can only succeed if conducted at a more global level. A hierarchy exists between different forms of law, with international agreements – once they have been ratified by a country's legislature – generally superseding national and local laws. The intensification of global trade, along with growing awareness of countries' economic, political, social and ecological interdependencies, supports this internationalisation of

? Should environmental policy be determined at the national or international level?

politics, especially where global problems such as resource depletion and pollution are involved (Speth and Haas 2006). Addressing problems of this magnitude in the absence of **global governance** mechanisms would be impossible.

Global governance:
Regulatory and supervisory functions fulfilled by authorities whose responsibilities supersedes national borders.

The United Nations, as the closest thing to a world government, has quite naturally taken a lead in this area, organising over the years a series of conferences that have helped to drive environmental concerns further up member-states' agenda. Table 4.1 offers a historical timeline of such events.

Table 4.1: Conferences that have set the global environmental policy framework

Year	Name	Issues/comments
1972	UN Conference on the Human Environment (Stockholm)	Population control; planning of human settlements/land use Launch of UNEP Whaling moratorium
1983-1987	World Commission on Environment and Development – Brundtland Report	'About the accelerating deterioration of the human environment and natural resources and the consequences of that deterioration for economic and social development.'
1987	Protocol on Substances That Deplete the Ozone Layer (Montreal)	Concern about holes in atmosphere's ozone layer; phasing out of CFCs
1992	UN Conference on Environment and Development (Rio de Janeiro)	'Earth summit' to 'rethink economic development and find ways to halt the destruction of irreplaceable natural resources and pollution of the planet' Patterns of production scrutinised for toxic substances Focus on public transportation/ alternative fuels/water scarcity
1997	UN Framework Convention on Climate Change (Kyoto)	'Overall framework for intergovernmental efforts to tackle the challenge posed by climate change' Emissions trading concept
2001	UN World Summit on Sustainable Development (Johannesburg)	Reconvened Earth Summit due to disappointing progress since Rio 1992
2004	Intergovernmental Panel on Climate Change (IPCC) - 20th session (Paris)	Scientific group charged by UNEP and World Meteorological Organization to assess human-caused climate change Findings paved way for 2006 Stern Review Report
2007	UN Climate Change Conference (Bali)	Successor to Kyoto
2009	G20 (London)	27. 'We agreed to make the best possible use of investment funded by fiscal stimulus programmes towards the goal of building a resilient, sustainable, and green recovery. We will make the transition towards clean, innovative, resource efficient, low carbon technologies and infrastructure….' 28. 'We reaffirm our commitment to address the threat of irreversible climate change, based on the principle of common but differentiated responsibilities, and to reach agreement at the UN Climate Change conference in Copenhagen in December 2009'
2009	Copenhagen Climate Change Conference	See Chapter 4 online case study

The problem for the UN is that it suffers from a lack of policing capabilities. Its conferences have often been criticised as talking shops lacking the power to implement policy centrally. This critique is surprising at one level, given many environmentalists' avowed preference for 'global networks of small-scale, self-reliant communities' (Patterson 2005). On another level, however, restrictions on the ability of this or any other central authority to dictate environmental policy is likely to please many if not most multinationals, as witnessed, for instance, at the 2001 Johannesburg conference when a group comprised of some of the world's leading MNEs declared that corporate codes of sustainable conduct should be enforced via voluntary self-regulation rather than by the UN or some other government body. Clearly, full-blooded cultural revolutions in companies seeking to create a greener future for themselves involves a different level of commitment than the one found in companies merely responding to government pressure. Both approaches have their use, however. Given the magnitude of the challenges facing companies today – 'only an Apollo-like effort, fusing technology with political will, can lead us to a low-carbon future' (Milliband 2009) – future managers can benefit from being conversant with the way that environment policy develops in both internal private but also external public spheres.

> **?** Should corporate sustainability efforts be voluntary or mandatory?

■ Towards a green new deal?

At the national level, green policy-making depends on a series of factors. One is local political leaders' personal conviction as to how much of a priority should be attributed to the ecological imperative. When US president Barack Obama stated that the bailout of failing American automakers had to be accompanied by (costly) measures accelerating their transition to more fuel-efficient models, he was accused of placing 'green issues before jobs' (Stewart *et al.* 2009). Of course, this criticism was at odds with Mr Obama's longer-term vision – one shared by the present book – that the only truly sustainable jobs are the ones that face up to the environmental challenge.

> **?** What is the arbitrage between protecting current jobs and preparing the transition to a greener future?

Another factor in green policy-making is the pressure that civil society places on government in a democratic regime. Above and beyond media campaigns waged by activist environmentalist groups such as Greenpeace or the World Wildlife Fund, it can be difficult gauging the general citizenry's attitude towards a particular green issue. A recent example from the industrialised world is the evolution in majority opinions (sometimes within one and the same constituency) towards key topics such as off-shore drilling or nuclear power. Moreover, even among those citizens who acknowledge the ecological imperative, there can be wide variations in attitudes about the legitimacy of the state doing something about it – as exemplified by the debate currently raging in America's 'greenest' city, Portland (Oregon) whether local authorities should have the right to proscribe plastic shopping bags, levy taxes on them or simply bolster local recycling channels. At one extreme, some voices would advocate that the green agenda be made 'the responsibility of every government department [and built] into every policy' (Hain 2007), i.e. that no governmental decision be made without an assessment of the environmental impact. At the other, complaints can also be heard about 'command-and-control regulations, like light bulb bans, that reduce prosperity and freedom' (Rauch 2009). There is some correlation between political parties' attitudes towards statist policies and their devotion to environmental causes but the link is imperfect. Environmentalist party politics remains a work in progress.

Managers would be wrong to belittle these discussions as sterile ideological debates. Depending on the extent to which a particular government acknowledges the ecological imperative, business conditions can vary markedly in the country. Companies will experience such variations in two ways: at the general level of the government's green spending budget; and in relation to the specific policy tools that it uses.

Green spending became a key topic in the wake of the 2008 credit crunch and ensuing recession. One interesting attitude in this respect is the one that former White House Chief of Staff Rahm Emmanuel expressed in a February 2009 You Tube video when he said that a good crisis should never 'go to waste' since it provides an opportunity to make changes that, albeit necessary in the long run, would be politically less palatable in normal times. Thus, in this view it is people's perception of the existence of a state of crisis that legitimises a government's decision to spend taxpayers' money on causes such as the ecological imperative. This explains the battle of the airwaves in many countries between voices lauding green spending as an economic stimulus package that also addresses the spectre of climate change – see UK scientist and government advisor David Stern's appeal for the immediate global disbursement of $400 billion in energy efficiency investments (Adam 2009) – and others who express doubt as to whether such spending constitutes an effective use of public monies (Samuelson 2009). Managers seeking insight into green policy frameworks would do well to follow the battle of ideas in this domain. With a few notable exceptions such as ex-Czech President Vaclav Klaus who famously spoke in 2007 of his disdain for 'green hysteria', there seems to be a broad consensus at the (inter-) governmental level that the ecological imperative is very real and that the transition towards sustainability will create jobs by achieving real economic value through a thriftier use of natural resources. Whether these words are supported by concrete action is, of course, another matter.

> **?** Should there have been be more or less green spending by government in the wake of the 2008 credit crunch?

Table 4.2 offers a sample of general green policy tools, listed in order of the extent to which each entails a market-based solution. As aforementioned, the differential implementation of such tools depends on a range of factors. Some are political in nature: leader attitudes; popular pressure; social institutions developed in response to new technologies' dangerous externalities (Dinda 2008). Others are more economic: levels of disposable income; state of innovation. The uncertainties characterising this rapidly evolving area of activity explain MNEs' growing demand for public affairs professionals specialising in environmental policy. This is yet another rapidly green service sector that it behoves business school graduates to explore.

Table 4.2: Main green policy tools used by state entities

Name	Discussion
Elimination of tariffs on green goods/services	Facilitate cross-border trade in green technologies and other energy-saving devices by minimising protectionist restrictions on imports
Carbon trading schemes (cap and trade)	Auction mechanism launched after governments determine allocations among sectors and decide whether to charge for permits and/or set a particular initial carbon price
Standards	Governments establish quantitative targets (emissions, fuel efficiency, etc.) and levy sanctions if they are missed
State sponsored R&D	Due to the expense and long payback period associated with green innovations, governments often provide financial, infrastructure and/or scientific assistance
Green taxes	Incentivise consumers to opt for greener products (cars) and/or behaviour (fuel taxes, airport taxes)
Green subsidies	Payments of varying intensities allowing operators to offer green products/services even when they are uneconomic at current price levels. Often monitored by an international body (WTO, EU) to prevent unfair advantage. Tax credits to hopeful entrepreneurs to spark inwards investment
Direct state investment	Government-owned and managed enterprises specialising in the creation/operation of a green service

Governments promote sustainable business not only directly but also through the policy framework that they formulate. One example is the 2008 decision taken by the German government to cut national greenhouse gas emissions by 40 per cent before the year 2020 versus 1990 levels. Studies indicated that whereas a 30 per cent reduction would be achievable without hampering economic growth or necessitating changes in lifestyle and less comfort (Hartmann *et al.* 2008), the higher target required higher taxation. Combined with Germany's decision to phase-out nuclear power and replace this with more expensive renewable sources, the net effect could be a possible fall in consumer disposable income and aggregate demand; a rise in state debt and long-term interest rates; and a squeeze on corporate margins.

Conversely, significant investments in public transportation in Germany – and other countries whose political culture welcomes the expansion of public goods – might in fact have an indirectly beneficial effect on corporate profitability. Moving away from a personal car culture, for instance, would reduce air pollution, with its negative effects on workers' health; reverse inefficient land use by promoting industrial clusters and proximity (thereby producing the positive externality of greater knowledge spillover between companies); and lessen the need for expensive roadworks that ultimately lead to higher CO_2 emissions. Durable public investment in mass transit would also create some certainty in the business environment. This should be a positive factor for many companies insofar it might justify significant investment in future technologies while enabling infant industries to achieve economies of scale more quickly than would otherwise be the case. The companies taking advantage of these changes would thrive in the new political economic context. On the other hand, parties paying higher taxes would need convincing. As such, a more neutral way of analysing the effects of direct and indirect national green policies is that they are likely to benefit some parties more than others. It is managers' task to position their companies so that they fall into the former category.

■ Obstacles and pathways

1 In economic theory, human self-interest is diametrically opposed to altruism.

   In reality, the two are not mutually exclusive and theory should evolve to reflect this.

2 Market pricing rarely reflects the depletion of finite resources.

Introduce substitution calculations into value assessment exercises.

3 Mitigation strategies seem too expensive compared to abatement approaches.

Redo calculations after internalising potential environmental liabilities.

4 International environmental law is an evolving discipline.

MNEs who can afford to hire specialists will benefit.

Case study: Making Britain's green and sceptr'd isle

In recent years, a broad consensus has emerged in the UK that national economic policy must be reconfigured along more environmental lines. This new paradigm has had a number of negative drivers: energy security fears; concerns about the rising cost of energy imports; and frustration because Britain is struggling to fulfil its EU commitment of producing 15 per cent of domestic energy from renewable sources by 2020. Alongside of this, there is the more positive goal of giving the UK a foothold in the new green economy, which some have predicted will account for as many as 1 million British jobs by the year 2017. What is particularly exciting about this latter prediction is that it also seems to offer the country a way out of the crisis of capitalism that many people sensed in the aftermath of the 2008 credit crunch.

Greening the British economy has turned out to be much easier said than done, however. The year 2009, for instance, was difficult for many UK renewables ventures. Headline problems included Danish company Vestas's closure of its Isle of Wight wind turbine blade factory (the only local producer of this kind of equipment, which is expected to play a key role in Britain's future offshore energy provision); Centrica and E.ON's freezing of a number of planned offshore wind farm projects (Macalister and Adam 2009); and the troubles experienced by the many smaller green power companies who had been counted upon to become the vanguard of the country's renewable energy drive. The real surprise, in fact, is that these teething problems were not more widely predicted – it is normal for new infant industries mobilising largely unproven technologies to struggle to gain market share at the expense of firmly entrenched companies benefiting from favourable competitive conditions, an example of which is conventional fuels' lower upfront production costs. The enthusiasm greeting the advent of a new green sector should not have blinded observers to the difficulties inherent to transformations of this magnitude. Inveterate optimists (or 'cheerleaders') are not particularly good servants of business.

Financial adventurism in the new industry – partially epitomised in green start-ups' relatively high debt-to-capital ratios – became one indicator of British eco-entrepreneurs' 'irrational exuberance'. There is a dangerous phase early in the life of all new companies when significant sums have to be invested in productive infrastructure even before enough cash flow is generated internally to finance such outlays. It is at this point that funding will be sourced from either equity capital or debt. The latter is more dangerous because creditors will ultimately require the loan principal to be repaid (irrespective of the borrower's cash position) and/or might refuse under certain circumstances to roll over short-term facilities. At the same time, entrepreneurs know that they can maximise their return on equity by borrowing as much as possible. Thus, where entrepreneurs are overly sure of themselves – as many green devotees were in the heady years preceding the 2008 credit crunch – they are apt to arrange riskier debt levels than is safe. It is their over-confidence that leads them astray.

With hindsight, it would have been more rational, in pure business terms, for the UK's new green energy ventures to have arranged a higher percentage of equity capital. The question would then be where entrepreneurs might access such funding. Traditionally, start-ups follow the venture capital model that prevails in the USA (see Chapter 10). This differs from established firms who often try to kick-start their new renewable divisions by transferring surplus funds internally. Both modalities exist in the UK. In a sector as risky yet strategic as renewables, however, there is a strong argument that the state can and maybe should become a prime source of funding. After all, energy is a generic commodity that drives most of a country's economic activity – without it, many businesses would fold. This makes energy crucial to national independence and security, hence the kind of public good for which state intervention is theoretically justified.

Against this background, there has been much scrutiny of the government's role in nurturing the UK renewables sector. Some voices have called for higher feed-in tariffs to accelerate British households' implementation of micro-generation from renewable sources. Others have scoffed at the relatively paltry aid given to companies engaged in the very expensive research that is a key part of all new technological development. It is worth noting that the UK's annual renewables subsidy has been around £1 billion in recent years. This pales in comparison with many of the country's other large spending items: the £75 billion that the UK needs to decommission ageing nuclear plants; the £25 billion cost of renewing its nuclear arsenal; or the almost £200 billion needed to bail out its banking sector. The first reality of economic policy is that there is always intense competition for budgetary resources. To succeed in the transition to environmental sustainability, a country must be willing to make this a priority objective – despite all the resistance that this might provoke. The rightwing UK Independence Party has been trying, for instance, to mobilise mass resistance to Britain's expanding investment in (subsidised) wind farms that, on a particularly auspicious day in 2010, produced a record 10 per cent of the country's overall electricity. The country's new Conservative government claims that it rejoices in such progress even as its spending cuts endanger the subsidies that made them possible. Revolutions never occur in a vacuum.

> ## Case study questions
>
> **1** Why did the environment rise up many countries' economic agenda in the 2000s?
>
> **2** Have Britain's new green industries experienced a smooth take-off?
>
> **3** How might Britain's new green sector be funded?

■ References

Adam, D. (2009), '$400 bn demand for green spending', *The Guardian*, 12 February.

Bell, S. and McGillivray, D. (2005), *Environmental Law*, Oxford: Oxford University Press.

Calcars (2006), 'Clean-tech advocates urge California global warming leadership', 21 August, available at www.calcars.org, accessed 3 January 2010.

Davidson, M. (2008), 'Wrongful harm to future generations: the case of climate change', *Environmental Values*, 17 (4).

Diamond, J. (2006), *Collapse: How Societies Choose to Fail or Survive*, London: Penguin.

Dinda, S. (2008), 'Technological progress towards sustainable development', *International Journal of Global Environmental Issues*, 9 (1–2).

The Economist (2009), 'Questioning the invisible hand', 17 October, p. 37.

Farrell, D., Nyquist, S. and Rogers, M. (2007), 'Curbing the growth of global energy demand', July, available at www.mckinseyquarterly.com, accessed 1 January 2010.

Foster, J., Brett, C. and York, R. (2009), 'The Midas effect: A critique of climate change economics', *Development and Change*, 40 (6).

Freeman, M., Haveman, R. and Kneese, A. (1973), *The Economics of Environmental Policy*, New York: John Wiley and Sons.

Goodin, R. (1999), 'Selling environmental indulgences', in J. Dryzek and D. Schlosberg (eds), *Debating the Earth: the Environmental Politics Reader*, Oxford: Oxford University Press.

Goodman, P. (2009), 'Emphasis on growth is said to be misguided', *The Observer*, 4 October, New York Times insert.

Greenwood, D. (2008), 'Non-market coordination: towards an ecological response to Austrian economics', *Environmental Values*, 17 (4).

Hain, P. (2007), *Collaborating Against Carbon*, SERA, Issue 72

Hale, B. and Grundy, W. (2009), 'Remediation and respect: do remediation technologies alter our responsibility?', *Environmental Values*, 18 (4).

Hardin, G. (1968), 'Tragedy of the commons', *Science*, 162 (3859), available at www. garretthardinsociety.org/, accessed 31 December 2009.

Hartmann, A., Riese, J. and Vahlenkamp, T. (2008), 'Cutting carbon, not economic growth: Germany's path, April, available at www.mckinseyquarterly.com, accessed 5 January 2010.

Hartzell, H. and Rust, J. (1990), *The Yew Tree: A Thousand Whispers: Biography of a Species*, Hulogosi Communications.

Hirschland, H., Oppenheim, J. and Webb, A. (2008), 'Using energy more efficiently: An interview with the Rocky Mountain Institute's Amory Lovins', July, available at www.mckinseyquarterly. com, accessed 1 January 2010.

4

Jones, V. (2009), *The Green Collar Economy: How One Solution Can Fix Our Two Biggest Problems*, San Francisco: HarperOne.

Keynes, J.M. (2007) *The General Theory of Employment, Interest and Money*, Palgrave.

Klein, N. (2009), 'What might the world look like if the bailout works? Like Sarah Palin', *The Guardian*, 31 July, p. 30.

Kovel, J. (2007), *The Enemy of Nature: The End of Capitalism or the End of the World*, London: Zed Books.

Kunz, M. and Sattler, S. (2009), 'Sie hätten früher Feierabend', *Focus*, issue 28, p. 43.

Macalister, T. and Adam, D. (2009), 'Warning over renewables as economic crisis leaves funding gap', *The Guardian*, 21 March, p. 38.

Mathews, R. (2008), 'Arcelor plans surcharge for US customers', *Wall Street Journal-Europe*, 28 April, p. 5.

McKibben, B. (2008), *Deep Economy: the Wealth of Communities and the Durable Future*, New York: Holt Paperbacks.

Meadows, D., Randers, J. and Behrens, W. (1972), *The Limits to Growth*, New York: Universe Books.

Milliband, E. (2009), 'One giant leap for a greener Britain', 20 July, available at www.guardian.co.uk, accessed 21 July 2009.

NEF (New Economics Foundation) (2006), 'Are you happy?', 21 November, available at www.neweconomics.org, accessed 1 January 2010.

Paterson, M. (2005), 'Green politics', in *Theories of International Relations*, 3rd edn, S. Burchill, R.Devetak, J.Donnelly, T.Nardin, M. Paterson (eds), Basingstoke: Palgrave Macmillan.

Pernick, R. and Wilder, C. (2007), *The Clean Tech Revolution: The Next Big Growth and Investment Opportunity*, New York: Harper Business.

Piranfar, H. (2009), 'Herd mentality and oil prices: implications for sustainability', *International Journal of Global Environmental Issues*, 10 (1–2).

Rauch, J. (2009), 'Ban the bulb? Not a bright idea', 10 October, available at www.nationaljournal.com, accessed 3 January 2010.

Romm, J. (2008), 'Why we never need to build another polluting power plant', 28 July, available at www.salon.com, accessed 14 January 2010.

Samuelson, R. (2009), 'Selling the green economy', 27 April, available at www.realclearpolitics.com, accessed 5 January 2010.

Siegle, L. (2010), 'Ethical living', *The Observer Magazine*, 19 September.

Smith, A. (2008) *The Wealth of Nations*, Wilder Publications

Speth, J. (2008), *The Bridge at the End of the World: Capitalism, the Environment and Crossing from Crisis to Sustainability*, New Haven, CT: Yale University Press.

Speth, J. and Haas, P. (2006), *Global Environmental Governance*, Washington DC: Island Press.

Stewart, H., Clark, A. and Seager, A. (2009), 'President's GM aid plan under fire', *The Observer*, Business & Media section, 31 May, p. 1.

Strahan, D. (2007), *The Last Oil Shock: A Survival Guide to the Imminent Extinction of Petroleum Man*, London: John Murray.

Wearden, G. and Pilkington, E. (2009), 'Nobel economics prize won by first woman', *The Guardian*, 12 October, p. 7.

5 Corporate Greening Strategies

Contents

Implementing the transition

Controls and measurements

Learning objectives

After reading this chapter, you will be able to:

- Drive top-down and/or bottom-up corporate greening initiatives
- Link organisational performance to environmental metrics
- Monitor external controls on companies' environmental behaviour

■ Introduction

For most companies, transitioning to a more ecological mindset is part of a broader corporate responsibility (CR) agenda. Theorists have long debated the role that business should play in attending to wider social and environmental needs with no direct relationship to the corporate bottom line. The main dividing lines in this debate are between economists such as Milton Friedman, with his minimalist view that it suffices for companies to act legally, versus partisans of the '**stakeholder** value' approach (Laszlo 2008), which holds that CR extends much further – especially in an era when states' diminishing legislative and financial resources prevent them from fully protecting the interests of their constituents, or indeed, of the planet as a whole.

Stakeholder: ■
Anyone affected, however indirectly, by an organisation's actions. Often understood to include employees, local governments, suppliers, consumers and host communities.

It is important to state openly that this book sides with the latter school, if only because Friedman's notion of legality is reprehensibly vague: depending on their size and the competitive pressures they face (Thornton *et al.* 2009), companies can and often will pressure a government into weakening green regulations that would otherwise reduce their short-term profits. Similarly and at a more cross-border level, many developing countries are so desperate for inwards investment (see Chapter 8) that they have no choice but to tolerate the environmental damage that comes with certain forms of international business. Lastly, there is the whole stewardship aspect of the ecological mindset: if companies do not protect environmental interests, who will?

At the same time, a number of obstacles feature on the corporate march towards a responsible future. Firstly, the stakeholder approach associated with a CR agenda can benefit many constituencies other than the environment. Indeed, for much of the 1990s, most discussion in this area concerned 'corporate social responsibility', a vision that mainly emphasised the duties that large companies like multinational enterprises (MNEs) have towards society. With few exceptions – such as BP's 1998 decision in to change its name to 'Beyond Petroleum' to signify a new focus on renewable energies – green issues used to be less central to multinationals' CR image than labour standards or human rights were. By the 2000s, however, this was no longer the case. Indeed, there is some evidence that ecological problems are now the crux of most companies' CR efforts – the cynical view being that this is because environmental problems affect the Global North, whereas labour problems are more severe in less developed countries (LDCs).

Discussing companies' motivations in adopting CR is useful since this indicates how far they might be willing to go in embracing the ecological imperative. The first problem is that whereas 'it is in the nature of moral obligations to be absolute mandates...most corporate social choices involve balancing competing values, interests, and costs' (Porter and Kramer 2006). Money spent on one ethically justifiable concern leaves that much less money to spend on another. If only for **opportunity cost** reasons, no strategy – environmental or other – can be considered free.

■ **Opportunity cost:** Cost of not doing something.

One of the questions this raises is whether managers will be more enthused about strategies that occur for positive reasons (i.e. where companies 'play to win') or for negative ones (i.e. where they 'play not to lose'). The problem is that these two orientations can be difficult to distinguish. For instance, greening will often help a company not only to comply with current regulations and avoid sanctions – a negative motive – but also to pre-empt future criticisms – a positive motive – and turn its foresight into a competitive advantage (Friend 2009). What is clear in today's business environment is that greening strategies will tend to be most attractive when they coincide with bottom line considerations. This too can be construed in different ways, however. Some companies will equate this with revenue expansion, which can involve, for instance, positioning themselves in new growth sectors such as clean energy (see Chapter 10). Others may focus on energy efficiency-related cost reductions (Hirschland *et al.* 2008), which can be substantial in this area, as exemplified by the $2 billion that US chemical giant Dupont is estimated to have saved between 1990 and 2006 through its accelerated energy savings programme. On the whole, it suffices that, in the famous words of General Electric CEO Jeffrey Immelt, 'green is green', i.e. that companies view environmentalism purely and simply as a new source of profitablity.

? To what extent is corporate greening a positive or negative strategy?

... greening strategies will tend to be most attractive when they coincide with bottom line interests.

Key issue

Alongside of this, there is the fact that going green can also enhance a company's reputational capital – as Chapter 7 will explain, customers tend to favour companies whom they consider ethical, even in sectors where the ecological imperative is comparatively less pressing. Conversely, companies accused of 'enviro-crimes' can suffer from a deteriorating brand image. There are a number of vociferous and often

NGOs: ■
Civil society associations created to deal with specific issues or promote a particular ethos or policy. International NGOs usually focus on problems that are cross-border in nature.

Corpocracy: ■
Regime where power is wielded mainly and conceivably solely by and for corporate interests.

Code of conduct: ■
Rules detailing accepted behaviour within an organisation.

? When, if ever, should a company's good environmental behaviour excuse its misconduct in this area?

media-savvy **non-governmental organisations (NGOs)** who see it as their mission to name and shame the **corpocracy** in general and environmentally irresponsible companies in particular (see *Web Resource 5.1*). Many large MNEs that were once quite willing to engage in public disputes with activist groups – Shell in Nigeria, Nestlé in Bangladesh – tend nowadays to opt for a more cooperative approach. This is because the sporadic consumer boycotts that result from bad environmental publicity cut into a company's revenues and affect its bottom line.

To prove their good faith in this area, many if not most large companies have spawned a profusion of environmental mission statements and **codes of conduct** in recent years, proclaiming their good intentions in areas that can range from a reduction in CO2 emissions to expanded recycling or the fight against pollution. Many of these assertions are sincere and accurate but others can be questionable, with some firms standing accused of using their codes to mask other, more dubious practices. In reality, most companies behave in ways that are both good and bad for the environment. McDonalds, for instance, can be commended for its purchases of sustainably sourced fish and for its package reduction efforts yet it has also been accused of buying beef from ranches built on the wasteland of the Amazon rainforest. Coca Cola has spent substantial sums on plastic recycling plants and water conservation policies yet has also been criticised for injecting wastewater into communal drinking sources in El Salvador and India. In general, the concept of companies' strategic greening remains a vague concept requiring further explanation.

■ Implementing the transition

EMS: ■
'Framework through which [a company's] environmental performance can be monitored, improved and controlled', (see http://www.envirowise.gov.uk/).]

Metrics: ■
Indicators chosen as measurement instruments.

Companies have different motives for pursuing green strategies. Analysts tend to distinguish between top-down initiatives where executives take it upon themselves to alter their company's mission statement, and more bottom-up approaches driven by change agents working on the corporate frontlines.

The former impetus will tend to be more procedural in nature, revolving around the implementation of **environmental management systems (EMS)** and performance **metrics** and reporting systems (Hitchcock and Willard 2009). The latter will be more diffuse, with devoted 'sustainability coordinators' working horizontally to raise awareness of the ecological imperative and **cascade** knowledge of best practices. A number of companies will have experienced a combination of these two drivers.

■ **Cascade:** Flow via a series of discrete steps.

A second analysis distinguishes between 'eco-defensive' behaviour emphasizing immediate economic benefits and considering environments investments solely as costs; 'eco-conformist' behaviour meeting requirements without ever exceeding them; and 'eco-sensitive' behaviour exceeding legal requirements and considering sustainability as crucial to a company's long-term survival' (Carroll 1979). This too is a useful insight since it speaks to the fact that companies' greening strategies can vary in terms of their speed of application, level of commitment and staging (see Box 5.1). It is important to remember that different organisations can have very different ways of implementing one and the same strategy.

1 Attractive pitches avoiding '1970s hippy nonsense'
2 Highlight concrete economic interests (savings, risk reduction, commercial benefits, lesser liability, better product design, differentiation)
3 Cement executive agreement for programme, including metrics
4 Set up internal/external partnerships to drive the programme
5 Hype successes as they occur.

Box 5.1: 'Getting leaders to lead' (adapted from Schendler 2009)

5

■ Sustainability from the top down

A number of studies have unsurprisingly shown that when a company's senior managers firmly support a sustainability strategy, its chances of implementation are greatly increased (Epstein 2008). This is because executive commitment, especially in centralised firms where headquarters exert greater top-down control, is likelier to institutionalise green approaches and help them to permeate a company's work culture. In the absence of 'whole system change' (Laszlo 2008), the risk is that some parts of the company will internalise the new paradigm but others will not, due to poor communications, managerial complacency, departmental isolation or staff apathy (Werbach 2009). In this case, those department heads who are recalcitrant or have a lesser sense of urgency will undermine their more proactive colleagues' chances of going green. In reality, senior executives are the only actors in a position to ensure that the whole of a company's value chain (from operations to marketing to finance) embraces green thinking.

Key issue   In the absence of 'whole system change'....the risk is that some parts of the company will internalise the new [green] paradigm but others will not.

The question then becomes why a CEO might suddenly choose to place sustainability at the core of his/her mission statement. Sometimes, the goal is to use green innovation as a platform for 'getting ahead of the pack' and creating products or practices that set the agenda in future markets (Nidumolu *et al.* 2009). In this view, the difficulty of complying with stringent green regulations is a good thing since it forces a company to remodel itself in a way that will ultimately increase competitiveness. On other occasions, however, the impetus is imitation and conformism. If a company's direct competitors or other global corporate icons convert to a more sustainable approach – overtly and with great fanfare – it becomes harder for executives not to follow suit. The same applies when charismatic non-business leaders declare an interest in ecology, one example being the recurring references to smart grids, alternative energies and green jobs during the 2008 US presidential campaign. Indeed, in a survey taken just before the credit crunch erupted, the majority of executive interviewees were predicting that over the next five years, the environment would be the main socio-political issue for both politicians and the general public (Bonini *et al.* 2008). It will be interesting to find out the extent to which this prediction survived the subsequent recession.

> **?** How did the 2008 credit crunch affect CEO attitudes towards corporate greening?

Executives' sense for the environment can also vary from one sector to another. If fossil fuel prices were to rise sharply, for instance, oil-consuming sectors such as automobiles and utilities would probably experience falling cash flows and stock market valuations (Brinkman *et al.* 2008), whereas companies in less energy-intensive sectors might be less affected. It would therefore be logical if executives in the former professions were more aware of the ecological imperative than their counterparts in the latter. Similarly, a CEO's primary green focus is likely to reflect their company's specific exposure: water quality will be a key concern for beverage companies whereas large supermarkets might tend to be more interested in lighting or refrigeration. It is rational for CEOs to concentrate their company's firepower on 'low-hanging fruit', i.e. improvements that might be achieved with a minimum of pain (Hoffman 2007). However, cherry-picking the easiest green projects increases the temptation to pass on other ones that are even more important but harder to carry out (Schendler 2009). The move to sustainability will always be a challenge – if it were inexpensive and easy, more companies would have been done it by now.

Still, as the people responsible for corporate strategising, executives are ultimately the ones who will be held accountable for their companies' green commitment. To the extent that the ecological imperative seems increasingly destined to constrain the kind of scenario planning work that is usually top managers' prime mission, it would be logical if they were the first members of their organisation to internalise the green imperative. After all, executives are usually supposed to devote much of their energy to retro-planning for the future by ensuring that all organisational structures and business systems are aligned with the direction they wish their company to advance. In reality, however, they vary widely in terms of future focus. A key factor at this level is people's attitude towards remuneration – as exemplified by the way in which ex-BP CEO Tony Hayward shrank his company's renewables division after taking over because the new activity's typically lower profit rate (see Chapter 10) was dragging on the group's short-term share price. Clearly, some managers are only 'prepared to integrate the environment in their economic decisions as long as this causes no hardship' (Bust 2002). It should not be forgotten that many of the world's most famous chief executives have been on the record voicing decidedly anti-green opinions (see Chapter 1). Ongoing corporate support for the climate change denial industry, or more recent attempts to eviscerate Californian legislation aimed at dissuading exploitation of Canada's carbon-dirty tar sands, provide ample further evidence of this point.

> **?** Why do CEOs vary in terms of their willingness to go green?

... some managers are only 'prepared to integrate the environment in their economic decisions as long as this causes no hardship'.

Key issue

At the same time, the fact that a particular CEO may be less committed than another to corporate greening might also translate the former's basic conservatism – in the sense of being resistant to change – rather than their specific rejection of the ecological imperative. There is an argument that executives' worldview in this area is often shaped, at least in part, by the particular accounting protocols applied in their companies. Where green outlays are booked as extraordinary, one-off project costs, they will often be equated with charges that should be minimised; but if they are categorised as capital expenditures, it is easier to conceive of them as an integral part of a company's ongoing mission. Indeed, this latter attitude appears to have been the one adopted by the growing number of companies who decided during the 2009 recession not to downsize their environmental capabilities, choosing instead to embed green specialists throughout their different corporate functions (Greener World Media 2010). Of course, it is one thing for CEOs to recognise the need for change but quite another to give mid-level managers the green light to implement it (MGS 2008). Indeed, in companies suffering from executive inaction (or hypocrisy), green gestures can even be quite token and even illogical – like when Ford's CEO spent $2bn on redesigning his company's iconic Rouge factory yet continued to support the production of inefficient gas guzzlers (Werbach 2009). At a certain level, corporate environmental policies cannot help but reflect broader organisational cultures (Dash *et al.* 2009). After all, regardless of executives' personal worldview, it is at the frontline operative level that policies will succeed or fail.

■ Employee buy-in

In some companies, the impetus for greater environmentalism actually starts with operatives and mid-level managers, who will then seek senior management's support to institutionalise the desired change. The question here is the level of pressure that staff members can bring to bear when, for whatever reason, their bosses manifest little interest in the environment (Blackburn 2008). The author recalls an episode in the early 1990s when, sharing a lift with a company executive, he excitedly laid out plans for setting up an office-wide paper recycling scheme, only to be chastised for not devoting his energy concentrating on 'what makes money'. Similarly, it often occurs that an employee aware of a problem requiring a simple environmental fix will communicate the problem and receive a vague promise that something will be done without managers issuing any firm instructions to make repairs. Even worse is when the employee tries to follow up on this inaction and is criticised as an irritant.

In cases such as these, employees can become disheartened and lose their sense of purpose. This can have serious consequences for a company, with a number of studies revealing a correlation between staff members' sense of loyalty and the employer's ethical (including environmental) profile. Conversely, disappointed employees may decide to fight against the ambient apathy by designing a bottom-up reorganisation of working practices without seeking prior managerial approval. Such initiatives will usually be limited by budgetary constraints and participants' lack of authority, with the employee activists usually compelled to re-engage at some level with their bosses. This second interaction might become more confrontational, however, with employees potentially having to seek help from a labour organisation – one example being the Green Workplaces Committee that the UK's Trades Union Congress has set up to help members. There are also instances of green employees complaining to shareholders – and in the worst-case scenario, organising strikes – to denounce a company's environmental inertia. In this latter scenario, the activist is at risk of being fired, although some protection is afforded nowadays in countries characterised by strong labour laws or if the dispute is construed as a health and safety matter.

> **?** How far are frustrated employees likely to go in response to employers' environmental inaction?

Key issue

... employees may decide to fight against the ambient apathy by designing a bottom-up reorganisation of working practices without seeking prior managerial approval.

5

Conflict of this kind is, of course, sub-optimal from everyone's point of view. There is a growing corpus outlining how staff members might convince management to focus more on greening strategies (see Box 5.1). The only real pitfall at this level is, once again, the risk that the company will be satisfied with one or two small measures such as a few extra recycling bins, paper-free processes, or automatic computer or lighting shutdown systems. These are all useful improvements but the fact that they help staff and management feel good about themselves may actually be counter-productive if this lessens people's hunger to engage in the deeper (and more expensive) actions that lead to a significant drop in a company's footprint: **retrofitting**; or carbon emission systems capable of achieving the massive reduction targets that some companies are hoping to achieve within a few short decades. Cheerleading in the wake of small changes may solidify cooperation between staff and management but it can also be an instrument that people use to wilfully blind themselves to the inadequacies of their own efforts.

■ **Retrofitting:** Adding new technological features to old platforms. Often refers to modernisation of building stock.

There are also occasions when the executive will set the tone but struggle to get operatives and mid-level managers to buy into the greening process. This kind of problem can arise because of employees' reluctance to change their working habits; a general disinterest in sustainability; or the sense that more environmentally-friendly procedures will make their working lives harder (i.e. if they are forced to use green chemicals that are weaker than the equivalent synthetic compounds; if energy-saving sprinklers produce lower water pressure, etc.).   In this case, the key to is to find some way of engaging staff members, which can often involve the tried and tested psychological ploy of offering people information and giving them responsibility for driving change so that they feel that they have a personal stake in it. One example is that way that Walmart employees have had since 2007 a system of 'Personal Sustainability Projects' encouraging them to determine environmental and health-related objectives and to disseminate knowledge in this field, not only at work but also in their private lives. Another is the award-winning energy consumption management programme that US retailer JC Penney has implemented, one aspect of which is the launch of an 'Energy Captain' portal intended to both inform employees and help them to exchange best practices. Indeed, frontline operatives are often the people with the most direct exposure to a company's resource use or pollution behaviour. As such, they will sometimes possess even greater understanding in these areas than senior managers. Even so, many might lack (or be disinclined to seek) knowledge on greener alternatives to the status quo. Thus, above and beyond the need to hone staff members' skill levels and accustom them to more environmentally attuned working processes, an in-depth green transition means finding a 'shared mental model' (Friend 2009). This can materialise, for instance, in employee forums focusing less on regulatory compliance issues and more on raising overall awareness. Of course, the problem with an approach of this kind – as with all change management – is that some people will find it patronising.

Insofar as green innovations can come from anywhere and anyone – and given the benefits of making staff members feel that they are part of the corporate governance process (Doppelt 2009) – some organisations set up cross-departmental task forces specifically charged with building sustainability into everybody's job description. Others will lodge sustainability subsections in each corporate division or else create a division dedicated to this goal (see Figure 5.1), one which may or may not be given cross-departmental oversight. The one constant is that organisational greening is never a linear, one-dimensional progression. Instead, it should be analysed as an uneven process requiring the involvement of different stakeholders, with each bringing their own perceptions and behaviours to the table (Rivera-Camino 2007).

Managers seeking to implement an in-depth green transition will necessarily be thinking in systemic terms instead of bolting sustainability on to existing structure. And yet, this latter approach can often seem more attractive. It certainly causes less uproar.

? Where should a company's green activities be lodged within its structures?

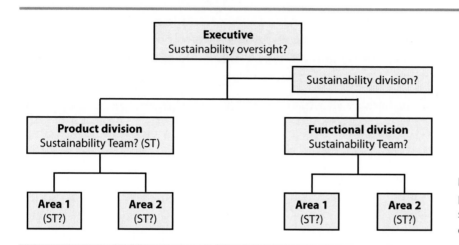

Figure 5.1: Different possibilities for lodging sustainability in a corporate structure

Interspersed sustainability teams will tend to work better in corporate cultures where adapted local strategies are considered desirable (see Chapter 8). Similarly, where an organisational culture is not conducive to top-down initiatives – for instance, in large firms where employees may feel more alienated from distant senior managers – extra incentives may be necessary before executive-driven greening strategies filter through. This usually means bringing Human Resource managers into the equation, to structure employees' sustainability training, model appropriate behaviour, track implementation and organise rewards (Hitchcock and Willard 2009). Some rewards will be pecuniary, with bonuses offered based on personal environmental performance. Examples include Sweden's Scandic Hotels, where employees are paid for reducing water consumption or generating less waste; US aluminium giant Alcoa, where some manufacturing units' compensation is linked with their success in lowering perfluorocarbon emissions; and Browning Ferris Industries, where one-third of some employees' remuneration is determined on an 'at-risk' basis reflecting how well they satisfy the company's landfill and solid and medical waste reduction goals (Greener World Media 2010). Even so, there is a growing trend is for companies to offer staff non-financial rewards, conceivably because less venal transactions are considered more coherent with an environmental ethos. Examples here include alterations to employees' work/life balance (flexitime arrangements involving fewer but longer days at the office); public transportation subsidies; employee-organised carpools or cycling initiatives; and above all, telecommuting ('home-working'). This latter solution is particularly prevalent in companies capable of providing staff with all the remote IT connections that they need in stay in touch from home. One example is Cisco, where the average employee telecommutes 2 days a week. This means fewer people go to the office at any one time, enabling the company to downsize its premises. On a more macro level, less commuting also means that a community emits lower total greenhouse gas emissions. On a micro-corporate level, some analysts (c.f. http://undress4success.com/) have even claimed that telecommuting can produce annual savings of up to $10,000 per employee.

Of course, ascertaining the extent of an employee's progress in helping the company to achieve its goals would be impossible in the absence of systems enabling comparative measurements. The maxim apocryphally attributed to management consultant Peter Drucker is very apropos at this point – namely that something can only be managed if it can be measured. This applies as much to corporate greening as to any other strategy implementation process.

■ Controls and measurements

The demarcation between internal metrics used for performance benchmarking purposes and external reporting attesting to company achievements can be somewhat artificial. Indicators devised internally can often be publicised externally. Conversely, many corporate auditing metrics were modelled after external guidelines, which might involve sectoral initiatives, national legislations or international codes of governance. In general, managers will want to concentrate on those environmental indicators that are most relevant to the specific fields where their company operates. Information overload is as much of a problem in Ecology and Management as it is in other disciplines, and despite understandable calls for maximum transparency to reduce 'greenwashing' (see Chapter 7) and communicate companies' real performance, the best audits tend to scrutinise a narrowly defined area in great depth instead of treating a wider range of data more superficially.

> **?** What resources should managers devote to gathering and measuring environmental data?

... managers will want to concentrate on those environmental indicators that are most relevant to the specific fields where their company operates.

■ Internal metrics

An initial problem that companies face in measuring their environmental performance is the absence of standardised international models (Kallio 2008). In some countries, government agencies can provide useful materials – two examples being the toolkits disseminated by the UK Climate Impacts Programme (www.ukcip.org.uk/) and the guidelines issued by Japan's Ministry of the Environment (http://www.env.go.jp/), as well as the Design for Environment protocol that the US Environmental Protection Agency (www.epa.gov/dfe/) has developed to induce the use of 'environmentally preferable chemistry' (see *Chapter 5 online case study*). Other useful protocols have been formulated by business associations such as the Greenhouse Gas Protocol Initiative (http://www.ghgprotocol.org/) – itself a partnership between the World Resources Institute and, crucially, the World Business Council for Sustainable Development (www.wbcsd.org/), a high profile 'CEO-led global association [providing] a platform for companies to explore sustainable development, share knowledge, experiences and best practices, and to advocate business positions on these issues in a variety of forums, working with governments, non-governmental and intergovernmental organizations'. Alongside of this, companies seeking to qualify for leading reporting groups such as the International Organization for Standardization (ISO) or the Global Reporting Initiative (GRI) can get input from these bodies about the green audits that they must undertake before and after joining. An example is the distinction found in ISO guideline 14031 between performance indicators monitoring operational or management actions and condition indicators measuring the status of an external environment. Lastly, many private consultancy firms such as Price Waterhouse Coopers (http://www.ukmediacentre.pwc.com) or Brown and Wilmans (www.bw-environmental.com/) sell toolkits to customers, similar to those from non-profit organisations such as the Institute of Environmental Management and Assessment (www.iema.net/) in areas such as 'effective data management', 'best practice in environmental auditing', 'environmental impact assessment', 'strategic environmental assessment'. The advice promulgated during such sessions (and in the growing number of guides written by environmental sustainability authors) usually revolves around ideal-type systems where companies 'track both relative and absolute metrics, capture data at multiple levels [and] collect the same information for the whole value chain' (Esty and Winston 2006). Managers interested in developing an understanding of environmental accounting principles will have no problem finding relevant sources nowadays.

The problem is subsuming these general recommendations into the kind of specific environmental management system (EMS) that more and more companies are looking to develop nowadays. Firstly, there can be problems accessing information (i.e. ascertaining the quantity of **embedded inputs** used to manufacture a particular good); allocating responsibilities (i.e. judging how much energy should be attributed to one sub-activity rather than another, related one) or mobilising scientific knowledge (i.e. deciding whether an impact study should inventory a company's stock of chemicals by their toxicity, sell-by date or substitution possibilities). A lack of operational knowledge can also be aggravated by the tendency within some companies to allocate insufficient human resources to measurement missions and rely excessively on external documentation rather than self-directed field interviews (Blackburn 2008).

Embedded inputs: ■
Total amount of energy or water consumed during the entire production process leading to the materialisation of a final product.

In addition, it also saves companies time and money if they concentrate on measuring their most significant environmental actions instead of the ostensibly less important ones. By definition, however, amalgamations of this kind introduce a bias into the calculations. A similar lack of precision can arise when managers are facing contingent environmental risks whose costs can only be assessed using relatively subjective parameters (Epstein 2008). Much work still needs to be done to merge traditional monetary accounting practices and more qualitative environmental audits.

Thirdly, grouping different corporate departments into a single environmental **balanced scorecard** may enhance summative analysis but this is no mean feat. A company's central goal of minimising environmental impacts might mean that some divisions will focus on manufacturing efficiency (machinery, load management), others on products (design features or lifecycle performance), others on packaging (materials, recycling) and others still on company-wide resource utilisation (energy, lighting, water) or pollution (liquid effluents,

Balanced scorecard: ■
Strategy tool used to measure performance based on a range of financial and non-financial parameters.

greenhouse gases). Amalgamating such disparate 'eco-audits' runs the risk of double accounting or, conversely, informational assumptions.

Despite these hurdles, many companies have made enormous progress in recent years towards the development of truly useful environmental metrics systems. Generally, such efforts have involved spending a great deal of time and money gathering baseline data and making a lifecycle assessment of the environmental footprint of the facilities, equipment and processes for each major use-type (Friend 2009). Note that auditing procedures of this kind are only feasible if the vast majority of employees commit to them, helping to design data collection systems, signify benchmarks, compare performance indicators – and above all, rethink and openly discuss the things they do that contribute to their environmental footprint (and why they do them). Yet staff members may not always be very motivated to help develop the new metrics system – with some viewing the work as unpaid overtime. Even worse, some employees may try to sabotage the process because of fears that tighter environmental accounting will make it harder for them to perform their jobs. Of course, it helps if everyone throughout the organisation receives psychological or material incentives to devise the environmental metrics. That way, frontline operatives are less likely to construe greening as a sneaky method found by executives to complicate work routines.

... it helps if everyone throughout the organisation receives psychological or material incentives to devise these environmental metrics.

Key issue

Despite the impossibility of generalising environmental metrics across different industries (and indeed within entire sectors), it is worth noting some of the more accomplished corporate efforts in this area. A leading example is the kind of **triple bottom line** reporting that French companies of a certain size have had to publish on an annual basis ever since France enacted its Nouvelles Régulations Economiques legislation in 2001. Box 5.2 shows the environmental data that the RATP Paris Transport Authority shares with counterparts when bidding on international contracts. By ascertaining different departments' environmental progress on a year-to-year basis and reproducing this information in a digestible form, RATP is able to use its metrics for both internal feedback and external communications purposes.

■ **Triple bottom line:** Idea that firms should report not only financial but also social and environmental outcomes; formulated by John Elkington in 1994.

Box 5.2:
Environmental indicators used by RATP Paris Transport Authority

- Air quality: average emissions, broken down by category
- Breakdown of bus fleet by fuel source (inc. clean energy)
- Noise pollution: complaints, actions taken
- Water usage: total consumption, industrial wastewater, disposal
- Physical waste: number of collection/sorting sites, types of waste, ultimate disposal
- Energy: total usage of electricity, fossil fuels, renewable sources
- Environmental innovation: research investments
- ISO 14001 certification: number of sites and employees involved in the process

A similar system is the 'Greenlist' sheet that US household brands company SC Johnson (www.scjohnson.com/) developed in 2001 to classify ingredients according to their environmental impact. All of the items that the company sells are subject to a stringent selection process aimed at reducing toxic materials. Products are given a rating reflecting their potential toxicity, with an explicit undertaking by SC Johnson to continuous improvement over time. The public is also able to hold the company to account, since product scores are posted openly. Note that this transparency is crucial to the process. Greenlist has been patented and is regularly reviewed by external scientific organisations. It has also won a number of awards. By gaining public approval, SC Johnson is seeking to bolster its green claims. It bears repeating that general cynicism constitutes yet another obstacle on the path towards corporate sustainability.

? How much credibility does a company gain by publicising its internal environmental metrics?

■ External reporting

As aforementioned, many companies' goal when implementing an environmental management system is not just to guide internal performance or monitor regulatory compliance but also (and possibly, above all) to demonstrate progress and accountability to outside stakeholders. The latter will often be comprised of consumers worried that a company's green claims are not substantiated. On other occasions, the interested stakeholders will be investors seeking to identify the environmental aspects of a company's business model, both to judge its growth prospects and determine potential risks or liabilities. External reporting also reassures regulatory agencies and can therefore stave off more stringent controls, especially in countries where environmental **disclosure** is not compulsory. Lastly, a number of NGOs who monitor

Disclosure: ■
Provision of information. Often comes in a specified form complying with legal requirements.

companies' ethical profile but lack the resources to gather reliable data themselves will count on specialist bodies to provide what they hope are objective appraisals.

Companies in turn are very aware that their reputational capital depends on the image that these and other stakeholders have of them. Where the two sides meet is in the agencies whose mission is to publicise objective third-party appraisals of members. Such agencies constitute a patchwork of bodies defined by geographic, sectoral or ethical principles. One way of categorising them is by distinguishing between reporting groups that mainly focus on processes versus eco-labelling organisations that are more geared towards product certification.

Environmental reporting groups

Joining a body of this kind is not without risks, if only because once this has happened, it is crucial that the company remain a member in good standing to avoid uncomfortable questions being asked why its standards have slipped. Moreover, companies trumpeting their environmental achievements always lay themselves open to criticism as to why they are not doing more. This, along with the costs and burdens associated with data compilation, explains why many small and medium-sized enterprises still only generate formal environmental reports when they feel that they absolutely have to (Gueben and Skerratt 2007). Moreover, the proliferation of reporting groups, with each guaranteeing different aspects of companies' environmental promise, can create confusion and undermine the value of membership – especially given fears that some companies only qualify because they hide crucial data about the environmental damage they cause (Porter and Kramer 2006) It therefore behoves companies to join reporting groups that themselves have impeccable credentials. In a sense, what they are trying to do is to bask in someone else's reflected glory.

... the proliferation of reporting groups, with each guaranteeing different aspects of companies' environmental promise, can create confusion and undermine the value of membership ...

Key issue

Different approaches have been taken to environmental reporting, depending on the needs and priorities of the parties involved (see Table 5.1). Companies will usually be asked to produce an organisational mission statement delineating objectives and previous performance (expressed in quantitative but also qualitative terms indicating compliance actions). Such reports will usually contain references to the company's measurement methodology. Lastly, it is also customary nowadays to vouch for the company's track record with affidavits signed by environmental ratings agencies such as ArEsE or BMJ in France, ERM in the UK or Innovest in the USA. Financial investors seeking to verify the sustainability credentials of a company in which they may be interested are particularly interested in the more technical output provided by agencies of this kind, or by the UK-based environmental research firm Trucost.

Table 5.1: Different focuses in environmental reporting (ACCA 2001)

Reporting methodology	Description (examples)
Compliance-based reporting	Prevalent in heavily regulated sectors like public utilities Example: Anglian Water (UK)
Toxic release inventory-based reporting	Mandated by law in certain countries Examples: IBM, Texaco, Monsanto (USA)
Eco-balance reporting	Detailed account of resource input/outputs Examples: Kunert (Germany), Ricoh (Japan)
Performance-based reporting	Improvement targets set for crucial areas Examples: BA, BT (UK), Novo Nordisk (Denmark)
Product-focused reporting	Declaration evaluating models' lifecycle effects Example: Volvo (Sweden)
Environmental and social reporting	Broaden scope to include social aspects Examples: Ben & Jerry's (USA), BP (UK)
Sustainability reporting	Triple bottom line including economic factors Examples: Shell (UK), Procter & Gamble (USA)

The world's largest voluntary reporting network is the UN Global Compact, which in January 2010 counted 5300 business participants from more than 135 countries. Companies sign up to the Compact to confirm their support for its basic principles, which include, alongside environmentalism, human rights, labour standards and corruption. The environment section features three central ideas, namely that members should support a precautionary approach to environmental challenges; actively promote greater environmental responsibility; and encourage the development and diffusion of environmentally-friendly technologies. The Compact can delist companies that fail to communicate progress on how they will achieve its goals. All the same, its enforcement capabilities remain relatively weak.

The world's three leading environmental reporting groups are the GRI Global Reporting Initiative (www.globalreporting.org/), the ISO

International Organization for Standardization (www.iso.org/) and the European Union's EMAS Eco-Management and Audit Scheme (http://ec.europa.eu/environment/emas/). The GRI is a large, 'multi-stakeholder network' of experts promoting triple bottom line disclosure within a 'Sustainability Reporting Framework'. The purpose is to give the public a full and transparent vision of the actions of its more than 1000 members (companies but also state agencies and NGOs). The ISO 14001 series 'offers a wide-ranging portfolio of standardized sampling, testing and analytical methods to deal with specific environmental challenges [such] as the quality of air, water and soil'. It is a highly reputed agency that certifies corporate processes from several other perspectives as well, including labour standards and general organisational governance. As for EMAS, this is a more regional body that registers companies once they 'conduct an environmental review … establish an effective environmental management system … carry out an environmental audit [and] provide a statement of environmental performance'.

A host of climate-change-specific reporting groups have also cropped up in recent years, reflecting the growing priority given to this particular issue. One example is investment bank Goldman Sachs's recent launch of the GS Sustain investment research firm, whose speciality is to analyse companies' future financial prospects in light of climate change factors. Another is the CDP Carbon Disclosure Project (www.cdproject.net/), a UK-based 'independent not-for-profit organization holding the largest database of primary corporate climate change information in the world'. The question mark hanging over bodies of this kind, however, is not only how many companies are willing to divulge data but the quality of the information provided. For instance, whereas 84 per cent of US companies listed among the FTSE Global 500 responded to the 2009 CDP survey, their average disclosure scores were quite mediocre (Greener World Media 2010). Indeed, representatives of an online database specialising in CR reports, CorporateRegister.com, have expressed concerns about US companies' reluctance to publish heretofore unreleased non-financial information or allow third party verifications. In green business as in other areas, statistics can be easily manipulated.

> **?** How reliable is the environmental information that companies provide to reporting groups?

Lastly, many branches of activity have set up schemes translating participants' adherence to behavioural principles instead of requiring them to report statistical performance per se. Examples include the BSR Clean Cargo group (specialised in sustainable logistics); the International Council of Toy Industries; the International Code of

Conduct on the Distribution and Use of Pesticides; and the Chlorine-Free Products Association. Similarly, the need to share knowledge about best practices has led to the creation of a wide array of sustainability associations, ranging from open bodies like the Green Business Network (providing assistance to SMEs in the USA) to more ad hoc entities that members join to develop or pool their knowledge in this area (see *Web Resource 5.2* for more on 'green business coalitions').

Eco-labelling

Studies have indicated that consumers find unsubstantiated environmental claims to be less credible than ones made by certifiably green brands (Phau and Ong 2007). Not only is it easy nowadays for consumers to access independent information about products, but given the extra sums that people have to pay for many green goods, it is often worth it for them to seek such information (D'Souza *et al.* 2007). Some potential customers trace endorsements by only consulting those non-profit organisations that they trust the most (NMI 2009). This has given birth to an entire industry in environmental certification (see Table 5.2), with some of the leading names in this field – like Energy Star or the Rainforest Alliance – clearly starting to influence consumer behaviour (see Chapter 7). Eco-labelling organisations 'protect consumers and sincere producers by undermining bogus claims and communicating credentials' (Friend 2009). By so doing, they stabilise the market for green goods.

Table 5.2: February 2010 www.ecolabelling.org list of certification categories

Category	Nr. of labelling bodies	Leaders
Buildings	64	LEED Green Building Rating System (USA)
Carbon	15	Carbon Trust Standard (UK)
Electronics	40	Energy Star (Canada/USA), EPEAT (USA)
Energy	31	Energy Label (EU)
Food	90	Demeter (global)
Forest products	36	Rainforest Alliance (USA)
Retail goods	74	Blue Angel (Germany)
Textiles	40	EcoLogo (Canada)
Tourism	28	Blue Flag (Denmark)
Misc. (marine, farms, factories)	79	Marine Stewardship Council (UK) Green Seal (USA) Soil Association (UK) Nordic Ecolabel 'Swan' (Scandinavia)

Normally, eco-labelling organisations focus on environmental metrics similar to the ones discussed above. The kinds of factors that they might highlight include the extent to which a product is made of recycled goods (or can be recycled itself); the care taken during its production to reduce energy, water or material use and to generate less pollution; its climate change impact, etc. ISO tends to differentiate between labels that simply put a stamp of approval on a product; ones that validate claimed attributes; and ones that confirm quality. Some third-party labels apply to specific companies or products, while others cover entire industries or product lifecycles – one example being the 'Chain of Custody' tracking mechanism that the Germany-based FSC Forest Stewardship Council (www.fsc.org/) has devised.

One of the problems with labelling is its potential for misuse. The FSC, for instance, relaxed its standards in the late 1990s and let members use the logo even if only 50 per cent of their paper pulp came from sustainable forests (as long as the words 'Mixed Sources' were added to their labels). Within a few short years, it became clear that companies such as Singapore's Asia Pulp & Paper, already criticised for its actions in the Indonesian rainforest, still qualified for the FSC logo (Wright and Carlton 2007). Instead of preventing misrepresentation, eco-labelling can, in the worst-case scenario, facilitate it.

? In the absence of an international standard, how reliable are eco-labels?

5

Another weakness relates to goods whose production is fragmented across a widely dispersed international value chain (see Chapter 8). It is not at all evident that the chain's prime contractor – the one interfacing with end users or else the eco-labelling organisation working on its behalf – possesses sufficient information on upstream suppliers' sustainability practices to guarantee the label's accuracy. This too undermines the credibility of the labelling process.

Lastly, it is worth noting that eco-labelling is a fixed cost that can be proportionately more expensive for SMEs having to amortise it over smaller volumes. This has led to the rise of a number of smaller labelling bodies such as Certified Naturally Grown, which specialises in produce from small North American farms, or Ecocert in France. It also explains why some companies are trying to convince the general public that their internal metrics are as valid as any external certifications. One example is US apparel maker Timberland, whose highly transparent 'nutritional label' – called the 'Green Index' – provides full information on its shoe products' environmental aspects. Similarly, in 2009, the giant beverage company SAB Miller, working in partnership with the World Wildlife Fund, published reports about the water footprint of its entire value chain in South Africa and the Czech Republic. In August of that same year, Tesco became the first British retailer to display the full carbon footprint for many of its own-label brands. Like SC Johnson does with its Greenlist metrics, these companies can hope to reduce the cost of environmental transparency by finding dual uses for information originally developed for a single purpose. By so doing, they cut the cost of going green and make the whole process seem less daunting.

■ Obstacles and pathways

1 Employees may feel alienated from top-down sustainability drives.

Apply change management techniques and give them a stake in the process.

2 Companies may go for 'low-hanging fruit' but shirk harder challenges.

Classify green targets by difficulty or timeframes and publicise rankings.

3 Amalgamating each division's environmental data can be daunting.

Create a data compilation body with cross-departmental competencies.

4 There is no global standard in environmental reporting.

If it is not too expensive, accumulate a diverse range of certifications.

Case study: Lenovo and its Greenpeace rankings

China's manufacturing boom over the past 20 years has been a mixed blessing for the country. On one hand, the standard of living has risen for tens of millions of citizens and Chinese companies are starting to feature towards the top of the Fortune Global 500 list of the world's largest multinationals. At the same time, the country's environment has suffered greatly as a result of its growth spurt. This can be explained by the energy-intensive nature of many industries whose global centre of activity has moved to China; the country's reliance on dirty coal as a prime electricity generation source; the relatively lesser diffusion of anti-pollution technology among Chinese firms; and a regulatory framework that places less stringent environmental demands on firms than is the case elsewhere – in part because continued poverty in the country means that policymakers focus more on economic development than sustainability.

Hence the general delight in March 2007 when Chinese computer maker Lenovo came top of a list compiled by the international NGO Greenpeace ranking the world's most environmentally-friendly electronics companies (Thurrott 2007). The rapid growth of computing since the 1980s has been a good thing for the environment in some respects, mainly because of the increased opportunities for virtual and/or remote transactions that consume less energy than traditional 'bricks and mortars' activities have done. This trend has severely burdened the environment in other ways, however: computer manufacturing consumes resources and generates pollution; information and communications technology requires enormous quantities of additional electricity; and the disposal of old equipment has created mountains of 'e-waste' (see Chapter 6). Trying to influence the behaviour of companies in this sector, Greenpeace published in August 2006 a 'Guide to Greener Electronics' ranking 'leading mobile and PC manufacturers on their global policies and practice eliminating harmful chemicals and on taking responsibility for their products once they are discarded by customers'. Because data mining is so expensive, the NGO did not conduct its own audits to support the new rankings but chose instead to recycle publicly available information, sometimes after seeking clarifications from the companies involved. In other words, the guide's value does not derive from the revelation of new data but instead from the imaginative way that it packages existing information (allocating composite scores to all companies based on particular weighted criteria) and also from the NGO's own credibility and fame.

For Lenovo to come top of the third rankings that Greenpeace published was a significant achievement, especially given the huge volumes of materials that the company had been processing ever since its acquisition of IBM's Personal Computing Department in 2005. Cognizant of the fact that its target markets outside China are more sensitive to the ecological imperative than its earlier customers back home had been, Lenovo began very conscientiously to flesh out its green profile. This included participating in the Hong Kong Rechargeable Battery Recycling Programme and establishing a Lenovo Asset Recovery Services (ARS) division to help customers 'manage their end-of-life technology equipment by providing computer take-back, data destruction, refurbishment and recycling' (c.f. lenovo.co.uk/news). The company's green reputation seemed secure, despite some criticism of the toxic substances that its manufacturing process uses. Lenovo's subsequent announcement that it would work to eliminate these substances within a few short years was supposed to consolidate its good Greenpeace score. The future seemed bright for Lenovo's new brand image as an environmental champion.

Just a few years later, things looked very different. Lenovo plummeted to 16th place in the December 2009 Greenpeace rankings, having been assessed a penalty point for 'backtracking on its commitment to eliminate PVC and brominated flame retardants (BFRs) in all its products by the end of 2009', a goal that it now hoped to achieve by 2012. The company continued to receive plaudits for its voluntary take-back programme and the good information that customers are given in the countries where this activity runs. It was also lauded for its use of recycled plastic. On the other hand, Lenovo fell short in terms of planning for greater renewable energy use or disclosing information about the modalities determining new models' compliance with Energy Star efficiency standards – and, more broadly, for its overall carbon footprint.

Having created expectations that it would become a green champion in the global electronics sector, Lenovo has discovered that initial success is a double-edged sword. As time passes, environmental standards tend to become increasingly demanding, and with competitors constantly fighting to improve their own rankings, companies cannot live on their laurels. Like most areas of international business, a green reputation is a battle that can never be won.

Table 5.3: Comparison of Greenpeace 'Guide to Greener Electronics' rankings

December 2009 ranking	Score	March 2007 ranking	Score
1. Nokia	7.3	1. Lenovo	8.0
2. Sony Ericsson	6.9	2. Nokia	7.3
3. Toshiba/Philips	5.3	3. Sony Ericsson/Dell	7.0
5. Sony/LG Electronics/ Apple/ Motorola/Samsung	5.1	5. Samsung/Motorola	6.3
10. Panasonic	4.9	6. Fujitsu-Siemens	6.0
11. HP	4.7	7. HP	5.6
12. Acer/Sharp	4.5	8. Acer	5.3
14. Dell	3.9	9. Toshiba	4.3
15. Fujitsu	3.5	10 Sony	4.0
16. Lenovo	2.5	11. LGE/Panasonic	3.6

Case study questions

1   Why has there generally been so much concern about the commitment of many young Chinese companies to sustainability?

2   What are the origins of Lenovo's environment commitment?

3   Who enforces Lenovo's ethical behaviour?

■ References

ACCA (Association of Chartered Certified Accountants) (2001), 'What is environmental reporting?', available at http://www.accaglobal.com/, accessed 15 February 2010.

Blackburn, W. (2008), *The Sustainability Handbook: The Complete Management Guide to Achieving Social, Economic and Environmental Responsibility*, London: Earthscan.

Bonini, S., Hintez, G. and Mendonca, L. (2008), 'Addressing consumer concerns about climate change', March, available at www.mckinseyquarterly.com, accessed on 4 February 2010.

Brinkman, M., Hoffman, N., and Oppenheim, J. (2008), 'How climate change could affect corporate valuations', October, www.mckinseyquarterly.com, accessed 2 February 2009.

Bust, T. (2002), 'Ford takes revamp back to its roots', *Financial Times*, 4 February.

Carroll, A. (1979), 'A three-dimensional conceptual model of corporate social performance', *Academy of Management Review*, **4** (1).

Dash, S., Bhal, K. and Udgat, J. (2009), 'Organisational culture and environmental responsibility: a study of textile industry in India', *International Journal of Indian Culture and Business Management*, **2** (3).

Doppelt, B. (2009), *Leading Change Toward Sustainability: A Change-Management Guide for Business, Government and Civil Society*, 2nd edn, Sheffield: Greenleaf Publishing.

D'Souza, Taghian, C., Lamb, P. and Peretiatko, R. (2007), 'Green decisions: demographics and consumer understanding of environmental labels', *International Journal of Consumer Studies*, **31** (4).

Epstein, M. (2008), *Making Sustainability Work: Best Practices in Managing and Measuring Corporate Social, Environmental and Economic Impacts*, Sheffield: Greenleaf Publishing.

Esty, D. and Winston, D. (2006), *Green to Gold: How Smart Companies Use Environmental Strategy to Innovate, Create Value, and Build a Competitive Advantage*, New Haven, CT: Yale University Press.

Friend, G. (2009), *The Truth About Green Business*, Upper Saddle River, NJ: FT Press.

Gueben, C. and Skerratt, R. (2007), 'SMEs and environmental communications: motivations and barriers to environmental reporting', *International Journal of Environment and Sustainable Development*, **6** (1).

Hirschland, M., Oppenheim, J. and Webb, A. (2008), 'Using energy more efficiently: An interview with the Rocky Mountain Institute's Amory Lovins', July, available at www.mckinseyquarterly.com, accessed 26 December 2009.

Hitchcock, D. and Willard, M. (2009), *The Business Guide to Sustainability: Practical Strategies and Tools for Organizations*, 2nd edn, London: Earthscan.

Hoffman, A. (2007), *Carbon Strategies: How Leading Companies Are Reducing Their Climate Change Footprint*, Ann Arbor: University of Michigan Press.

Kallio, T. (2008), 'The Janus face of sustainable foreign direct investments', *Progress in Industrial Ecology, An International Journal*, **5** (3).

Laszlo, C. (2008), *Sustainable Value: How the World's Leading Companies Are Doing Well By Doing Good*, Stanford, CA: Greenleaf Publishing.

MGS (Mckinsey Global Survey) (2008), 'How companies think about climate change', February, available at www.mckinseyquarterly.com, accessed 3 February 2010.

5

Nidumolu, R., Prahalad, C.K. and Rangaswami, M.R. (2009), 'Why sustainability is now the key driver of innovation', *Harvard Business Review*, available at www.hbr.org.

NMI (National Marketing Institute) (2009), 'LOHAS consumers want proof and third-party verification', 5 May, available in www.environmentalleader.com/, accessed 9 May 2009.

Phau, I. and Ong, D. (2007), 'An investigation of the effects of environmental claims in promotional messages for clothing brands', *Marketing Intelligence & Planning*, **25** (7).

Porter, M. and Kramer, M. (2006), 'Strategy and society: the link between competitive advantage and corporate social responsibility', *Harvard Business Review*, available at www.hbr.org.

Rivera-Camino, J. (2007), 'Re-evaluating green marketing strategy: a stakeholder perspective', *European Journal of Marketing*, **41** (11–12).

Schendler, A. (2009), *Getting Green Done: Hard Truths from the Front Lines of the Sustainability Revolution*, New York: Public Affairs.

Thornton, D., Kagan, R. and Gunningham, N. (2009), 'When social norms and pressures are not enough: environmental performance in the trucking industry', *Law & Society Review*, **43** (2).

Thurrott, P. (2007), 'Lenovo tops in environmental friendliness', available at www.windowsitpro.com/, accessed 10 October 2008.

Werbach, A. (2009), *Strategy for Sustainability: A Business Manifesto*, Boston, MA: Harvard Business Press.

Wright, T. and Carlton, J. (2007), 'Why green logo may mean little', *Wall Street Journal-Europe*, 30 October.

6 Green Operations

Learning objectives

After reading this chapter, you will understand how to:

- Modify corporate operational processes using green engineering principles
- Reduce the data function's environmental footprint
- Redesign manufacturing schemes to produce fewer 'non-product' externalities
- Cut waste during products' post-industrial handling

■ Introduction

Some observers feel that the production side is where companies are most likely to achieve the most progress in terms of environmental sustainability (Vogel 2005). This is because operations-related greening efforts have the dual benefit of not only optimising internal processes but also positioning companies in the market for **clean technology** (see Chapter 10). Implementing green operations is easier said than done, however. At the practical level alone, there are already a number of obstacles to overcome, ranging from the high cost of rebuilding a firm's industrial apparatus to many front-line operatives' reluctance to engage in some of the gruelling and even unhealthy tasks associated with green operations (Schendler 2009). Other hurdles are more conceptual in nature, first and foremost being the ecological inertia affecting people who do not react well to change and are therefore incapable of internalising green operations' holistic principles. Indeed, many sustainability writers evoke the need for a new mental model focused on reducing the flow of physical goods throughout the whole of the industrial economy, with upstream professionals' role no longer revolving around material performance per se but seeking instead to create functionalities that will help customers to achieve their ultimate goals. This subtle shift would have vast consequences: appliance makers might provide refrigeration instead of refrigerators; utilities heat and lighting instead of electricity. Essentially, the shift would entail piloting corporate production functions as if they were service activities fostering the kind of lessor–lessee relationship to which customers are already accustomed, for instance when they fly on an airplane or stay in a hotel (Richards and Frosch 1997). Of course, this kind of service mindset will be very foreign to many manufacturing specialists.

It may soon become more widespread, however, given growing evidence of the responsibility that traditionally 'brutal' production processes bear for the frightful ecological challenges facing Planet Earth today. The manufacturing function stands accused, ever since the Industrial Revolution, of participating in a 'commoditisation of nature', with industrialists imposing harsh and unadapted synthetic processes on a vulnerable ecosphere instead of working within the boundaries of sustainability (Braungart and McDonough 2009). Thus, the obsolescence built into many products – or the wastefulness of chemical and engineering practices where an estimated 90 to 95 per cent of all material inputs are consumed and rejected during the

Clean technology: ■
Set of industrial principles where energy or power are generated in an environmentally friendly manner.

? How amenable are industrial engineers to operational greening?

production process without figuring in the final product – constitute clearly unsustainable ways of organising industry. Notwithstanding the strength of old habits, there is a broad consensus today in favour of the mass greening of companies' physical activities.

The manufacturing function stands accused, ever since the Industrial Revolution, of participating in a 'commoditisation of nature'.

Key issue

Hence the growing relevance of key green constructs such as life-cycle assessment, recyclability, total environmental impact – and where possible, zero waste. A good example of a company that has almost achieved this ambitious goal is pioneer modular carpet manufacturer Interface, for whom less than 1 per cent of the 400 million pounds of raw materials purchased in 2009 ended up in landfill (Greenbiz 2010b). Of course, such recycling targets will suit some products – goods that have longer lives such as carpets or houses; require frequent upgrades such as software or appliances; or are harder to dispose of such as chemicals or minerals – more than others (Friend 2009). In general, however, the general green business paradigm of focusing on holistic, long-term consequences more than on specific, short-term goals is as applicable to industrial operations as it is to any other corporate function.

6

■ Knowledge management

The fundamental goal of any ecologically harmonious production operation is to optimise the use of material and energy inputs while minimising the generation of environmentally damaging outputs. This credo, widely known as **eco-efficiency**, has long been recognised in business literature, dating back to the mid-20th-century writings of Buckminster Fuller, an advocate for designs that imitate nature and offer 'more for less'. At the same time, it is noteworthy that other leading environmental thinkers have criticised eco-efficiency, accusing it of being a conservative concept that perpetuates bad behaviour by alleviating the harmful effects of brutal production processes instead of eliminating them. In this latter view, what is required is a wholesale reconstruction of upstream activities, a new industrial model in which sustainability is embedded in processes instead of added on as an afterthought.

■ **Eco-efficiency:** Organisational process characterised by lower material and energy intensities, less toxicity, greater recyclability and maximal use of renewable inputs.

? How useful is eco-efficiency if the overall production system is unsustainable?

Clearly, designing operations to be green from the very outset is a more coherent approach in environmental terms, as well as one that is easier to implement and probably less expensive. Still, this ideal does not speak to the reality of the world's existing infrastructure, which has been largely designed according to the bad old principles of imposing industrial solutions on the ecosphere. Even if there is good cause to support green visionaries' call for non-toxic 'closed loop' industries producing durable and recyclable products, it is important to remember that, for most managers, operational greening mainly means recognising which improvements to their existing apparatus are feasible under current circumstances. Hence the need to explore how companies manage knowledge about green operational concept before seeing how these precepts are implemented across the value chain.

■ Design

To say that companies look to 'design' as a catalyst for operational greening is a broad statement given the different connotations associated with this term. Recent studies have indicated, for instance, that many companies now apply green design approaches to products, components and packaging, but that fewer seek to redesign their manufacturing processes along green lines (Carbone and Moatti 2008). If this were confirmed, it might indicate that managers prefer acting upon their companies' interfaces with external partners such as suppliers or customers instead of greening their internal processes – possibly because external changes are less disruptive than internal ones. Having said that, the two spheres are not entirely separate given the feedback mechanisms that link a company to its marketplace. Whether an idea begins inside or outside a firm is usually less important than its ultimate proliferation. Moreover, whether or not a 'Design-for-Environment' (DfE) strategy highlights products or processes, certain overarching principles will always apply. Suffice it to say that for most companies, green design is a multi-criteria decision-making process (Choi *et al.* 2008).

Some observers view the rise of green design as a successor to the 'quality revolution' that has had such a major impact on the production-marketing cycle in recent years (Hitchcock and Willard 2009) – especially since the 1970s, which saw the global diffusion of a Japanese management model often referred to as the 'Toyota Production System' (see below). One similarity between the quality and the green approaches is that both involve goods that are likely to be more expensive to produce and hence harder to sell, yet offer companies sufficient operational benefits to justify this risky positioning. Another is the criticism levied at many industrial companies' longstanding habit, especially where a mass production system is involved, of trying to lower costs by accepting lower quality inputs – a business decision in which the short term betrays the long term. One principle shared by all ecological designers is that green operations necessarily mean preferring quality, in its different manifestations, over cheapness.

The main precept underlying green design is that corporate operations and/or products should imitate natural processes as far as possible. Ecological literature is unanimous in its praise of energy-efficient eco-systems such as forests or aquatic environments, usually characterised by their diversity and interdependence; reliance on sunlight or other locally supplied inputs; reuse of waste; and husbandry of existing resources. Green design approaches will usually try to replicate such interplays. One example is the field of 'biomorphism', where designers try to imitate 'intelligent patterns'. This is exemplified by the Genware research laboratory's invention of 'living' curtains that draw signals from external noise and lighting levels and uses them as signals altering product behaviour in a way that mitigates the need for further action (Steffen 2008). Similar work is being done in the field of nanotechnology, exemplified by the recent invention by scientists in Berkeley (California) of energy-generating micro-fibres that create 'smart clothes' deriving energy from normal human motion. More conceptually, there is the widely lauded 'biomimicry' approach developed by the renowned biologist Janine Benyus who wonders at the marvels of natural engineering, characterised by spider webs that are stronger than Kevlar, termites that maintain body temperatures under a blazing desert sun and mussels that create tremendously sticky glue in an aquatic environment – all achievements that surpass what human industry realises with its traditionally brutal (and energy-inefficient) 'heat, beat and treat' processes. According to Benyus, biomimicry takes 'nature's best ideas and then imitates these designs and processes to solve human problems' (www.asknature.org). It has already led to a number of concrete outcomes, exemplified by the winglets that Boeing places on its 737 aircraft to lower air resistance (imitating the flight apparatus of bats); swimming suits whose contact with water replicates sharks' swimming dynamics; and even 'neo-biological' experiments aimed at getting living organisms to produce the kind of performances normally associated with inanimate objects (i.e. getting viruses to store

6

> **?** Are there any sectors of activity where green design principles do not apply?

power in the way that a battery does). The broadest application of this approach is the design work being done to get buildings – and possibly entire urban districts – to operate like forests (see Chapter 9).

Key issue	Ecological literature is unanimous in its praise of energy-efficient eco-systems such as forests or aquatic environments... Green design approaches will usually try to replicate such interplays.

Chief among the schools of green design, however, is the 'cradle-to-cradle' concept largely attributed to an American designer, William McDonough (see Figure 6.1). The starting point for this revolutionary vision is the author's disdain for 'end-of-product' recycling solutions that are expensive, ecologically unsafe and useless in solving the health problems that traditionally arise when people handle products made from hazardous substances. McDonough started with a criticism of most industries' longstanding pattern of seeking economics of scale via standardised inputs, with companies flooding their manufacturing processes with a whole range of contaminants that are supposed to achieve certain desired outcomes while neglecting to incorporate a number of other (more ecological) considerations. To replace this paradigm, he has come up with an entirely new approach to design, one where goods are conceptualised from the very outset as a function of their environmental footprint. His starting point is to differentiate between **biological nutrients** that can be returned seamlessly into the natural environment at the end of a product's life, and **technical nutrients** comprised of substances such as synthetic chemical compounds or materials and minerals whose disposal would be toxic to the ecosphere. Substances in the former category are called 'products of consumption' because they can become nutrients for further lifecycles after their initial usage, i.e. there is a safe 'open loop' interaction between their initial manifestation as a product component and their subsequent appearance as product waste. Technical nutrients, on the other hand, are dangerous and should not be released into the ecosphere. They need to function in a 'closed loop' where they can serve as reusable 'products of service' fulfilling a particular design function time and again for a range of different products or services. Obviously the ideal is to design products that avoid toxic inputs, but if this is impossible, the key is to separate biological from technical nutrients so that each can follow its own 'metabolism'. The fundamental advice here is for companies to correctly inventory everything that goes into

Biological nutrients: ■
Natural inputs into the production process.

Technical nutrients: ■
Synthetic inert inputs into the production process.

their production processes – and everything that comes out. The goal is to phase out waste entirely.

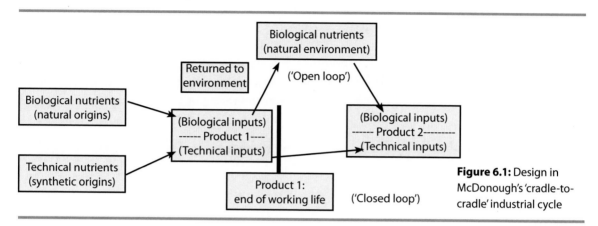

Figure 6.1: Design in McDonough's 'cradle-to-cradle' industrial cycle

Unfortunately, McDonough's vision constitutes an ideal that few companies are in a position to implement without abandoning their existing product ranges or production facilities. As a result, most green design initiatives currently focus on less ambitious objectives that can be targeted either individually or in combination. This includes: minimising the generation of waste (hazardous or other) throughout a good's lifecycle; **lightweighting** materials; extending products' useful life via **upgradeability**; and enhancing end-of-life disassembly (Blackburn 2008). The choice of which of these goals is to be prioritised within a particular production unit depends on a host of factors: the company's general innovativeness and/or technical capabilities; **lifecycle costing** analysis revealing the opportunity costs of greening one part of the value chain as opposed to another; the extent to which the cost of environmental investments can be passed on to customers; and whether the DfE effort is more oriented towards new product development or else towards the modification of older products (Bevilacqua *et al.* 2007). In addition, numerous 'trade-offs will have to be made weighing health and safety attributes and consumer desires for convenience against packaging, energy use, and recycling requirements' (Friend 2009). Green design reforms do not occur in a vacuum.

Along these lines, one of the best ways for contemporary companies to optimise their green design efforts is by keeping abreast of current best practice. This will sometimes involves internal (organisational) learning, exemplified by Dutch electronics giant Philips's habit of choosing a

■ **Lightweighting:** Engineering initiatives aimed at reducing the mass of materials comprising a manufactured item.

■ **Upgradeability:** Ease with which an object can accommodate modernisation.

■ **Lifecycle costing:** Total cost of an item once all expenditures are accounted for, particularly relating to the minimisation of its environmental footprint (pollution permits, disposal, safety measures).

6

green flagship in each product category, maximising its environmental attributes and then applying these innovations across all other product lines (Hitchcock and Willard 2009). More often than not, however, a company will have to look outside for useful design knowledge. Several information platforms have been created towards this end, one being www.designersaccord.org, a participatory forum where designers can access a community of peers with a particular sustainability interest. Note that the ecological ethos generally places great emphasis on shared intelligence, because this embodies its ideal of harmony and group-interest (see Chapter 1) but also because data exchanges are arguably a more eco-efficient way of achieving technological progress than if each company were to engage its own material resources in a separate research and development programme. Of course, there is no doubt that the desire for competitive advantage means that many managers will continue to preserve the confidentiality of their discoveries, whether green or of another variety. The fact remains, however, that data sharing in a bid to optimise operational behaviour is widely viewed as a second pillar of environmental knowledge management.

? Why should managers be any more willing to share environmental knowledge?

Key issue

... data exchanges are arguably a more eco-efficient way of achieving technological progress than if each company were to engage its own material resources in a separate research and development programme.

■   Data exchanges

There are several ways in which IT can be used to green corporate operations. As aforementioned, one of the main challenges in minimising the toxicity of a company's inputs or outputs is gaining real knowledge of its actual material flows, a process that is particularly complicated if discussions with suppliers focus more on commercial and product performance, as is historically the case, than on chemical attributes. Data capabilities help at this level by inventorying substances found in a product's value chain and assessing the environmental impact at a level of scientificity surpassing the understanding of many of the operational managers who would otherwise be called upon to exercise oversight. Secondly and as discussed in Chapter 5, more and more companies are implementing environmental management systems (EMS) that offer information on the optimal cross-departmental utilisation of resources. These are corporate versions of the **smart grid** technology that is revolutionising many economies' power distribution

Smart grid: ■
Energy distribution network that uses information technology to optimise power allocations and reduce wastage.

networks (see *Web Resource 6.1* and *Chapter 6 online case study*). Their goal is to ascertain possible synergies and spillover effects in sectors such as heating or lighting. An EMS will centralise information and optimise operational resource allocation better than any one manager could ever hope to do, especially given individuals' tendency to focus on their own interests. Thirdly, data exchanges underpin many of the environmental 'balanced scorecard' approaches that companies have increasingly started to implement (see Chapter 5) in a bid to get their various departments to move incrementally towards greater sustainability. Famous examples include global clothing giant Nike or US office furniture maker Herman Miller, where repeated cross-departmental information exchanges have had the effect of motivating designers, procurement officers and manufacturing managers to demand greener operational solutions from one another. In this, like all areas of business, innovation tends to occur more quickly when people are allowed to borrow ideas from colleagues (Werbach 2009). Lastly, note also the use of IT to drive some of the 'just-in-time' lean manufacturing algorithms that are being used to increase the eco-efficiency of corporate logistics and inventory management practices (see discussion below on Toyota Production System).

Data capabilities help ...by inventorying substances found in a product's value chain and assessing the environmental impact at a level of scientificity surpassing the understanding of many ... operational managers.

Key issue

6

Otherwise, data exchanges have also become a key tool for greening corporate data centres. The background to this issue is the rapid rise in the amount of energy (specifically electricity) consumed by these units, not to mention the separate but related problem of the e-waste they have to manage. By some estimates, the number of servers in US data centres, for instance, is currently growing by about 10 per cent annually, due to the networking and data storage effects of customers' demand for more real-time services and companies' adoption of more technologically-intensive working practices (Forrest *et al.* 2008). The carbon footprint implications of this trend are very worrisome.

At the same time, a great deal of knowledge already exists regarding potential modalities for increasing data centres' energy efficiency. The main ideas are that companies need to make a more intensive usage of whatever computer infrastructure they possess (i.e. avoiding surplus capacity and sizing equipment to fit actual and future use); optimise energy-hungry cooling systems via smarter data centre layouts and better inter-terminal connectivity; implement 'cloud computing' whenever possible to reduce single workstations' memory requirements; and cut consumption by installing Energy Star-certified systems that rely on LCD display technology or shut down automatically when terminals or peripherals go unused for too long. Of course, this latter proposal will be undermined if some employees are unwilling to look beyond their own convenience – which is the transcription of organisational ecological inertia at the level of frontline operatives. The same limitation applies to some of the **dematerialisation** possibilities (paperfree offices, telecommuting workers) that smart computing enables – as Chapter 5 indicates, the transition towards corporate sustainability is as much a matter of staff members adhering to the new paradigm as an issue of defining new procedures. There is great optimism regarding IT's future role in corporate greening initiatives – with several commentators asserting that if used wisely, the IT function's own greenhouse gas emissions will ultimately represent no more than a tiny proportion of the total quantities that it eliminates elsewhere (Boccaletti *et al.* 2008) – the very definition of an eco-efficient solution. Yet such predictions are rooted in the idea that managers will necessarily focus as much on computing's green possibilities as on its other functionalities. This confidence is only justified if the ecological imperative receives as strong a reception from companies' more inwardly-oriented production specialists as it does from its more outwardly-focused marketing managers. Given some evidence that many companies' sustainability efforts are mainly driven by considerations of commercial positioning, it is not certain that this will be the case.

Dematerialisation: ■
Virtualisation.

■ Value chain functions

The holistic paradigm underlying all ecological thinking is also (and possibly mainly) relevant to the corporate value chain. This is best encapsulated in a construct called 'industrial ecology', where an overview is taken of all of the physical operations relating to a product over the course of its lifecycle in an attempt to ascertain different modalities for minimising net resource utilisation or pollution (see Figure 6.2). Some descriptions of this approach see it as equating economic organisation with the workings of a forest, which consumes as few new inputs as possible (basically ambient sunlight and rainfall) and reuses any waste generated by system participants as nutrients sustaining the lives of others. Thus, the industrial cluster near Middlesbrough in Northern England – where the waste from a local chemicals factory is used to heat large greenhouses, whose outputs then feed back into the original plant – constitutes a small step towards industrial ecology. The benefits in this one case are multiple, not only for the companies involved but also for society as a whole, insofar as the arrangement reduces the need for expensive imports shipped from afar (see Chapter 8). However, it is just as clear that new value chain linkages of this kind will only be feasible if there is a modicum of coordination between participants and/or if collective infrastructure (heating pipes, etc.) can be developed. The question then becomes who should take responsibility for such installations.

? Can 'industrial ecology' be achieved without government intervention?

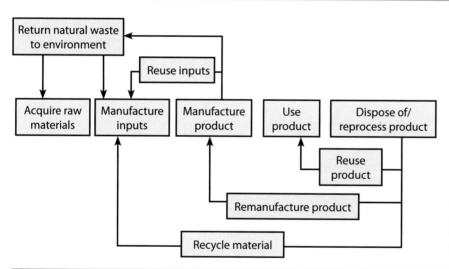

Figure 6.2: Lifecycle product value chain (adapted from Blackburn 2008, p. 51.)

6

Thus, it is often the quality of the overall coordination that determines a green value chain's chances of success. According to some analyses, eco-efficiency gains may be easier to achieve for the whole of an industrial system than at the level of one element therein (Richards and Frosch 1997). Yet there are also risks in adopting a macro-organisation defined primarily by the ecological **symbiosis** between 'co-located' industries – first and foremost being that this entire organisation is vulnerable to one of the partners going out of business or, indeed, not generating the useful waste on which the others rely. Furthermore, it is not at all evident that the by-products generated by one member of a cluster can be used by its partners, nor that companies should or will

■ **Symbiosis:** Interdependent relationship.

decide to locate facilities somewhere based primarily on proximity to firms with compatible waste streams. Depending on the specific level within the product value chain, other business objectives – mainly return costs – will as often as not be considered more pressing.

Key issue	... it is often the quality of the overall coordination that determines a green value chain's chances of success.

■   Upstream

Managers vary widely in terms of the particular value chain operation that they are most likely to subject to a greening process. Accepting that larger companies with a deeper and older strategic commitment to environmentalism can and will cover a wider range of activities when embarking upon this trajectory, recent studies have indicated that the leading areas for operational greening are logistics (i.e. journey reductions); followed by sourcing/manufacturing (i.e. green materials) and lastly product design and reverse logistics (Carbone and Moatti 2008). The focus of the operational greening will also tend to vary by sector of activity. There is evidence, for instance, that companies with capital-intensive operations are more interested in energy and water consumption than service providers who might prefer measures attracting potential consumers. On the other hand, multinationals with globally decentralised manufacturing and distribution functions will, quite logically, be more interested in logistics. All in all it is difficult generalising about the ultimate goals of contemporary companies' operational greening efforts, notwithstanding Christopher and Towill's laudable attempt (2001) to distinguish between 'agile' green value chains that are flexible hence more useful in unpredictable circumstances, and 'lean' variants that are resource-efficient hence better in less volatile mass markets. What remains is a straightforward approach analysing different value chain stages in chronological order, moving from upstream procurement to downstream recycling.

Sourcing

At the very start of the corporate value chain, there are the inputs (raw materials or intermediary components and modules) that companies acquire from suppliers. Attempts to green a company's procurement operations can be complicated first and foremost by how hard it is to ascertain suppliers' environmental footprint – combining upstream with downstream data – with any degree of precision, especially where hybrid products mixing different categories of inputs are involved. This is all the harder given the international scale upon which many supply chains are being developed nowadays (see Chapter 8).

There are numerous examples today of companies cooperating with another to overcome this opacity problem. Sometimes this will involve shared data exchange platforms (e.g. www.footprintnetwork.org/). On other occasions, a powerful contractor might impose its own data requirements on supply chain partners, who find themselves forced to divulge information that they might otherwise view as confidential for fear of losing the account. One example is the Green Supply Chain Program that giant California utilities company PG&E announced in June 2010. Another is Walmart's GreenWERCS Chemical Screening Tool, which charters the human health effects of the chemical substances in the goods that it carries – information that has become crucial to this retailer following reports that toxic substances may have been present in some of the toys that it imported from China. As always, the quality of a business decision depends on the quality of the information upon which it is based. It is important to remember that operational greening remains a relatively new activity in which decisions are as often rooted in calculated guesses as in hard facts.

6

It remains that quality knowledge is essential to prime contractors, if only because regulations increasingly hold them accountable for the overall liability of the products transiting through their value chains (Bacallan 2000). Similarly and as aforementioned, there is the reputational damage that companies can suffer if their partners engage in behaviour deemed environmentally damaging – as exemplified by the pressure put on Nestlé in early 2010 after one of its palm oil suppliers was accused of illegal deforestation practices. In addition, the high **non-product ratio** (NPO) characterising many consumer or high-tech products (see Figure 6.3) means that up to 60 per cent of the carbon footprint of companies in many sectors – and up to 80 per cent of retailers' footprints – can be inherited from upstream suppliers (Brickman and Ungerman 2008). Lastly, the simple risk of having to handle wastefully bulky incoming packaging can be costly to a company – and even dangerous to its employees – when hazardous goods are involved. In short, most companies that are serious about achieving operational sustainability must do this in conjunction with their supply chain partners.

■ **Non-product ratio:** Percentage of inputs that are transformed over the course of a production process into waste.

Key issue

... quality knowledge is essential to prime contractors, if only because regulations increasingly hold them accountable for the overall liability of the products transiting through their value chains.

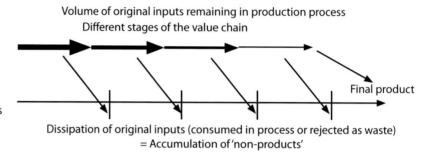

Volume of original inputs remaining in production process
Different stages of the value chain

Final product

Figure 6.3: Non-product ratios rise as goods are transformed into final products

Dissipation of original inputs (consumed in process or rejected as waste)
= Accumulation of 'non-products'

This kind of relationship increasingly involves a prime contractor offering suppliers positive or negative incentives to enhance their environmental performance (Nidumolu *et al.* 2009). One leader in this respect is Walmart, which in recent years has given thousands of its suppliers worldwide some very specific directives regarding its expectations in terms of carbon emissions, packaging, preferred chemicals or energy-efficiency. Other companies, such as US office products chain Staples, seek to source a growing proportion of their paper or wood stocks from sustainably managed forests. Textiles giant Levi Strauss, on the other hand, focuses more on its suppliers' water consumption. Lastly, note recent studies indicating that a number of companies have started to redesign their supply chains around logistics aims such as lower transport costs per pallet, lower handling costs (or CO_2 emissions) per pallet, lesser lead times and improved on-shelf availability – measures requiring deep linkages between partners up and down the chain (Research Recap 2008).

Prescriptions of this kind are often amalgamated within Environmentally Preferable Purchasing (EPP) specifications, many of which first develop under the aegis of public agency tender policies (OGC 2008). In such arrangements, it is customary for supply contracts to contain sustainability conditions that the prime contractor will monitor via LCA-based environmental management systems. For these procedures to be effective, however, increasing amounts of knowledge must be shared, relating to materials' toxicity but also potentially to component design functions that might constitute the supplier's core competency – in which case, collaboration will only occur if sufficient trust exists. This will depend in turn on the nature of the relationship between the partners (strategic or market-based) and if the suppliers have been ISO 14001 or Green Seal certified. At an advanced level of integration, some prime contractors will even sponsor 'materials pools' providing the necessary green infrastructure to preferred suppliers who are currently incapable of manufacturing a particular input along green lines. One example is the supply network that Nike, Harley-Davidson and Ford have developed jointly because they all want access to previously unavailable types of sustainable leather (Greener World Media 2009). In general, inputs designed to be interchangeable at the final product or end user level tend to be more eco-efficient than more specialised goods.

Production

The footprint directly associated with goods and services' actual physical production can be divided between the profile of the facilities hosting this particular stage of the value chain, and the actual industrial or other operations being implemented. In terms of facilities, Chapter 9 offers specific analyses on upgrade and redesign initiatives affecting lighting systems and, more broadly, buildings as a whole. The main goal here will almost always be to achieve savings and/or cut costs by using less energy. There are a number of other, less structural measures that staff members can implement more easily, however, as long as management encourages green awareness and initiative (see Chapter 5). Examples of simple but effective actions include monitoring drafts from doors and windows, as per the Close the Door campaign targeting retailers in London's main commercial district (Hickman 2009); keeping ambient room temperatures lower (an average 1°C drop can translate into something like 8 per cent lower annual heating bills); switching off non-essential equipment; or using bicycle couriers instead of motor vehicles when dispatching parcels across a city (Slavin 2007). Note that more and more countries have government agencies like the UK's Carbon Trust offering companies – especially SMEs – both advice and beneficial loans so as to accelerate their installation of energy-efficient devises such as condensing boilers or LED lighting. The key factor of success at this level is the company's willingness to overcome any inertia and allocate human resources to pilot such schemes.

At a more structural level, large companies are increasingly investing in 'energy management software' enabling them to get real-time information about their consumption and make adjustments accordingly (Greener World Media 2010). Hi-tech projects of this nature

6

are often big enough for senior managers to view them as something strategic (see Chapter 5). A recent example is IT specialist Engenuity Systems's sale to McDonalds of a series of devices that will constantly adjust lighting and temperature levels to the actual needs of the fast food retailer's facilities' – a control system that McDonalds hopes will help cut its $1.5 billion annual energy bill by up to 14 per cent. It is this kind of practical operational investment that can be assessed using traditional financial return indicators.

Companies' attempts to green their production processes should also be analysed on a more conceptual plane, however. Whereas earlier analysts would usually focus attention on pollution prevention or process certification possibilities enabled by ISO 14001, there is more talk today about a crossover between green manufacturing and high quality – the kind of NPO waste minimisation focus that is also found (see Box 6.1), in 'lean' manufacturing regimes such as the Toyota Production System. TPS seeks to reduce the overall volume of material throughputs – a very green ambition – via a whole host of mechanisms. These include 'just-in-time' inventory management; a 'kaizen' search for continuous improvements; plus 'jidoka' human automation, where people determine process speeds by prioritising maximal quality and minimal defects. The net effect is the 'rightsizing' of outputs, with manufacturing entities producing fewer units but more durable ones. The science of waste management meshes seamlessly with eco-efficiency precepts.

? Asides from ROI, what measures can be used to validate green operational investments?

Box 6.1: 'Muda' categories of wasteful industrial processes (Ohno 1988) – Muda is a Japanese term for 'waste', as used in lean manufacturing and agile software development

- Overproduction (exceeding customer demand)
- Time lost waiting (at production or delivery level)
- Movements (sub-optimal ergonomics)
- Surplus stocks (of inputs or outputs)
- Defects (time and cost of rework)
- Over-processing (performing beyond requirements)
- Transportation (unjustified conveyance)

Industrial companies are constantly seeking greater (eco-)efficiency, if only because this contributes directly to their bottom line – always a strong argument for going green. One recent example is the $2billion that Korean steelmaker Posco spent building a furnace that would directly convert raw coal and iron ore into pig iron without going through a second transformation stage that is traditional in such processes – with this shortcut reducing costs and pollution (Ramstad 2008). Other advances pertain to improvements in general machine design technology, enabling devices made out of stronger, lighter and more flexible parts, hence capable of nearly zero tolerances. One example here comes from the new nano-tubes that are being made out of a non-toxic substance called fullerene and used in conductors, semiconductors and insulators such as the kind found in sensors or photovoltaic cells (Steffen 2008). Similarly, there is the work being done at Chicago's Gas Technology Institute, which tries to speed up glassmakers' old-fashioned sand melting process via enhanced heat recovery methods (Zachary 2008). Note as well the significant value chain **knock-on effects** when green innovations involve intermediary goods that subsequently become components in a number of end products. Industrial glass, for instance, is used in everything from windows for buildings and cars to containers for liquids, screens for computers and cell phones or hybrid products like fibreglass and fibre optics. The effects of changes implemented at an earlier stage of the value chain are amplified by their diffusion later on.

■ **Knock-on effect:** Where events occurring at the upstream level of a sector's value chain affect its downstream phases.

■ Downstream

Many operational greening efforts are stimulated by downstream concerns about a producer's sustainability profile, especially in cases where the public has fears about the toxicity of its physical processes (see Chapter 4). Recent examples include demands made of US consumer goods company Johnson & Johnson in 2009 to remove two potentially carcinogenic chemicals from its baby shampoo line and other personal care products (Greener World Media 2010); or the changes that California cleaning products company Clorox has made to its signature bleaching product to alleviate public anxiety. On other occasions, companies pre-empt potential criticism by taking it upon themselves to remove toxic substances from products and replace them with innocuous substances – a prime example being Sony Ericsson's early decision to remove brominated flame retardants and polyvinyl chloride from its main electronics products. Improvements of this kind can be less self-evident that they first seem, however. For instance, in the same way as Porsche has moved towards ceramic brake pads, Ford and Volkswagen no longer use asbestos on their brake pads but have replaced them with antinomy sulphide. There is no assurance, however, that these substitutes are better than the original inputs (Braungart and

McDonough 2009). The value of a greening effort is rarely exclusively physical but often depends as well on the public's perceptions of this action.

Packaging

One of the most visible problems in global waste management is the mountain of packaging that is one ugly feature of today's consumerist societies. Packaging is also an upstream topic where it relates to shipments of raw materials and industrial components, although the assumption can be made that such operations are largely **utilitarian** in nature and have been pared down to reflect functional needs. At the downstream interface with end users, however, there is a longstanding pattern of companies viewing product packaging as a marketing tool, thereby wasting vast quantities of paper and other wrappings (see Table 6.1). Improvements in this area are relatively easier than elsewhere, however, and it is by reducing packaging that many companies have actually started their operational greening efforts.

Utilitarian: Designed solely to fulfil a practical function.

Table 6.1: US packaging trends (Greener World Media 2010)

	Packaging use: thousands of tons per billion dollars of GDP	Paper intensity: thousands of tons of paper per billion dollars of GDP (Source: American Forest & Paper Association)
1998	N/A	9.84
2001	N/A	8.58
2004	6.20	8.31
2005	6.09	7.88
2006	6.09	7.76
2007	5.87	7.32
2008	5.47	6.77

Fundamentally, the main ways that companies can diminish the net volume of packaging that they produce involve intensifying the use of recycled, biodegradable or bio-based materials or creating designs (and/or incentive schemes, such as deposit returns) that help consumers dispense with packaging altogether. Conversely, there is an argument in favour of sturdier packaging that can be reused, sometimes after cleaning. Lastly, some efforts focus on simply designing packaging to be smaller.

Key issue

... the main ways that companies can diminish the net volume of packaging they produce involve intensifying the use of recycled, biodegradable or bio-based materials or creating designs...that help consumers dispense with packaging altogether.

The business press is full of stories about companies adopting one or the other of these approaches. Measures taken by the Quizno fast food chain, for instance, include the introduction of catering lunch boxes made of 100 per cent recycled paperboard, plastic lids made of 30 per cent post-consumer recycled PET bottles or pulp salad bowls made from renewable sugarcane – not to mention 100 per cent compostable wax-coated paper cups or napkins made from 100 per cent recycled material and fibres (Gunther 2010). The Swedish furniture Ikea, on the other hand, employs 'air hunters' seeking unused spaces in its current packaging with a view towards reducing overall volumes (Werbach 2009). Computer giant Dell has recently taken to inserting biodegradable bamboo to cushion its packaging, replacing non-recyclable and potentially toxic Styrofoam. European container maker Rexam – like its American counterpart Ball (GreenerDesign 2010) – has invested enormous sums in recent years in technologies enabling it to both light-weight cans made out of aluminium or other metals, and increase the recycled plastic component of its bottles and lids. Conversely, drinks manufacturers like Anheuser or Coca Cola have, respectively, saved money and burnished their green credentials by introducing containers that are more resource-efficient and/or make greater use of recycled inputs – epitomising the range of motivations driving corporate greening initiatives. In a similar vein, it is worth noting eBay's recent decision to offer sellers 100,000 reusable green shipping boxes made of FSC-certified and recycled materials.

6

Logistics

Value chains are affected at every level by the logistics function, which integrates different stages in what can be globally referred to as supply chain management. Categorising this activity as downstream is somewhat arbitrary, and it is important to remember that earlier stages in a good's overall value chain represent the final customer interface for companies specialised in raw material or component activities. As such, it is useful to simply apply a relatively broad term such as 'distribution' when describing goods' general physical movements.

To a certain extent, distribution volumes (meaning the amount and distance of goods transported) reflect other strategic decisions, first and foremost being a company's chosen configuration – namely, whether manufacturing units are situated close to supply sources or consumer markets; if a transportation hub approach is being used; and to what extent the company outsources production locally or internationally. MNEs that have opted for dispersed configurations will necessarily have a larger distribution footprint. For agricultural products, this is encapsulated in **food miles** – a topical debate pitting ecological versus development priorities (see Chapter 8).

Food miles: Distance a foodstuff has travelled from its place of production to its place of consumption.

Reducing companies' footprint in this area generally involves two kinds of actions. Firstly, at an industrial level, the shipments can be redesigned to weigh less – one suggestion being that detergent manufacturers should not move product in bulk form but instead as concentrated pellets (Braungart and McDonough 2009). More strategically, increasing the interchangeability of supplies or parts can reduce the overall need for transportation. Secondly and above all, against today's general backdrop of rising fuel prices, saturated infrastructure and pollution concerns, the transportation sector itself has become a major battleground for operational improvements. It is at this level that many companies first encounter the ecological imperative, regardless of whether they own their own fleet of vehicles or, increasingly, outsource this function to specialist third party logistics providers – who might mix ('co-mingle') different customers' shipments and travel with fuller loads, a solution that is more eco-efficient in macro terms. Logistics specialists are responsible for many headline green innovations because the services they provide are so energy-dependent and polluting. One noteworthy example is FedEx, which is updating its aircraft – and using fuel consumption software to further enhance performance – while installing solar power capabilities that might be used one day to power its new hybrid truck fleet (Nidumolu *et al.* 2009). More generally, vehicle operators are increasingly implementing 'telematic' software to manage fleet use – 'right-sizing' vehicles to load sizes, reducing idling and re-routing itineraries – in a way that will cut both fuel usage and greenhouse gas emissions. Note that this trend seems to have slowed down in 2009 due to the effects of the recession (Greener World Media 2010). This is the basic dilemma of operational greening: such processes usually end up saving companies money; but committing to them can be very costly.

Key issue

Logistics specialists are responsible for many headline green innovations because the services they provide are so energy-dependent and polluting.

The same observation applies to reverse logistics, also known as recycling. This is the final stage of the value chain and one that is quite specific to sustainable business. As discussed above, a fundamental green paradigm is that products which cannot be reused at the end of their working lives are wasteful hence costly, if not to the company itself then to society (and the ecosphere) as a whole. Yet setting up appropriate recycling systems can be quite challenging. On one hand, the activity is not always economically justified in market pricing terms (see *Web Resource 6.2*). On the other, many items (such as plastics or paper) tend to lose some of their flexibility or strength attributes when recycled and can only be restored through the addition of chemicals that are not only costly but environmentally-unfriendly, defeating the purpose of the whole exercise to some extent. In addition, there is the aforementioned technical difficulty of handling different waste streams comprised of product disposals that mix 'biological' with 'technical nutrients' – not all of which are certain to be present in the amount or quality that makes them useful, especially given the obsolescence planned into many less standardised product components (Gonzales and Adenso-Diaz 2006). Lastly, note the legal uncertainty that companies face if, as envisioned in 'extended stewardship' approaches, their liability were to extend past the end of their products' working lives.

Nevertheless, recycling has clearly become one of the most iconic of all operational greening efforts. Sometimes the tone for this activity is set by government policy, one example being Germany's Duales System Deutschland (DSD) scheme requiring all companies to establish recycling schemes for any packaging they produce. This would be prohibitively expensive if companies paid for the operation themselves – especially where high volume, mass goods are concerned – hence the development of a Grüner Punkt (green dot) alternative where participants pay a licence fee reflecting the variable costs of recycling the different materials they produce (see Table 6.2) before getting DSD to take charge of waste collection on their behalf. Note that putting a green dot on packaging has the added benefit of reminding customers that the company in question is helping to fund the national recycling system – a sign of good corporate citizenship.

6

Table 6.2 : September 2008
green dot packaging tariffs
(www.gruener-punkt.de)

Type of material	Euros/tonne
Glass	1.00
Paper/cardboard	3.00
Tin plate	5.00
Aluminium	13.00
Plastics	17.00
Composite cardboard	13.00
Other composite materials	13.00
Natural materials	2.00

On other occasions, it is economics that drives a company's recycling efforts, specifically when older components are used to 'remanufacture' goods. Some studies have indicated that product recovery motivations of this kind – broken down more or less evenly between recycling/refurbishment and recycling/reuse following cleaning or refurbishment – account for more than half of all reverse logistics (Carbone and Moatti 2008). This has become big business in some cases, one example being the December 2009 announcement by US equipment manufacturer Caterpillar that it had agreed to a joint venture with a Chinese partner named Yuchai offering global services including the remanufacturing of Yuchai diesel engines and components along with Caterpillar diesel engines and components – all adding to the more than 100 million pounds of end-of-life iron that Caterpillar already recycles annually.

Operations of this sort – which, by their very nature satisfy green engineers preference for 'closed loop' solutions – are facilitated when the product components in question are designed from the very outset with recyclability in mind. One example here is Xerox, the photocopier specialist, which designs equipment to ensure that as much as 60 per cent of all parts are retrieved from earlier models (Blackburn 2008). Xerox invests heavily in components' durability to ensure that they can be reused – a policy that, when combined with the company's active product take-back scheme, is said to save several hundred million dollars a year. Other companies' recycling efforts focus on design measures facilitating products' end-of-life disassembly. This can include labelling parts for easier identification or else engineering them to be functionally interchangeable. Lastly, in more consumer-oriented sectors such as computer ink cartridges, the key is to peak customers' interest in recycling schemes that – given the small size and ostensibly low value of the object in question – may not seem worthwhile. One way of doing this is to turn sales counters into collection points. More conceptually, companies can portray their achievements in this area – less waste generated or sent to landfill; more waste re-treated; support for schemes like Grüner Punkt or for NGOs like the Grassroots Recycling Network (www.grrn.org/) – as evidence of their green credentials. In this way, marketing becomes the main driver behind many recycling schemes (indeed, behind many corporate greening operations). Whether this is criticisable or just a statement of fact is another question.

> **?** What are the implications of a larger market for remanufactured goods?

Obstacles and pathways

1 Operational greening seems expensive.
   Programme cost projections should be adjusted to reflect future savings.

2 The company lacks knowledge about operational greening.
   Knowledge garnered from past quality approaches can often be applied.

3 There is a lack of information about components' environmental footprint.
   Set up green procurement systems featuring data exchanges.

4 Recycling is complicated by mixture of 'biological' and 'technicial' nutrients.
   Product designers and end-of-pipeline system engineers must consult regularly.

6

Case study: BASF has a brand new bag

Not unsurprisingly, the chemicals industry has long been blamed for the parlous state in which Earth's ecosphere finds itself today. On one hand, this attitude can be attributed to the sheer number of high-profile events involving the uncontrolled spillage of lethal chemicals into the environment – including, as already discussed, terrible incidents that have occurred at Minimata Bay (Japan), Love Canal (USA), Bhopal (India), a number of European rivers or Abidjan (Africa). On the other hand, the sector's poor reputation also reflects the responsibility that it bears for producing substances whose overall 'bio-accumulation' in the ecosphere has reached a point where the effects can no longer be diluted through natural processes.

The related disposal problem manifests in the mountain of non-biodegradable plastic waste overwhelming landfills and aquatic systems worldwide – as exemplified by the Great Pacific Garbage Patch (see http://www.greatgarbagepatch.org/). One avenue being explored by an increasing number of retailers is whether to ration the distribution of plastic bags at supermarket checkout counters, thereby encouraging customers to discard unwanted and excessive packaging (Smithers 2009) and/or migrate towards new reusable bags. The problem is that many consumers continue to require free plastic bags and, above all, that distributors still use these items for product transportation or conservation purposes. As such, the sector is still in desperate need of resolving end-of-life disposal issues in relation to consumer plastics – explaining why German chemicals giant BASF (www.basf.com) has in recent years made this one of its main missions.

Since 1998 and using the trade name of 'Ecoflex', BASF has been marketing a product line of rubbish bags and disposable packages comprised of entirely biodegradable polyesters made from petrochemical raw materials. In 2006, the base product was enhanced with renewable raw materials including corn-derived polylactic acids to create a bio-plastic product called Ecovio, which biodegrades within a few weeks under certain conditions (such as those found in industrial composting systems) to leave no harmful residues behind. Advertised as 'water and tear-resistant, elastic and printable', Ecovio's 'hybrid strength' allows it to comply with food safety requirements and therefore be used as packaging for products (such as laminated film, wrapping paper, drinks cartons, fast food packaging, drink cups but also certain foam applications) that might otherwise face a risk of contamination from messaging ink. Like Ecoflex, it is 'toxicologically safe' and compares well in performance with standard, low-density, non-biodegradable polyethylene plastic. In other words, it satisfies sustainability criteria while providing the functionalities that business requires – the very definition of a useful green innovation.

To deal with ongoing doubts about bio-plastics' longevity, BASF is constantly looking for ways to enhance product performance. It conducts these studies transparently, stating openly, for instance, that Ecovio may be slightly more vulnerable to the ageing process than some of its rival products. The company continues to experiment with alternative renewable materials (such as starch made from potatoes, or cellulose made from wood), making it likely that the Ecoflex trade name will continue to dominate industrial headlines in the years to come – all the more so since BASF is simultaneously exploring methods of shortening its industrial polymerisation process, an operational improvement that would have the direct environmental benefit of reducing energy costs. This dual focus means that bio-plastics are expected to experience much higher growth rates than traditional polymers, increasing their total share of the enormous global market in plastic goods – a success not only on a commercial plane but also in green operational terms, with bio-plastics becoming one of the first product lines to be designed entirely according to 'cradle-to-cradle' lifecycle assessment principles.

BASF benefits from a first mover advantage despite the growing competition that it faces in the bio-plastics sector – including from interesting SMEs such as French provincial packaging company Jean Bal, specialised in eco-friendly thermoforming methods. A recent 'Sustainable Value' poll (Greenbiz 2010a) awarded BASF joint first place in environmental performance alongside the industrial gases giant Air Liquide. It is true that BASF's top achievements have been in areas that do not necessarily relate directly to the Ecoflex bio-plastics product line – including water and energy use – but this can also be analysed as an indication that the company is seeking to green all of its operations, not just packaging. All in all, given the promising outlook for bio-plastics' possible applications (ranging from thermal insulation for buildings to components for appliances or even automobiles), BASF is quite comfortable in committing to the new business line. At the same time, there has been growing criticism in recent years of the global diversion of many food sources (such as the corn that BASF uses to make Ecovio) for industrial or energy reasons, due to fears about the possibility of insufficient food production to sustain the world's growing population. Thus, there is a risk that companies like BASF whose new activities rely on biological inputs will be accused of taking food off people's plates and typecast as eco-villains. This would be ironic given the company's environmentally-friendly intentions when it first decided to increase its sourcing of biodegradable renewable materials. It does reveal an important lesson, however, namely that all actions involve an expenditure of energy and therefore have some environmental footprint. In bio-plastics like other areas of human endeavour, there is no such thing as a free lunch.

Case study questions

1 Why do so many environmentalists criticise the chemicals sector?

2 What is the particular problem associated with plastic shopping bags?

3 How is BASF trying to use science to solve this problem at an operational level?

■ References

Bacallan J. (2000), 'Greening the supply chain', *Business and Environment*, **6** (5).

Bevilacqua, M., Ciarapica, F. and Giacchetta, G. (2007), 'Development of a sustainable product lifecycle in manufacturing firms: a case study', *International Journal of Production Research*, **45** (18–19).

Blackburn, W. (2008), *The Sustainability Handbook: The Complete Management Guide to Achieving Social, Economic and Environmental Responsibility*, London: Earthscan.

Boccaletti G., Löffler, M. and Oppenheim, J. (2008), 'How IT can cut carbon emissions', October, available at www.mckinseyquarterly.com, accessed 5 March 2010.

Braungart, M. and McDonough, W. (2009), *Cradle to Cradle: Re-Making The Way We Make Things*, London: Vintage Books.

Brickman C., and Ungerman, D. (2008), 'Climate change and supply chain management', July, available at www.mckinseyquarterly.com, accessed 5 March 2010.

Carbone, V. and Moatti, V. (2008), *Greening the supply chain: preliminary results of a global survey*, ESCP-EAP Paris.

Choi, J., Nies, L. and Ramani, K. (2008), 'A framework for the integration of environmental and business aspects toward sustainable product development', *Journal of Engineering Design*, **19** (5).

Christopher M. and Towill D. (2001), 'An integrated model for the design of agile supply chains', *International Journal of Physical Distribution & Logistics Management*, **31** (4), 235–246.

Forrest, W., Kaplan, J. and Kindler, N. (2008), 'Data centers: how to cut carbon emissions and costs', November, available at www.mckinseyquarterly.com, accessed 5 March 2010.

6

Friend, G. (2009), *The Truth About Green Business*, Upper Saddle River, NJ: FT Press.

Gonzales, P. and Adenso-Diaz, B. (2006), 'Reverse logistics practices in the glass sector in Spain and Belgium', *International Business Review*, **15** (5).

Greenbiz (2010a), 'BASF ranked most efficient chemical firm, Dow finishes last', 24 February, available at www.greenerdesign.com, accessed 4 March 2010.

Greenbiz (2010b), 'Interface 1 per cent shy of zero waste operations', 23 March, available at www.greenbiz.com, accessed 29 September 2010.

Greener World Media (2009), *State of Green Business 2009*, available at www.greenbiz.com, accessed 5 February 2010.

Greener World Media (2010), *State of Green Business 2010*, available at www.greenbiz.com, accessed 5 February 2010.

GreenerDesign (2010), 'From can lids to wine bottles, Ball is changing the shape and weight of packaging', 22 February, available at www.greenerdesign.com, accessed 5 March 2010.

Gunther, M. (2010), 'Unwrapping Quizmos' greener packaging', 23 February, available at www.greenbiz.com, accessed 5 March 2010.

Hickman, L. (2009), 'Reversing retailers' open door policy hinges on public campaign', 23 December, available at www.guardian.co.uk, accessed 5 March 2010.

Hitchcock, D. and Willard, M. (2009), *The Business Guide to Sustainability: Practical Strategies and Tools for Organizations*, 2nd edn, London: Earthscan.

Nidumolu, R., Prahalad, C. and Rangaswami, M. (2009), 'Why sustainability is now the key driver of innovation', *Harvard Business Review*, **9** (September), 57-67.

OGC (Office of Government Commerce) (2008), 'Buy green and make a difference', available at www.ogc.gov.uk/, accessed 6 March 2010.

Ohno, T. (1988), *The Toyota Production System*, New York: Productivity Press.

Ramstad, E. (2008), 'Posco forges a better path to iron', *Wall Street Journal – Europe*, 29–31 August, p. 3.

Research Recap (2008), 'Greening of supply chains has benefits too', 11 June, available at www.researchrecap.com, accessed 6 March 2010.

Richards, D. and Frosch, R. (1997), *The Industrial Green Game: Implications for Environmental Design and Management*, available at www.nap.edu, accessed 5 March 2010.

Schendler, A. (2009), *Getting Green Done: Hard Truths from the Front Lines of the Sustainability Revolution*, New York: Public Affairs.

Slavin, T. (2007), 'Small business, big footprint', *The Observer Green Business Guide*, 25 November, p. 6.

Smithers, R. (2009), 'Too much packaging? Leave it with us, Tesco tells shoppers', *The Guardian*, 1 April, p. 10.

Steffen, A. (2008) *World Changing: A User's Guide for the 21th Century*, Harry N. Abrams, Inc.

Vogel, D. (2005), *The Market For Virtue: The Potential And Limits Of Corporate Social Responsibility*, Washington DC: Brookings Institution Press.

Werbach, A. (2009), *Strategy for Sustainability: A Business Manifesto*, Boston, MA: Harvard Business Press.

Zachary, G. (2008), 'The ancient art of glassmaking, minus the waste', *The Observer*, 27 July, *New York Times* insert, p. 5.

7 Green Marketing

Learning objectives

After reading this chapter, you will be able to:

- Isolate green consumers' varying motivations
- Identify obstacles to green purchasing
- Apply classical marketing mix analysis to green business lines

■ Introduction

Ecology and Management students are generally well advanced in their business studies, justifying this chapter's assumption that readers need no introduction to the principles of marketing. Those seeking to review basic concepts in this discipline can refer to useful texts such as *The Busy Manager's Guide to Marketing* (Donaldson 2009).

At one level, the traditional marketing aim of increasing consumption conflicts with the environmental goal of reducing resource utilisation. Beyond these contradictory aims, however, there are many areas where standard marketing concepts can be applied within a green framework. The first step is to determine in which way green marketing resembles or differs from other branches of the discipline.

> **?** How mainstream can green marketing ever hope to become?

Marketing analysts have long spoken of an 'essential tension between environmentalism and modern mass consumption' (MacKoy *et al*. 1995). This is rooted in the basic conflict between the anti-materialist values that have traditionally animated the green movement (see Chapter 1) and the financial and/or consumerist definition of success prevailing in many societies today. The effect is often to undermine the credibility of **green marketing** from the outset. It bears repeating that much of the world continues to see the ecological imperative as less of a priority than this book (and presumably, its readership) does.

Green marketing: ■
Where companies offer products or services that are largely defined by their environmental benefits.

Such scepticism is unsurprising at two levels. Firstly, for many consumers facing a purchasing decision, the environment is still a secondary consideration (Esty and Winston 2006). Whether this apathy is a consequence of potential buyers' financial or socio-economic conditions, cultural values or other factors, the fact is that green consumption remains the exception rather than the rule (Peattie and Crane 2005).

Secondly, many green activists are averse to the kind of marketing that, while proclaiming a company's good intentions, still induces people to consume ever greater quantities of material goods, sparking further resource depletion and pollution. A number of companies stand accused of a manipulative, **greenwash** approach where they gloss over their activities' overall ecological cost by overstating a few token gestures (see *Chapter 7 online case study*). Several websites have been created specifically to expose the inconsistencies in certain companies' environmental claims. *The Guardian* newspaper runs one such site in the UK, regularly featuring stories such as the one published on

Greenwash: ■
Where companies' advertising overstates the extent of the environmental activism.

2 April 2009 when Swedish furniture retailer Ikea was taken to task for publicising that 5.8 per cent of all of its customers in France use public transportation to visit its retail outlets in that country – while neglecting to mention that the company's decision to build out-of-town increases everyone else's automobile use. Skewed representations of this kind aggravate the lack of credibility from which green marketers already suffer. Overcoming this hurdle will require a more realistic dialogue between companies and consumers. This is not something that can be resolved in the short-term, but it appears to be the only way to help green marketing transcend its currently marginal status.

? How sincere is green marketing?

■ Green consumption

Since one of the main goals of any marketing drive is to implant in consumers' minds the idea that a company shares their values so they feel at ease with themselves when purchasing its goods, companies will necessarily struggle when advertising their green credentials to consumers who are oblivious to the ecological imperative. Green marketing enthusiasts often argue that companies should proactively 'push' potential consumers towards greener behaviour (Grant 2007) but this kind of top-down approach will only resonate with consumers if they see it as relevant to their immediate concerns.

Yet different customer groups find different things relevant at different times. It is true that since the late 20th century, an ever-greater number of consumers have signalled a desire to engage in purchasing acts that align with their sense of social responsibility. The idea that economic actors might be driven by **altruistic** attitudes has led to the rise of 'cause-related' or **social marketing** (Kotler and Lee 2005; see *Web Resource 7.1*), or the notion that companies can market to social partners in a way that enhances global welfare by achieving certain non-business goals: a social justice agenda, and an ecological one.

■ Altruism: Sense of greater concern for the welfare of others than for one's own immediate (material) self-interest.]

7

■ Social marketing: Commercial efforts by companies to affect consumers' behaviour in a way that will enhance the broader social good.

■ Segmenting green consumers

Ethical marketing broadens people's sense of self-interest to include strong elements of communitarianism. It asks potential customers to behave in an altruistic way that may not correspond to what they perceive as their immediate material interest but satisfies other longings (Grant 2007). The problem is that this approach creates a conflict between self-interest and group-interest that is akin, in psychological terms, to the divide between the id and the superego. Such confusion is particularly unsettling when promises are made that seem distant in time (depletion of fish stocks by 2050, fear of global warming by 2100) or place (melting of polar ice caps, droughts in Australia). A major challenge for green marketing is how to educate consumers to favour products offering long-term benefits that accrue to society as a whole instead of short-term benefits that accrue to themselves. Indeed, there is much debate whether this can be accomplished without a revolutionary shift in global cultural values.

Key issue	A major challenge for green marketing is how to educate consumers to favour products offering long-term benefits that accrue to society as a whole instead of short-term benefits that accrue to themselves.

One further complication is that green consumers do not represent a unified whole but an accumulation of segments with variable environmental needs and perceptions (Finisterra do Paço 2009). Students will be aware from their general marketing classes of the different socio-economic, demographic and cultural variables that companies use to define target populations. One of the problems with a new field such as green marketing is the lack of knowledge about consumer attitudes in this regard. Recent studies have discovered both that women tend to buy more eco-products than men (Lee 2009) and that men are more positive towards green purchases than women (Mostafa 2007). It is true that the former study covered a Hong Kong sample whereas the latter was undertaken in Egypt – understanding international variations in ecological sensitivities is a key goal for the bigger MNEs that have been the main drivers of green marketing in recent years (see Chapter 8). In the same way that consumer segmentation works best when broken down into micro-markets (Proverbio *et al.* 2008), green consumption behaviour also benefits from differentiation. Having said that, many commonalities do exist between global segments, resulting in part from the incipient trend towards a hybrid global culture following the globalisation of modern communications (Dahl 2002). To a large extent, international green marketing means ascertaining how far a company's approach in one market can be transplanted to another (see Chapter 8).

The difficulty is that differentiated analyses that work at one point in time may be less successful at a later date. Hence the proliferation of market research that companies commission in this area. Spring 2009, for instance, saw the publication of a major report co-written by the Deloitte consulting group and the US-based Grocery Manufacturers Association (GMA), entitled 'Finding the green in today's shoppers: sustainability trends and new shopper insights'. Covering a large sample of green grocery shoppers, the study discovered that although Americans from all walks of life are interested in green products, buyers tend to be older, wealthier and better educated than the average consumer. Less price-sensitive and apt to greater brand and store loyalty, green consumers shop more often and buy larger quantities than most shoppers. In short – and contrary to popular mythology – many green consumers display characteristics that are very much at odds with the monk-like or hippy qualities commonly attributed to them.

Clearly, social and/or green marketing will be more effective with consumers whose internal value systems view the satisfaction of community and personal needs as being equally rewarding. Thus, there is also a strong generational aspect to green consumption. Studies have revealed the so-called 'Millennial' generation's particularly high level of environmental awareness (Gaudelli 2009). This has not necessarily translated into widespread green consumption by this segment, however, with younger consumers often frustrated by the high price of green goods. At the same time, there is every possibility that as the Millennials age, their purchasing power will increase and translate into higher demand for such products, especially given the proliferation of **LOHAS** consumers.

■ **LOHAS:** Acronym for Lifestyles of Health and Sustainability, a market segment focused on health and fitness, the environment, personal development, sustainable living, and social justice, see http://www.lohas.com/.]

7

■   Green intentions vs. green purchases

Companies often find themselves facing consumers who have been somewhat sensitised to the ecological imperative and have a vague desire to do something about it, without this always translating into concrete purchases. The Deloitte/GMA study of green shoppers revealed a 'leakage' process where 95 per cent of all consumers said they would buy a green product in the abstract but only 75 per cent were actually aware of one; 63 per cent sought it; 47 per cent found it; and 22 per cent ultimately bought it. There are several reasons for these results: a general lack of information regarding green alternatives; insufficient assortments requiring improved in-store locations and point-of-sale communications; and above all, the fact that customers generally lack a 'willingness-to-pay' extra for green products.

One of the lessons from these findings is that green products will only succeed if their sustainability argument does not replace their performance argument but supplements it. With few exceptions, green products tend to be sold at a premium, either because their innovation costs (and absence of industrial scale) warrant a mark-up or because sellers want to take advantage of their rarity value. This price constraint is a constant factor in green marketing. Customers who are already amenable to green arguments might take cost in stride but for everyone else, it can be an insurmountable obstacle.

Key issue

With few exceptions, green products tend to be sold at a premium...
Customers who are already amenable to green arguments might take cost in stride but for everyone else, it can be an insurmountable obstacle.

Bonini and Oppenheim (2008) have devised a model (see Figure 7.1) that breaks customer-perceived obstacles to green purchasing down into successive stages. After becoming aware of the existence of a green alternative within a particular category of goods – and educated as to its potential benefits – consumers need reassurance that the new product will perform as well as traditional alternatives (e.g. the reluctance of 'petrol-heads' to purchase electric cars). They must also sense that it can be relied upon to fulfil its promise. This is a significant hurdle, particularly when greenwash aggravates potential consumers' cynicism. Then comes the hurdle of price, often the difference between the 'normal' surcharge that budding green consumers might expect to pay and the high sticker prices charged by retailers seeking to maximize margins on novelty items. Lastly, there is general concern about the availability of green products, with many customers rightly or wrongly presuming today that because green products are not sold everywhere, they are too hard to find in sufficient quantities to be considered staple products that can be replenished as need be.

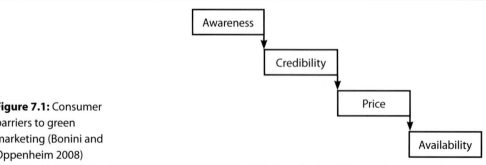

Figure 7.1: Consumer barriers to green marketing (Bonini and Oppenheim 2008)

Lastly, in addition to the problems identified in this model, it is also worth mentioning the discomfort that many consumers feel with the 'sharing' ethos that is part of many green consumption experiences, especially where services are involved. One example is 'liftshare.com', an online platform where strangers are supposed to come together to share automobile journeys, thereby reducing their overall carbon footprint. Given the highly individualistic nature of consumption in many modern societies, it can be jarring to consumers to enter a green marketing universe that stresses communitarianism more than personal enjoyment. The sum total of these obstacles explains why green consumer segments remain so limited to this day.

■ Corporate green marketing approaches

Studies have shown that the green consumption resonates more among people with an ethnocentric culture (i.e. who believe that their values are universal) and/or who already engage with the ecological imperative (Paladino 2005). Such consumers will proactively demand green solutions – unlike other, less engaged segments, where the impetus for green marketing must come from the company itself. This distinction between companies 'pushing' a new message (see Figure 7.2) or being 'pulled' by signals from the market is a key dividing line in contemporary international business analysis (Sitkin and Bowen 2009).

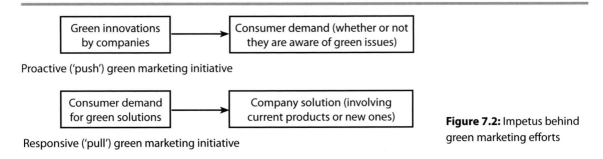

Proactive ('push') green marketing initiative

Responsive ('pull') green marketing initiative

Figure 7.2: Impetus behind green marketing efforts

7

■ 'Push' vs. 'Pull' marketing

A responsive 'pull' strategy has a greater chance of succeeding due to the fact that the promised benefits correspond to preferences that the market has already made explicit. At the same time, since a company's rivals will also pick up on these signals, it is harder to charge a premium. Such strategies therefore tend to cover high volume/low return commodity products, one example being the kinds of corporate promotional products (fridge magnets, caps, T-shirts) that the Australian firm Haul sells, made solely out of recycled materials. Conversely, in proactive 'push' marketing, the company is in a position to achieve a first mover advantage with its new idea and can therefore demand a higher price. This strategy applies to more innovative green products exemplified by the fuel-efficient, high-tech line of printers that Korean manufacturer Samsung's Indian subsidiary has started marketing in recent years. Of course, because the innovator can never be sure whether the new product will resonate among potential buyers, proactive initiatives also tend to fail more often. This is quite normal in economic terms, since the higher return generated when the company has developed a new idea should also come with greater risk. At the same time, companies proactively positioning themselves as green innovators are more likely to benefit from a **halo effect** because their first mover status helps them to define their image in consumers' eyes. This partially offsets the greater risk associated with 'push' initiatives.

Halo effect: ■———
Where a company gains marketing goodwill in certain areas because consumers appreciate its actions in others.

Key issue

... companies proactively positioning themselves as green innovators are more likely to benefit from a halo effect because [of] their first mover status.

With many market segments remaining relatively ignorant of (or apathetic towards) the ecological imperative, companies often feel that they have no other choice than to pursue a 'push' approach in this field. The first step then becomes educating potential consumers about the benefits of green consumption. This can be quite difficult at a psychological level, however. Lacking previous knowledge on how innovative green products work, potential buyers' initial reaction will often be one of incredulity. The degree of resistance that companies encounter at this level depends on whether the consumer is being asked to accept a green product that offers specific quantifiable benefits, or a green brand, which is a more emotive choice (see Figure 7.3).

? How feasible is it to educate people to 'consume green'?

Figure 7.3: Proactive vs. responsive green marketing matrix

	Companies marketing a green product	Companies marketing a green brand
Consumers already sensitised to the ecological imperative	Responsive 'pull': volume markets driven by competitive arguments such as price	Responsive 'pull': company hopes for 'halo effect' helping to sell other products
Consumers not yet sensitised to the ecological imperative	Proactive 'push': argument focused on material benefits such as lower 'lifecycle' costs	Proactive 'push': long-term project to educate potential future customers

Companies can overcome reactions of incredulity with messages containing at least one element familiar to consumers. For consumers – especially from the LOHAS segment – a new green product's health-related benefits can fit the bill. On other occasions, the company will want to invoke a lifecycle costing (LCC) arguments, asking buyers to reason in terms of the savings that the green product offers over the long run. Because this is more of an intellectual argument than an emotional one, however, its potential use is limited in mass consumer markets. On the other hand, intellectual green arguments are likely to be better received in B2B sectors where the customers are themselves professionals and therefore accustomed to approaches such as LCC.

■ The green marketing mix

From their general marketing classes, students will be familiar with standard marketing mix parameters such as product, price, promotion, place (the 'four Ps'). The section below applies these tools in an environmental context.

Green products

There are various ways of categorising green products. One is to distinguish between items that generate no direct environmental benefits themselves but are manufactured according to environmental principles and others whose green benefits are realised by the end user upon consumption. Other comparators include products' health and safety profile, the amount of waste (including packaging) with which they are associated and, as aforementioned, their lifecycle costing. Different green arguments will have varying impacts on different target markets.

7

Different green arguments will have varying impacts on different target markets.

Key issue

B2B green products

General Electric (www.ge.com), a diversified group best known for its industrial strengths, provides a prime example of the kinds of green products that industrialists might offer professional customers. In 2005, GE launched a new environmental solutions division called 'Ecomagination', which was given the mission of marketing industrial systems to enhance customers' operational and environmental performance. As demonstrated in Table 7.1, the division operates an extremely broad portfolio of sustainable products. It positions itself vis-à-vis the competition by calculating the savings that customers can make in energy consumption and carbon emission terms. It also publishes its own targets for reducing greenhouse gas emissions and water usage.

Table 7.1: Partial list of green industrial products offered by GE (http://ge.ecomagination.com/site/#ecel)

Category	Product name	Function and/or description
Water	Advanced Biological Metals Removal Process (ABMet)	Protects the environment from excess levels of nitrate, selenium and other heavy metals found in wastewater streams from power plants, mines and agricultural sites
	Waste-to-Value Solution	Converts organic industrial waste into renewable resources
	Pro and Titan Reverse Osmosis	Removes over 99 per cent of salt contaminants from brackish water sources in industrial plants. Operates with low energy membranes producing savings of above 45 per cent
Energy	Zonal™ Combustion Optimization System	Sensors and proprietary software with optional adjustable burners, airflow and coal flow dampers…Improves [power plant] efficiency, reliability and availability while cutting emissions
	DLN 2.6+ Combustion System	Reduces gas turbine NOx emissions to between 9 and 15 parts per million
	Gasification Combined Cycle	Converts coal into a high-value, cleaner burning fuel… Cuts key power plant pollutants by as much as 50 per cent
Transportation	CFM56-3 Time on Wing (TOW) Upgrade	Modifies key components of the CFM56-3 engine to cut maintenance costs, raise fuel efficiency and lower levels of greenhouse gas emissions
	China Mainline Evolution locomotive	Cut emissions and is more fuel-efficient than most locomotives in China today
	DusTreat Road Dust Control Treatment	Controls fugitive dust from unpaved plant, mine ramps and haul roads.
Lighting	Compact Fluorescent Lighting (CFL)	Over 90 per cent of GE's CFLs are ENERGY STAR®-qualified
	Tetra® LED Lighting Systems	Commercial signage and architectural lighting…. energy savings, long life, reduced maintenance

To achieve these targets, GE invested more than $1 billion in clean technology R&D in 2007, with $1.5 billion budgeted for the year 2010. The main areas of focus were renewable-energy, transportation and water use and purification. Business has been good, with the company predicting that Ecomagination should increase revenues from $14 billion in 2007 to $25 billion by 2010. With this drive, CEO Jeffrey Immelt has moved his company beyond the days when his predecessor, Jack Welch, used to downplay GE's environmental responsibility, for instance, for the chemical pollution of New York State's Hudson

River (Esty and Wilson 2006). Today, the company is perfectly placed for the large contracts that the US government will put to tender over the next few years as the Obama Administration implements its campaign promise to restore American infrastructure via green energy grid projects. It is also well placed to bid on contracts for similar green construction projects overseas. Note the main rivals with whom GE will be vying in the global green utilities sector: ABB from Switzerland; Siemens from Germany; and Mitsui from Japan. All have learned to re-engineer their existing industrial systems and/or design new ones in a way that maximises environmental benefits. Furthermore, all derive green marketing benefits from this positioning.

B2C green products

Green products translate public concerns about the ecological imperative at the level of people's individual consumption. This is exemplified by the response to the decision taken at the 1987 UN conference in Montreal to reduce the global production of ozone-depleting CFC chemicals. In line with this new policy, companies worldwide, led by the giant American conglomerate Westinghouse and European white goods specialist Electrolux, designed a whole new range of refrigerators with coolant systems using a less hazardous chemical compound called HCFC. Within a few short years, consumers had accepted HCFC refrigerators as the sector standard.

> **?** How different is it marketing green products B2B or B2C?

Another example from the same period involved babies' diapers (nappies). In response to public concerns about the growing mountain of used, non-biodegradable diapers being sent to landfill, consumer product manufacturers including Procter and Gamble in the USA or Unilever in Europe began experimenting with 'super-absorbent' polymer that could produce the same functionalities as the product's existing components but required fewer material inputs. As was the case with refrigerators, consumers were relatively quick to migrate to the new green standard. Within a short period of time, however, concerns were being expressed regarding the new diapers' disposability. This is a recurring problem in the field of green marketing, with new products often responding to the environmental issues associated with past product generations but raising their own issues in turn.

One example of this dilemma is the recent rise of online information services. If people get their news online, this will reduce the use of paper, hence deforestation and pollution from paper mills. At the same time, reading online consumes electricity and above all requires portals like PCs, iphones or the Amazon Kindle – all of which are produced using material inputs. Like most economic decisions, green products often involve compromises between conflicting solutions.

On some occasions, however, green products can be deemed an unmitigated environmental success, particularly where they result from real technological progress. For instance, the biodegradability of different forms of plastic – materialising in the mountains of polystyrene and non-recyclable trash or shopping bags that accumulate in nature or on waste disposal sites (di Benedetto and Chandran 1995) – has long been an area of real concern for environmentally-conscious consumers. Facing this polystyrene problem almost 20 years ago, McDonalds and Burger King tried to win favour with the public by phasing out their old foam containers and replacing them with paper or cardboard-based substances that were often made from recycled materials. As aforementioned, in and of itself this positioning would not have sufficed to assure revenues – but when implemented in conjunction with the companies' normal marketing promises, they were effective as an additional sales argument. Along the same lines, the shopping bag market has in recent years witnessed a similarly positive development in B2C green marketing. Complementing grocers' efforts to get shoppers to voluntarily abandon carrier bags (see Chapter 6), new names such as Australia's Envirotrend or the UK's Greengrocer have created a thriving sector involving the design and sale of fashionable bags made out of recyclable or organic materials. Associating green products with elegant overtones is one of the approaches that contemporary companies use to get consumers to transition to the new product ranges. In this portrayal, it is chic to be green.

Key issue	Associating green products with elegant overtones is one of the approaches that contemporary companies use to get consumers to transition to the new product ranges. In this portrayal, it is chic to be green.

Green consumer durables

The green household appliance sector offers many examples of successful green consumer durables. There have been a number of breakthroughs in this area, derived from the creation of new product lines (e.g. eco-kettles launched by Product Creation Ltd, a small UK design company) or from an improvement in existing ones (e.g. energy-efficient Samsung or Sony televisions that switch off automatically). Further examples of green consumer durables include telecommunications (e.g.

solar-powered mobile phone chargers, handset recycling networks) and personal computers (e.g. low power systems; energy-efficient mice from Apple; or cooling technology from Sun Microsystem). All of these products have in common the fact that they are conducive to messaging that appeals simultaneously to consumers' emotions (trendiness) and rationality (lower LCC, reduced energy consumption). Clearly, this dual argument enhances the new products' chance of success.

Green consumer perishables

The psychology associated with green perishables differs from durables since the promised benefits accrue first and foremost to the buyer instead of society as a whole. Moreover, buyers often see perishables as very personal items, an intimacy that is at odds with the sharing ethos that is otherwise an intrinsic part of green marketing's altruistic emphasis. This personalisation should have the effect of making the act of purchasing this category of goods less unusual, in that green perishables speak to self-interest much in the same way as their non-green counterparts do. It is for this reason that some of the earliest green products to have experienced mass success are perishables. Examples include organic, pesticide-free foodstuffs (i.e. cereals or snacks from MNEs such as General Mills; juices from SMEs such as Innocent; vegetables and fruit from local cooperatives) or 'natural' health and beauty products (ranging from cosmetics to bath and skin care or vitamins).

Green pricing

Green products' generally higher point-of-sale pricing partially reflects the fact that many companies will take advantage of their novelty value to impose premium pricing. Furthermore, few green products have achieved sufficient production scale to lower costs, triggering the virtuous circle of broader consumer interest leading to further economies of scale. Lastly, many green products have fundamentally higher return costs due to the care taken during their manufacturing phase to use higher-quality inputs, internalise the cost of any waste generated and provide reverse logistics facilities enabling end-of-life recycling. As detailed in Chapter 5, the value system adopted by a truly green company means that price competition will not even necessarily be viewed as a priority. Quite the contrary, the focus may be on ensuring that all of the environmental costs associated with an item's sourcing, transformation, commercialisation and ultimate disposal are fully accounted for in its price. Unlike their non-green rivals, green products are supposed to incorporate not only all ecological costs for the com-

7

pany but also for society as a whole. Where price alone is concerned, this puts them at a competitive disadvantage (see Table 7.2).

Selling expensive goods implies a niche positioning, since consumers will only migrate to the new product if they can afford to and something helps them to overcome the price barrier. Even among segments that are interested in green products and can afford them, the higher retail price is an obstacle that can only be overcome if consumers' psychological state at the time of the purchase is conducive to this. Populations where demand is inelastic to price are few and far between. The question is whether this condemns green products to a permanent minority status.

Key issue

Selling expensive goods implies a niche positioning, since consumers will only migrate to the new product if they can afford to and something helps them to overcome the price barrier.

Companies marketing green products must pursue specific avenues to overcome their price disadvantage. The most direct approach involves organising point-of-sale promotions reminding potential purchasers why they should be willing to pay more – with recent research indicating that the themes generally invoked on these occasions include the idea of supporting 'fair trade, fitness, healthy living, healthy eating, organic produce, sustainability, employment policies, charitable giving, and support for local communities' (Jones *et al.* 2007). Such appeals will be most effective if they mix emotional, brand or cause-related appeals with more reasoned arguments detailing concrete benefits (Hartmann 2005). Both registers can be useful, and indeed might be necessary where products feature a substantial **green premium**.

Green premium: Surcharge paid for a green product over a non-green product offering the same functionalities.

Table 7.2: Comparison of green and non-green retail prices (convenience sample, North London grocery store, May 2009)

Item	Green price (£)	Non-green price (£)	Green premium (%)
Potatoes (kg)	1.72	0.97	+77.3
Carrots (kg)	1.32	0.87	+51.7
Yoghurt (container)	0.45	0.29	+55.2
Chicken (kg)	4.89	2.79	+75.3
Detergent (wash)	0.194	0.175	+11

Although research has indicated that for some potential consumers the main barrier is not the green premium but insufficient awareness of green choices (Roche *et al.* 2009), intuitively it is clear that the higher the premium, the greater people's reluctance to buy green. The extent of their reluctance will depend on the product in question. A host of studies have analysed, for instance, the surcharge that rent tenants are willing to pay to inhabit green buildings; that green utilities customers will countenance; or that purchasers of different kinds of consumer perishables or durables are prepared to accept. Some have found respondents willing to pay anything between 10 per cent and 33 per cent more than they would for non-green equivalents. It would not be particularly meaningful to attempt an exhaustive list of what people consider commercially acceptable green premiums, however. Different factors come into play at this level: consumers' cultural values and demographic characteristics; prevailing socioeconomic conditions; the extent to which consumers have already been educated in LCC valuation, etc.

> **?** Why are green price premiums so high?

One example of the kind of lifecycle costing education that helps consumers to overcome the green premium barrier is the way that many solar heating companies prepare potential buyers psychologically before revealing their systems' considerable price tags (see: eight-page technical insert placed by 'Solarworld' in the May 2009 issue of German magazine Der Spiegel). Marketing communications in this area often start with in-depth analyses of the ecological imperative (global warming, rising fuel prices) followed by a discussion of potential targets' current energy bills and resource consumption behaviour; an assessment of possible future bills based on energy price forecasts; and calculations identifying the long-term savings that can be achieved by switching to solar systems. It is only at the end of this long LCC process that the new system's price is revealed. This approach reduces the psychological shock from which potential green customers are bound to suffer when discovering the high initial outlay that they are being asked to make.

7

Different factors affect people's mindset in a purchasing situation. One is the persuasion work that the company has done to prepare the moment. Another is the physical (or virtual) context of the place where the purchase takes place. This latter factor explains why 'place' is typically the third parameter in the standard marketing mix toolbox.

| Key issue | ... [LCC-based education] ... reduces the psychological shock from which potential green customers are bound to suffer when discovering the high initial outlay that they are being asked to make. |

Green places

Given green marketing's anti-gigantism ethos and antipathy to huge out-of-town shopping centres, it is unsurprising that green retail originally centred on small local stores or cooperatives often staffed by environmental devotees trying to escape the corporate lifestyle. Even today, specialist outlets still account for a disproportionately large percentage of all green product sales. They are no longer as dominant as they used to be, however, with almost all of the world's leading retail chains starting to offer green product ranges to a greater or lesser extent. Whether these ranges are interspersed with non-green goods in store sections defined by product category, or sold separately in dedicated green (or **organic**) sections, depends on whether management's main priority is normalize customers' overall transition to greener consumption or else to sharpen the store's reputation as a green provider.

Organic: ■
Grown without any
synthetic additives.

Green retailing has also developed a number of idiosyncratic distribution channels.

Guerrilla marketing

In this case, big budget campaigns based on high profile mass media vehicles are replaced by small innovative 'weapons' that are not normally associated with marketing but which – in line with environmentalism's proximity ethos – fit directly into consumers' standard day-to-day routines (Levinson 2007). In effect, this approach involves marketing specialists applying eco-friendly principles to their own medium. An example is Curb (www.mindthecurb.com/), a UK publicity agency that only uses natural vehicles such as 'clean advertising' (stencilling washable messages on random public surfaces); 'logrow' media moulding shrubs, plants, turf and other natural elements; sand or snow tagging; 'solar art' (using magnifying glasses to direct natural light); and woodcarvings.

Some analysts describe all online communications as a form of green guerrilla marketing insofar as they view the Internet as a non-traditional advertising medium. Whether or not this is accurate, the World Wide Web is a preferred host for many green communications. This can involve the viral marketing of environmentally-friendly brands as well as the sustainability sections that most MNEs' websites feature nowadays. There is also the way that environmentalists use guerrilla marketing actions to mobilise crowds. Note 'carrotmobbing', where groups of shoppers arrange online to descend all at once on stores that have agreed to reduce their environmental footprint. In one such instance, 300 shoppers spent $9276.50 in just a few hours at local San Francisco retailer K&D Market to reward it for promising to use 22 per cent of the day's turnover to improve its lighting systems and hazardous waste disposal processes (Taylor 2008). Success stories like this one bolster optimists' view that companies should view the ecological imperative first and foremost as an opportunity to redefine their business models in a way that directly benefits the bottom line.

Online green marketing can be used to publicise not only physical retail outlets but also e-commerce stores, which can reasonably claim to produce many green benefits, first and foremost being the resources that buyers and sellers both save by avoiding in-store purchasing, which generates transportation costs for customers and inventory and operating costs for retailers. Similarly, e-commerce requires less packaging and paper than traditional physical merchandising, in part because many goods (such as iTune songs or jpg files) are digitised and delivered electronically. Companies such as Amazon or Dell, part of whose supply chain operations are conducted online, also benefit from lower costs due to enhanced communications (see Chapter 6). Lastly, in pure advertising terms, online marketing is coherent with green values since the messages are being diffused via resource-thrifty media such as e-mail and other web-based solutions instead of using paper (Ahmed and Sharma 2006).

Shared platform experiences

Often web-based but also occurring in non-virtual (i.e. physical) spaces, this kind of marketing involves green consumers coming together specifically to enact certain environmental principles. The aim is generally to minimise waste and reduce consumption by sharing services and/or recycling. Rooted in a collaborative ethos, these are often small and medium-sized schemes where monetary transactions play a lesser role than usual - asides from the organisers pocketing small membership fees as a reward for hosting and marketing the service. Examples include the growing number of non-profit municipal auto and bike-share schemes where members book a vehicle for a limited period of time. A similar example from the recycling sector is the service organised by the grassroots network 'freecycle.org', whose nearly 7 million members worldwide 'gift' unwanted items to one another instead of throwing them away. Also worth mentioning is the website www.whatdoidowiththis.com, which encourages construction sector professionals and hobbyists to recycle surplus materials. This latter service is slightly different, however, since it is run on a for-profit basis (albeit with profits accruing to platform participants instead of to the organiser).

Because schemes of this nature are self-directed and usually not very lucrative, few are of major interest to big corporations. At the same time, by using this approach to build **brand tribes** (Cova *et al.* 2007), companies can foster potential customers' self-awareness as green consumers, laying foundations for a sense of identity that might subsequently turn into a commercial relationship. An example is the business model developed by UK company Worn Again, whose physical operations involve recovering ('upcycling') discarded goods, redesigning them in workshops located in Portugal and Britain before marketing them online. Worn Again is a for-profit company, although a percentage of its earnings are given to an organisation called Anti-Apathy that offers 'guilt-free fashion ... crowd-powered online platforms for change [and] sustainable lifestyles' (http://antiapathy.org/). By linking its home page with this other website, Worn Again is enlarging the psychological space where potential consumers can develop the sort of value system that will ultimately induce them to consume the kind of green products that it commercialises.

Brand tribes: Communities of consumers defined by their shared loyalty to (and often experiences with) a brand.

Key issue

... enlarging the psychological space where potential consumers can develop the sort of value system that will ultimately induce them to consume the kind of green products that it commercialises.

Eco-sponsoring of this kind (see *Web Resource 7.2*) is one of the most efficient tools used in proactive green approaches where, as aforementioned, the impetus for the business opportunity comes from the company itself. It can also be categorised as a kind of green promotion – the final and probably most widely discussed parameters in the (green) marketing mix toolbox.

Green promotions

In a world where some multinationals' revenues exceed the gross domestic product of entire national economies – thus where the consequences of corporate activities extend well beyond the commercial sphere alone – companies can only truly legitimise their power in the long run if they are viewed as responsible members of the communities in which they operate. Green marketing sends out concrete signals that a particular company is not only cognizant of stakeholders' ecological concerns but also proactive about improving the environment. This attitude has been shown to have real benefits for a company's brand image, thus its bottom line. McDonalds offers a prime example of this sort of **green redemption**. Denounced for decades for the allegedly directly or indirectly negative effects of its fast food business model, the company now receives spontaneous praise from leading environmentalists (Juniper 2008) appreciative of its green re-branding programmes. McDonalds' actions in this area have included the decision to turn cooking oil into bio-diesel to fuel its fleet of company trucks or to sell coffee with sustainable certification from the Rainforest Alliance, a respected international activist group (Barkham 2008). The latter example is particularly symbolic for a giant multinational whose meat procurement policies used to be highly criticised by green activists as contributing, however indirectly, to the destruction of the Amazon rainforest. McDonalds' green makeover means that it receives less negative press nowadays. This enhances its overall reputational capital and helps consolidate existing consumers' loyalty.

■ **Green redemption:** Where a company that once suffered from a reputation of environmental destruction restores its brand image through green (marketing) actions.

In a pure marketing sense, however, promotion refers to a whole range of communications initiatives, including point-of-sales actions, internal corporate communications and external advertising. It is this latter aspect that is most apparent to (and has the most effect on) potential green consumers.

Back in the early 1990s, as more and more companies began promoting their green credentials, expressions like 'bio-degradable' and even 'recyclable' or 'refillable' were relatively new and would often be misused by companies. In the United States, a body called the Federal Trade Commission responded by issuing a series of guidelines requiring companies not to overstate a product's green promise and to clarify whether the stated benefits actually reflected the inputs used for its production, the effects of its consumption or the nature of its packaging (Polonsky 1995). Despite these early steps towards a code of conduct for green promotions, the explosion in environmental advertising over the past 20 years meant a wave of exaggerated and sometimes false green claims, often involving vague associations with the terms 'sustainable', 'organic' or 'greenest in its class' (Tibbetts 2008). Such behaviour has undermined green promotions' credibility for many potential customers, reinforcing their reluctance to adopt green consumption patterns

7

that already suffer from the dual handicap of being expensive and new. This can be aggravated by the risk of 'green fatigue' if the target audience has been overly solicited with environmental messages.

Key issue	... a wave of exaggerated and sometimes false green claims......[has reinforced potential customers'] reluctance to adopt green consumption patterns that already suffer from the dual handicap of being expensive and new.

Given the other obstacles that green marketing faces, companies cannot afford this added hurdle of scepticism. One way that they have tried to overcome it is through eco-labelling (see Chapter 5). The crucial factor at this level is that the environmental message be crafted in a way that fits the circumstances. Companies can appeal to consumers' rationality; social responsibility; subjectivity; and/or material interest. The effectiveness of each emphasis will vary in time and place. For instance, if an advertisement focuses on emotionality and oversimplifies the rational aspect of the green purchasing decision, consumers may feel belittled in their role as citizen-consumers (Frame and Newton 2007). Conversely, if a green promotion is too complex or political, its message may not be accessible to enough people – with studies revealing that objective, knowledge-based LCC arguments can create negative reactions to an advertisement, even as they improve the credibility of the brand and company involved (Molina-Murillo and Smith 2009). In short, the tonalities that companies use in their green promotion – whether bucolic wildlife-based literary references, neutral science, passionate manifestos, catastrophic subtexts or calm persuasion (Allen 1990) – are crucial to marketing success.

Environmental messages tend to indicate different combinations of strategic positioning (see Table 7.3). For instance, a company with a damaged green reputation in need of repair might choose to combine a green brand focus with appeals to the wider social benefits of environmentally-friendly behaviour. One example is a May 2009 advertisement by German engineering company Siemens showing a child standing in front of an aquarium and asking whether it is possible to wash water. Neither this strapline, nor the explanation provided for it (that the company is responsible for municipal purification processes in Singapore) relates directly to a kind of product that one of the magazine's readers might consider buying. They do solidify Siemens's technical reputation, however, while enveloping its general brand image in a (green) halo – a benefit that the marketing department will have considered crucial following the ethics scandal that had rocked the company earlier in 2009. Similarly, green promotions by companies such as BP, Shell or Exxon Mobil highlighting their renewable energy research may be partially driven by a desire to counter criticisms of their past environmental behaviour.

Conversely, companies might choose to highlight their brands' green credentials while appealing to consumer self-interest when they want to overcome their reputation as relative newcomers to the field of sustainability. One example is a May 2009 advertisement run by British supermarket Asda showing employees discussing how cost savings achieved in areas such as packaging and fuel efficiency might feed through to lower retail prices. Note that such advertisements generally combine generic social branding with personalised green promises. This is because the complexity of green marketing often requires newcomers to play on several registers at once if they are to gain consumers' attention.

Product-specific advertising identifying green benefits for society as a whole tends to be used by companies offering a more expensive range of goods or services, and who therefore have very little chance of appealing to consumers' self-interest. This register is also appropriate for 'popular, well trusted brands [with] the potential to build on the relationship that they have with customers' (Aitken 2007). Examples include campaigns by the Eurostar train service between Paris and London detailing plans to further reduce per-passenger CO_2 emissions on a transportation mode that is already much greener than its rivals (planes, passenger cars). For this company, green promotion is more of a way to consolidate and extend its current marketing positioning rather than a radical shift in focus.

Lastly, product-specific green advertisements focusing on consumer self-interest are often found in saturated markets where differentiation requires as personal a promise as possible. Thus, one specificity high-lighted in Procter and Gamble Europe's 2008 Ariel detergent, namely that it washes clothes at lower temperatures, appealed to consumers' desire for lower utilities bills more than to the idea of society as a whole consuming less energy. To a certain extent, personal promises are more relevant to products that are intimate to an individual, and/or where the target segment has not been identified as being particularly sensitive to altruistic arguments.

7

Table 7.3: How companies position their green promotions depends on their particular marketing needs

	Brand focus	Product-specific
Appeals to social benefits	Need to repair image	Less price-sensitive
Appeals to consumer self-interest	Newcomers	Saturated markets

The above categorisation is not exhaustive, largely because hybrid positions are always possible. For example, companies may need to position themselves in a certain light in some markets but differently elsewhere. One example is the way that energy giant Shell positioned its Pura zero-sulphur diesel liquid in Thailand, where cities can be very smoggy and customers sensitive to arguments highlighting the product's clean aspects, versus the Netherlands, where consumers are more sensitive to arguments stressing engine power (Esty and Wilson 2006). There are also situations where a company will promote some but not all of its products in a green light. An example of this is the choice that Toyota made in 2009 to run a US advertisement showing its Tundra trucks driving through flames under swooping helicopters – an image contrasting sharply with the green reputation associated with Toyota's Prius hybrids. To some extent, promoting non-green images is a luxury that can only be afforded by companies that have already consolidated a sufficiently green reputation.

Consumers' receptiveness to a green promotion will also depend on the extent to which they view it as fact-based or, to the contrary, as manipulative. This wariness is very much part of the zeitgeist of cynicism characterising today's consumers. It has been encapsulated in a new marketing concept – the '99 to 1' rule, or the accusation that some companies devote 99 per cent of their promotional efforts to green product lines that constitute a mere 1 per cent of their actual portfolio. It is cognitively confusing for consumers to believe in companies (or products) that are green in a few respects and non-green in most others. Such confusion has led to a rising number of complaints to regulatory watchdogs worldwide concerning instances of greenwash. A recent example was when UK's Advertising Standards Authority demanded that Renault withdraw an advertisement because it exaggerated the benefits of a vehicle that the company calls 'economical ecological' and classifies as part of its so-called Eco2 scheme – without defining what these terms actually mean (Stewart 2008).

... ['greenwash'] accusation that some companies devote 99 percent of their promotional efforts to green product lines that constitute a mere 1 per cent of their actual portfolio.	**Key issue**

Similar cases involving the same government body have included actions launched against discount airliner Ryanair for stating that 'aviation accounts for just 2 per cent of CO_2 emissions' when the British figure is 5.5 per cent; against Shell for claiming that it uses its waste CO_2 to grow flowers when this only accounts for 0.325 per cent of the company's overall emissions; and against Toyota for claiming CO_2 emissions savings on its Prius hybrid vehicles that reflect average US driving distances rather than European ones (Tibbetts 2008). All of these cases have had the effect of undermining the general credibility of green promotions – a bad proposition in an area where marketing already has enough obstacles to overcome.

■ Obstacles and pathways

1 Potential customers may not be motivated by a social marketing ethos.

   Position the product so that it combines self-interest and altruism arguments.

2 Green products are comparatively expensive.

   Marketing effort must include investment in lifecycle costing education.

3 Green products are given a relatively small share of total shelf space.

   Augment in-store promotions, possibly to the detriment of the mass media budget.

4 Consumers are often cynical about veracity of green claims.

   Devise communications that are more factual and technical in nature.

7

Case study: Wal-mart eats its greens

One of the more striking examples of the search for green redemption is the re-positioning of US giant Wal-mart, the world's leading retailer. For many years, the company had undergone severe criticism from a variety of sources, crystallising most notably in a scathing 2006 documentary called 'Wal-mart – the High Cost of Low Price'. Much of the negative publicity in this film revolved around the retailer's social practices, often relating to its famously anti-union policies, low-wage culture and pressure on poor overseas suppliers. Its environmental misconduct also received some attention. For instance, in 2004 the US Environmental Protection Agency levied a fine of $3.1 million on Wal-mart for Clean Water Act violations in multiple states – the largest ever penalty for a retailer – with one local authority ordering the company to pay a further $1.15 million in 2005. In the spring of that same year, activist groups set up a website (http://Wal-martwatch.com/) in a bid to launch 'public education campaign to challenge the world's largest retailer, Wal-Mart, to become a better employer, neighbor, and corporate citizen'. This website highlighted the aforementioned fines and listed a series of other environmental problems for which Wal-mart was blamed, including air pollution, stormwater runoff violations and oil storage disputes. The company's main challenges in terms of its sustainability image may have been centred on labour standards at the time, but its green image also needed repair.

In a 2005 speech about '21st century leadership', Wal-mart CEO Lee Scott admitted that apart from the need for more recycling and less waste, he used to consider the environment as one of Wal-mart's lesser concerns. After witnessing the devastation of Hurricane Katrina and receiving advice from McKinsey that the company should proactively seek to become 'a role model on a significant societal issue', Scott changed course and embarked on a series of high-profile green initiatives. The new policy included reducing Wal-mart's use of food product packaging, increasing the fuel efficiency of its fleet of delivery trucks and selling a wider selection of green products such as organic food or energy-efficient light bulbs. The company actively sought environmental advice from leading non-governmental organisations such as the Environmental Defence Fund (http://www.edf.org/). It also started to communicate increasingly green messages, running for instance a web-based clip in 2009 showing normal employees speaking to the camera to explain how the group's sale of 'more than 260 million compact fluorescent light bulbs [has eliminated] the need for3 coal-fired power plants'.

All of these actions can be classified as ecological and would therefore justify that Wal-mart position itself as environmentally-friendly without being accused of greenwash. Yet critics continued to denounce the company, affirming that the new initiatives were little more than token gestures. This scepticism largely reflected the size of Wal-mart's footprint. The extra 28 million metric tons in CO_2 emissions resulting from the new stores that the company is planning to build by 2013 far exceed the 2.5 million metric tons in savings that it was hoping to achieve through the aforementioned measures (Mitchell 2007). More generally, Wal-mart's business model has been accused of being fundamentally energy-inefficient: relying on goods sourced from all across the world; requiring shoppers to drive additional distances to visit out-of-town store locations; and operating outlets that consume great quantities of energy in comparison with other retailers. Wal-mart has also continued to suffer bad publicity due to the many acres of land spoliated by the stores that it opens and sometimes subsequently abandons. In short, despite the green re-make upon which Wal-mart has embarked, it has not yet fully consolidated its reputation for environmentalism.

This will have been frustrating to management, but instead of highlighting Wal-mart's progress, Lee Scott stated in an amazing interview with the Wall Street Journal dated 14 March 2008, that 'we are not green', averring that his company did not 'have a clue' about how it would meet its goal of 'eliminating waste and providing 100 per cent renewable energy'. The general public could react to this admission in several ways. People more inclined to view Wal-mart in a positive light would be reassured by Scott's honesty and view the interview as proof that he eschews greenwash and is trustworthy. By summer 2010, for instance, environmentally-conscious manufacturers such as cleaning products specialist Seventh Generation that used to purposefully avoid selling through Walmart had reversed their stance and were cooperating with the company. Others would react with scepticism, however, in the belief that Scott's statement merely reinforces the argument that the giant retailer's business model is fundamentally non-green. Because people tend to have a longer memory of misconduct than of good behaviour, Wal-mart will need years of constructive green marketing to repair its image. By definition, environmentalism requires long-term commitment.

Case study questions

1 Why has there been so much criticism of Wal-mart's ethics over the years?

2 Why and how did CEO Lee Scott re-position Wal-mart in 2005?

3 How has the new positioning affected Walmart's image?

7

■ References

Ahmed, N. and Sharma, S. (2006), 'Porter's value chain model for assessing the impact of the internet for environmental gains', *International Journal of Management and Enterprise Development*, **3** (3).

Aitken, L. (2007), 'Wiping out greenwash', *The Guardian, Media*, 19 November, p. 9.

Allen, E. (1990), *Green Ink*, World Wide Fund for Nature.

Barkham, P. (2008), 'The big McMakeover', *The Guardian*, section G2, 28 January , p. 6.

Bonini, S. and Oppenheim, J. (2008), 'Helping "green" products grow', October, available at www.mckinseyquarterly.com, accessed 23 April 2009.

Cova, B., Kozinets, R. and Shankar, A. (2007), *Consumer Tribes*, Oxford: Butterworth Heinemann.

Dahl, S. (2002), *Communication and Culture Transformation: Cultural Diversity, Globalization and Cultural Convergence*, ECE Europacom.

Deloitte and Grocery Manufacturers Association (2009), 'Finding the green in today's shoppers: sustainability trends and new shopper insights', April, available at www.deloitte.com, accessed 12 May 2009.

Di Benedetto, C. and Chandran, R. (1995), 'Behaviors of environmentally concerned firms: an agenda for effective strategic development', in M. Polonsky and A. Mintu-Wimsatt (eds), *Environmental Marketing: Strategies Practice, Theory and Research*, London: Haworth Press.

Donaldson, B. (2009), *The Busy Manager's Guide to Marketing*, Oxford: Goodfellow Publishers.

Esty, D. and Winston, A. (2006), *Green to Gold: How Smart Companies Use Environmental Strategy to Innovate, Create Value and Build Competitive Advantage*, New Haven, CT: Yale University Press.

Finisterra do Paço, A., Raposo, M. L. B. and Filho, W. (2009), 'Identifying the green consumer: A segmentation study', *Journal of Targeting, Measurement and Analysis for Marketing*, **17** (1).

Frame, B. and Newton, B. (2007), 'Promoting sustainability through social marketing: examples from New Zealand', *International Journal of Consumer Studies*, **31** (6).

Gaudelli, J. (2009), 'Generate insight: confused teens choose "less expensive" over "green"', 22 April, available at www.marketingcharts.com/, accessed 8 May 2009.

Grant, J. (2007), *The Green Marketing Manifesto*, John Wiley & Sons.

Hartmann, P. (2005), 'Green branding effects on attitude: functional versus emotional positioning strategies', *Marketing Intelligence & Planning*, **23** (1).

Jones, P., COmfort, D. and Hillier, D. (2007), 'What's in store? Retail marketing and corporate social responsibility', *Marketing Intelligence & Planning*, **25** (1).

Juniper, T. (2008), 'How McDonald's finally got green', 30 November, available at http://www.guardian.co.uk/, accessed on 2 May 2009.

Kotler, P. and Lee, N. (2005), *Corporate Social Responsibility: Doing the Most Good for Your Company and Your Cause*, John Wiley & Sons.

Lee, K. (2009), 'Gender differences in Hong Kong adolescent consumers' green purchasing behavior', *Journal of Consumer Marketing*, **26** (2).

Levinson, J. (2007), *Guerilla Marketing: Easy and Inexpensive Strategies for Making Big Profits from Your Small Business*, 4th edn, Boston, MA: Houghton Mifflin (Trade).

Mackoy, R., Calantone, R. and Droge, C. (1995), 'Environmental marketing: bridging the divide between the consumption culture and environmentalism', in M. Polonsky and A. Mintu-Wimsatt (eds), *Environmental Marketing: Strategies Practice, Theory and Research*, London: Haworth Press.

Mitchell, S. (2007), *The impossibility of a green Wal-mart*, 28 March, available at www.grist.org, accessed 11 May 2009.

Molina-Murillo, S. and Smith, T. (2009), 'Exploring the use and impact of LCC-based information in corporate communications', *The International Journal of Lifecycle costing*, **14** (2).

Mostafa, M. (2007), 'Gender differences in Egyptian consumers' green purchase behaviour: the effects of environmental knowledge, concern and attitude', *International Journal of Consumer Studies*, 31 (3).

Paladino, A. (2005), 'Understanding the green consumer: an empirical analysis', *Journal of Customer Behaviour*, **4** (1).

Peattie, K. and Crane, A. (2005), 'Green marketing: legend, myth, farce or prophesy?', *Qualitative Market Research: An International Journal*, **8** (4).

Polonsky, M. (1995), 'Cleaning up green marketing claims: a practical checklist', in M. Polonsky and A. Mintu-Wimsatt (eds), *Environmental Marketing: Strategies, Practice, Theory and Research*, London: Haworth Press.

Proverbio, S., Smit,S. and Viguerie, S. P. (2008), 'Dissecting global trends: An example from Italy', March, available at http://www.mckinseyquarterly.com/, accessed 26 September 2008.

Roche, C., Manget, J. and Munnich, F. (2009), 'Capturing the green advantage', 7 May, available www.environmentalleader.com/, accessed 8 May 2009.

Sitkin, A. and Bowen, N. (2010), *International Business: Challenges and Choices*, Oxford: Oxford University Press.

Stewart, B. (2008), 'Advertising environmentalism – is it just greenwash?', 31 March, available at www.independent.co.uk/, accessed 10 May 2009.

Taylor, T. (2008), 'Meet the carrotmob', *The Guardian*, 18 September, p. 18.

Thurrott, P. (2007), *Lenovo Tops in Environmental Friendliness*, Penton media, available at www.windowsitpro.com/, accessed 10 October 2008.

Tibbetts, G. (2008), 'Green ad complaints at record level, says watchdog', *Daily Telegraph*, 26 April.

7

8 Ecology and International Business

Learning objectives

After reading this chapter, you will be able to:

- Identify how the ecological imperative impacts upon international business

- Set MNEs' greening of their strategies and supply chains within an international context.

- Set economic emergence within an environmental context .

■ Introduction

One of the main trends characterising business life in recent decades has been greater internationalisation, encapsulated by a considerable rise in the proportion of total economic activity being conducted on a cross-border basis (Sitkin and Bowen 2010). Given that the sum total of global trade accounts for more than one half of total wealth creation in many of the world's leading economies nowadays, robust analysis of the evolving relationship between Ecology and Management is only possible if the international aspects of this equation are taken into account. This is especially important given the significant variations in national approaches to green business. Whether this involves the environmental aspects of organisational efforts by multinational enterprises' (MNEs) efforts or the more structural problems associated with international business itself, it is only by taking a global view that it becomes possible to apprehend the full scope of the ecological challenge that most companies face at home and abroad.

At one level, there is little question but that different national cultures tend to embody a wide variety of attitudes towards corporate responsibility (CR) in general and the environment in particular. Comparative analysis of countries' varying affinities with the ecological mindset is clearly a relevant field of study (see *Web Resource 8.1*), albeit one that is probably more useful in an anthropological study of environmentalism than in a management textbook. On another level, international business speaks to many of the questions raised in Chapter 4's discussion of green economics and politics. For instance, it is always useful to question to what extent a political regime acknowledges the ecological imperative at a given moment in time, if only because this provides some measure of the constraints and/or opportunities that managers are likely to face when doing business in that country. As an example, it is not unjustified to suggest some connection between the ecological inertia characterising the administration of former US President George W. Bush and the way in which leading US automakers fell behind Toyota in the race to develop environmentally-friendly motor vehicles (see Chapter 1). Conversely, the presence of Green Party representatives in Germany's governing coalition over the same period of time (early 2000s) goes a long way towards explaining the country's success in nurturing a solar panels industry, largely driven by state-subsidised feed-in tariffs system that created incentives for consumers to migrate towards renewable energy (see Chapter 10). Yet it would be wrong to take too static a view of any country's long-term predisposition towards creating a framework conducive to the expansion of green business. It is also in the USA that many of the breakthrough technologies enabling the clean energy sector's take-off are being achieved. As for Germany, the country's undeniably strong green credentials do not prevent domestic carmakers from continuing to manufacture over-powered vehicles exacerbating the already substantial environmental footprint of its major heavy industry. No nations are unadulterated environmental heroes or villains.

> **?** Are some cultures fundamentally greener than others?

... it is always useful question to what extent a given political regime acknowledges the ecological imperative [to get] some measure of the constraints and/or opportunities that managers are likely to face [here].

Key issue

■ Multinational enterprises and the environment

The sheer size of many of today's leading MNEs means that it is worth studying the environmental implications of their actions, irrespective of the framework created by a particular national government. This is especially true in light of the considerable role that mega-firms play in shaping environmental law (Levy and Newell 2004) through their lobbying activities and also because they can and often do threaten to invest elsewhere if local regulations become too stringent and/or costly. Thus, the relative power of MNE executives vis-à-vis a national governments is one factor determining the dynamics of green international business. Other relevant considerations include the profitability demands that shareholders put on a particular MNE (in part a function of national attitudes towards the role of business in society); incentive schemes devised by governments to catalyse companies' green transition; the benefits associated with an environmentally-friendly brand image in different cultures; and/or managers' personal value systems. The sum total of these influences has translated into a patchwork of green performances worldwide, at both a strategic level and in terms of MNEs' physical operations.

8

■   MNEs' green strategies

Chapter 5 has already identified links between certain organisational structures and the way in which a company's staff members might view the world. International business literature contains a whole subset of studies devoted to MNEs' dilemma of whether to centralise strategic decision-making in their global headquarters or decentralise authority to the subsidiary level (Sitkin and Bowen 2010). One of the advantages of the latter approach is that decisions made closer to local markets tend to be more adapted to customer demand. Conversely, where decisions are centralised, the MNE will benefit from a more coherent global policy, albeit one that may be less suited to the specificities of their different national markets (see Figure 8.1). With regards to green business paradigms, MNE structure can be a double-edged sword, depending on whether the ecological imperative is being pushed by global headquarters or pulled by local managers (and/or customers).

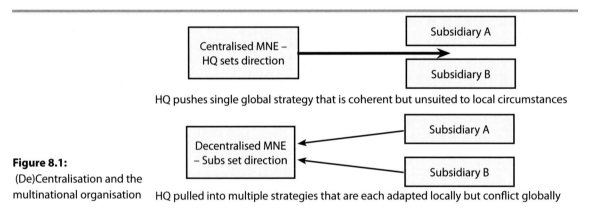

Figure 8.1:
(De)Centralisation and the multinational organisation

Analysis at this level is complicated by the fact that green demand is stronger in some markets than in others. MNEs regularly find themselves in a position where they must decide whether to seek the highest common denominator and offer better quality but more expensive green products (and operations) everywhere at the risk of pricing themselves out of certain markets – or the lowest common denominator where they concentrate on less environmentally-oriented segments at the risk of disappointing greener customers in some locations. In an ideal world, the MNE would tailor its offer to different markets but this is not always practical, if only because adaptations of this sort make it harder for companies to achieve the economies of scale that have become such a key factor of competitive advantage in so many markets today. Indeed, there is an argument that all else remaining equal, MNEs whose executive bodies fully embrace the ecological imperative are best advised to pursue their greening strategy out of global headquarters, since implementation requires a holistic overview that is difficult to drive out of local offices.

A second and related deep trend affecting MNE organisations in recent years has been operational fragmentation, with entities in some locations being asked to specialise in a given production, assembly or sales function, depending on the site's specific comparative advantages. This has resulted in an explosion in the volume of intra-firm trading, which according to some estimates accounts nowadays for up to 60 per cent of all international business volumes. In turn, this puts upwards pressure on most MNEs' environmental footprint, in part because expanded intra-firm trading patterns have increased resource use for packaging and transportation purposes. Fragmented supply chains' environmental performance is also more difficult to analyse, if only because data monitoring may not be commensurate on different sites. Add to this the rapid expansion in international **outsourcing**, where companies ship inputs purchased from external partners increasingly located on the other side of the world, and it is clear that many MNEs' entire value chains are being developed with little or no regard for the ecological imperative. Reshaping MNE configurations along green lines – for instance, by **nearsourcing** supplies and migrating towards the cross-border transfer of knowledge rather than physical goods – is a monumental effort that could only be decided and implemented by global level executives insofar as they are the only managers with sufficient authority over their group's overall resource base.

> **?** Are today's extensive MNE networks necessarily less energy-inefficient?

> ■**Outsourcing:** Where a company buys the supplies that it needs for its products or services from an outside company instead of making them itself.

> ■ **Nearsourcing:** Where a company moves to procure supplies from a provider located closer to them.

.. [fragmented global supply chains and] increased intra-firm trading patterns have increased resource use for packaging and transportation purposes.

Key issue

8

This is not to say that intermediate steps cannot be taken to introduce greening strategies within today's fragmented paradigm. One example is the way in which some firms, such as Dow Chemical, have introduced **internal waste tax** systems to ensure that each business unit takes responsibility for its pollution behaviour and pays a notional fine to a central clearing body as compensation (Epstein and Roy 1998). Another is the internal carbon trading system that BP set up to motivate units worldwide to alter their environmental behaviour. Of course, schemes of this kind can be high problematic in decentralised organisations where the centre lacks the power to impose and police them.

> ■ **Internal waste tax:** Invoicing system where the different entities comprising a multidivisional company pay notional fines for the waste they produce.

More debatable is the exact unit within the group where the MNE should centre its environmental standards and reporting activities. At one level, headquarters is arguably the entity that should ascertain which units might engage in widely recognised quality processes such as ISO14001, and indeed whether qualification for the award should be organised on an MNE-wide basis or at the level of specific units. In terms of reporting, however, the absence of a single international environmental disclosure standard means that local subsidiaries may be in a better position to identify local stakeholders' legal, cultural or business expectations and devise the relevant metrics based on this. Again, different companies' preferred solutions will depend on whether they have a global environmental coordinator working out of headquarters or local supervisors operating within each regional or national unit.

Comparisons of MNEs' reporting behaviour do reveal significant variations across the world. CorporateRegister.com, a website dedicated to tracking such information, has discovered for instance that whereas only a slightly higher percentage of European companies engage in non-financial reporting than their US counterparts do, they are much likelier to rely on external auditors (see Chapter 5) – an approach that, according to GRI guidelines, constitutes best practice in this domain. This would intimate that the quality of environmental information provided by European companies is superior insofar as it has been compiled by a third party who necessarily has less of an interest in manipulating the publication for greenwash reasons than the company itself might have. Another recent study (Moore and Wen 2008) has determined that US sustainability reporting seems relatively more focused on general ethics, whereas a higher proportion of European (and to a smaller extent, Asian) MNEs focus on the environment. Explanations for this discrepancy might include longstanding concerns in the USA about corporate governance issues, whereas Europe and Asia – with their higher population densities – are more concerned by resource depletion and pollution. In sum, given these regional variations in reporting emphasis, managers in MNEs originating from different parts of the so-called developed world are likely to be oriented towards different kinds and levels of environmental engagement.

Key issue | .. managers in MNEs originating from different parts of the ...world are likely to be oriented towards different kinds and levels of environmental engagement.

The same applies in the developing world, whose changing economic circumstances might be expected to affect leading local companies' attitudes towards the ecological imperative. Some researchers have found that at the current stage of China's economic development, short-term economic considerations remain more important than sustainability concerns to many managers worried that environmental reporting will be a costly enterprise that lacks credibility and betrays confidentiality (Rowen and Wehrmeyer 2001). At the same time, other more recent studies of China's larger and more profitable firms have discovered a growing willingness to disclose environmental information (Zhang *et al.* 2009), intimating a positive correlation between acceptance of the ecological imperative and a company's confidence in its own survival prospects. It will be useful in coming years to monitor the relationship between national economic development trajectories and local companies' green strategies – the kind of analysis currently being undertaken by bodies such as the Social Investment Research Analyst Network (www.siran.org/).

■ MNEs' green operations

As demonstrated in Chapter 6, a growing number of firms are trying nowadays to augment their eco-efficiency through a partial or complete revamp of their value chains. One vehicle towards this end is the so-called 'industrial ecology' approach based on clusters where the heat or waste products produced by one company become inputs for another. For practical reasons, such arrangements depend on upstream suppliers and downstream purchasers of goods (raw materials, components or finished products) operating next to one another. However, today such proximity tends to be the exception rather than the rule. This is because of a trend towards longer supply chains (Figure 8.2), grounded in many MNEs' calculation that the higher transportation costs associated with longer distance value chains will have less of a bottom line effect than the gains derived from sourcing inputs produced in distant low-cost countries.

8

	Nearby supplier in high cost country 1	Distant supplier in low cost country 2
Manufacturing costs	M1	M2
+ Logistic costs	+ L1	+ L2
= Total return costs	= T1	= T2

Figure 8.2: The calculation at the heart of long distance supply chains is that T2<T1

Expressed otherwise, today's ubiquitous delocalisation drive is explained not only by international cost differentials but also by the efficiency of modern logistics. Conversely, it would be hard to justify the predominantly extensive configurations typifying most MNEs today if either of these factors no longer applied. The question then becomes how long the current situation can be expected to last. The first component in the equation – namely major international variations in manufacturing costs – is largely a reflection of countries' different stages of socio-economic development, a topic that supersedes the scope of our book. The second is very relevant to us, however, since it raises the question of whether today's efficient (hence inexpensive) logistics are causing MNEs to generally underestimate the real **frictional costs** of trade. One example is the way that many supermarkets calculate that it is worth shipping out-of-season fruit worldwide so that consumers can access their favourite varieties all year long. Accumulating **food miles** in this way only makes business sense if shipping costs remain negligible. This will depend on two factors in turn: productivity performances in the international logistics sector; but even more crucially, fuel prices. If these rise as quickly as predicted based on the variables analysed in Chapter 2, the cost of today's extensive supply chains will soon outweigh their benefits.

Frictional costs: ■
Costs relating to the transfer of economic actors from one sector to another, often because the former has faltered due to the arrival of new technology.

Food miles: ■
Calculation of how far a foodstuff has travelled from its place of production to its place of consumption.

In a world of prohibitively expensive energy, MNEs can be expected to engage in a wholesale shortening of their international value chains, a trend that is already being witnessed in industries such as textiles where there is growing concern about the business risks associated with distant transcontinental outsourcing (problems guaranteeing just-in-time deliveries, greater time-to-market) – not to mention the inverse correlation between a supply chain's length and a company's ability to monitor it. A likely corollary of this restructuring process is that MNEs would want to redefine their subsidiaries' assigned missions, with many groups moving from a fragmented 'global' production logic based on function-specific units serving the whole of the group to a more 'multi-domestic' strategy where each national (or at least regional) entity is responsible for its entire value chain, reducing dependency on long distance imports. Such changes would probably affect the nature of international trade itself, with the trade in **intangibles** – data packages characterised by an insignificant drain on logistics resources – accounting for a greater proportion of cross-border flows than they do today. MNE managers' interactions would also become increasingly based on

Intangibles: ■
Immaterial, non-physical assets such as patents or brand image.

video-conferencing and longer term overseas assignments as opposed to today's energy-intensive routine of repeated short-term travel.

In a world of prohibitively expensive energy, MNEs can be expected to engage in a wholesale shortening of their international value chains.

Key issue

More broadly, international managers who start to integrate these kinds of ecological adaptations into their personal planning will be better attuned to the future and enjoy a competitive advantage over career rivals. The main problem for these pioneers would be convincing their peers of the need to implement the changes before the prime justification for them – prohibitive logistics costs – becomes patently obvious. As always in green business, the mooted advantage of seeking first mover advantage runs up against people's reluctance to accept the cost associated with this – an arbitrage that itself depends on prevailing attitudes in the local business culture regarding short-term versus long-term rewards.

Such variability in managers' attitudes towards the greening of international business – and the ways in which this can be achieved – can be witnessed on several levels. Recent studies (e.g. Carbone and Moatti 2008) have, for instance, detected meaningful variations in the organisation of cross-border supply chains based on MNEs' region of origin, an indication that green business strategies are formulated in specific contexts. It was discovered that North American companies' supply chain focus centres more on issues such as water – as might be expected given the frequency of droughts in parts of the USA – whereas their European counterparts concentrate more on packaging and resource husbandry (also unsurprising given the region's comparative lack of natural resources). Japanese firms, on the other hand, seem more interested in future pollution risks, translating the famously long-term orientation of this particular business culture. Note as well the link uncovered between companies' supply chain greening efforts and the level of national regulation: more regulated contexts tend to be associated with cost-cutting; whereas less regulated ones are more conducive to innovation and differentiation. Such typologies are not absolute but, as aforementioned, what they do indicate is the primacy of the national framework in determining a company's approach to the ecological imperative. Based on this evidence, green business means different things across the world.

8

? Why and how do MNEs' green efforts vary in different parts of the world?

■ International dilemmas

In absence of a 'World Environmental Organisation' with powers equivalent to those wielded by the World Trade Organization (WTO) – and given that most multinational environmental agreements (MEAs) lack any real policing powers – the environmental frameworks within which companies operate continue to be primarily defined at the national level and depend therefore on the attitude of a particular national regime at a given point in time. This is exemplified by shifts in US policy, where President Barack Obama's 2009 appointment of such high-profile environmentalists as Nobel Prize winner Steven Chu to cabinet level position as Secretary for Energy creates a very different green business framework than the one formulated by his predecessor George W. Bush, famous for instance for resisting moves to legislate higher automobile fuel efficiency standards (a stance that the new Administration has also reversed). In general, MNEs' perceptions of different markets worldwide will depend on signals indicating whether or not the local political regime is actively pursuing a long-term strategy for attracting green investment (i.e. streamlined planning procedures for renewable energy projects, subsidies, feed-in tariff schemes, etc.). Insofar as countries send out different signals at different times, MNEs are tempted to engage in green behaviour to a lesser or greater extent in each.

Key issue	... the environmental frameworks within which companies operate continue to be primarily defined at the national level and depend therefore on the attitude of a particular national regime at a given point in time.

The question then becomes why the international community has not developed a unified green business framework to promote full commitment to corporate environmentalism everywhere. There are three obstacles to this kind of convergence. Firstly, given the enormous variation in countries' ability to apprehend the pollution or energy efficiency performance of companies operating locally, monitoring any global agreement appear impracticable. Secondly, no global consensus exists regarding sanctions for ecological misconduct, making it is far too easy (and cheap) in some countries for companies to commit enviro-crimes. Lastly, it is unclear how to allocate responsibility for repairing cross-border environmental damage for which no single culprit has been identified. In this case, countries might not cooperate to solve the problem but decide instead that national interest lies in 'free-riding', i.e. trying to get partner countries to pick up the bill for any problems that arise, for instance, by denying responsibility. Such rent-seeking calculations are a further obstacle to governments developing the sorts of frameworks that are likely to spark green business practices – as witnessed most poignantly in the two key areas of international relations that are trade and economic emergence.

■ Trade and the environment

It is important to appreciate the high level of support from which international trade generally benefits, having been historically viewed by many if not most economists, politicians and business leaders as a source of wealth creation and efficiency. Trade theories based on notions such Ricardo's theory of comparative advantage or the 'international division of labour' have bolstered the widespread idea that trade in and of itself is a good thing. Much less airing has been given, however, to the environmental implications of the associated exploitation of natural resources; the extra pollution caused by trade's long-distance transportation of goods; or the biodiversity impoverishment resulting from many countries having to specialise in **monoculture** cash crops. Even in discussions about moralised trading systems such as **fair trade** (see *Web Resource 8.2*), relatively little attention is paid to the potentially negative effect on the environment.

> **■ Monoculture:** Where an agricultural production region specialises in a single plant genus.

> **■ Fair trade:** Markets organised to ensure that the producer receives a living wage, even if this involves consumers paying more than the market minimum for the goods.

This conflict of paradigms became very apparent during the 1990s when the World Trade Organization – a leading **intergovernmental organisation (IGO)** that is an unabashed advocate of free trade – sanctioned the US government for having restricted shrimp imports from Vietnam because of the insufficient care for turtles caught up in shrimping vessels' nets. In general, the WTO views itself as a single-issue body focused on trade alone, and considers that environmental coordination is better handled through other vehicles such as MEAs (Holtby *et al.* 2007). Moreover, even reputedly greener IGOs such as the European Union vacillate in terms of their willingness to prioritise the ecological imperative – as witnessed by the EU's 2009 decision to add anti-dumping tariffs on the price of the energy-efficient compact fluorescent light bulbs that the Italian group Targetti was importing from China, effectively hampering the launch of this niche despite its environmental benefits. Cases such as these make it clear that despite their ostensible concern for all things green (the WTO has, for instance, long established what it calls a 'Trade and Environment Committee'),

> **■ IGO:** International body created by nation-states, often for coordination purposes, to deal with cross-border issues.

8

> **?** Should the WTO dilute its free trade mission because of the ecological costs?

Global governance: ■
Where regulatory and supervisory functions are fulfilled by authorities whose responsibilities supersede national borders.

some of world's largest **global governance** institutions are still reluctant to make ecological well-being more of a priority than trade.

One argument often heard at this level is that free trade induces a company to locate its production activities in a country where they will benefit from a competitive advantage. This is then supposed to enhance overall productivity and therefore reduce waste, itself a positive outcome for the environment (Newell 2005). A frequent example here is the idea that growing tomatoes in North Europe during the winter requires greenhouses that will waste more energy than the amount consumed transporting such goods from warmer climes. Of course, this argument does not speak to the possibility that North European consumers might accept to only access produce that is in season – a solution that would have an even lower environmental footprint.

Along similar lines, there is the argument that offsetting international business activities' environmental externalities by imposing trade sanctions on foreign companies who display insufficient regard for the ecological imperative would lower global well-being. The idea here is that controls of this type should therefore only be implemented at a good's point of production or consumption, thus within a national instead of a global framework (Griffin 2003). The hope is that by working through very narrowly focused international bodies such as the International Whaling Commission or the United Nations Environment Programme (UNEP) – or by forcing suppliers to undergo certification processes organised by recognised standards authorities in the buyer's region of origin (exemplified by the EU's REACH programme for safe chemicals) – it is possible to address environmental problems without undermining the globalisation dynamic that many view as a leading vehicle of wealth creation. In this entire school of thought, the environment is viewed as an add-on consideration for companies, a simple adjunct whose marginal cost must be minimised at all costs.

There are just as many voices doubting that environmental concerns can ever be addressed adequately without real convergence in global policies (Figure 8.3). When US President Bill Clinton negotiated the NAFTA trade agreement in the 1990s, he tried to stop companies from profiteering from Mexico's looser regulatory framework by inserting environmental protection clauses into the treaty. This attempt to prevent **regime arbitrage** largely failed, however, due to Mexico's inability to police green legislation that was somewhat foreign to its business culture. Otherwise, there is the claim that institutions such as the UNEP – and many of the MEAs established to attack specific

Regime arbitrage: ■
Where multinational enterprises put pressure on a national government to relax regulations under threat of investing elsewhere.

concerns, including the UN Convention on Biological Diversity or the FAO International Treaty on Plant Genetic Resources for Food and Agriculture – are instruments furthering the current **neo-liberal** paradigm whose diffusion is responsible for elevating profitability to the number one goal of public policy (Brand *et al.* 2008) before considerations such as the ecological imperative. The accusation here is that MNEs use compliance with (sometimes token) measures as a smoke-screen to avert potential critics' attention from their fundamentally un-green production organisation. Others view most IGOs as 'toothless' and are concerned that relegating green policy-making to the national level might worsen the power imbalance between those who benefit and those who suffer from environmental externalities (Boyce 2004). The thinking here is that most environmental problems (pollution) but also solutions (biodiversity) have cross-border effects, implying that regulation must necessarily be trans-boundary as well.

■ **Neo-liberal:** Belief in a minimal interference of government in the economy.

Key issue

... [some] voices doubt that environmental concerns can ever be addressed adequately without real convergence in global policies.

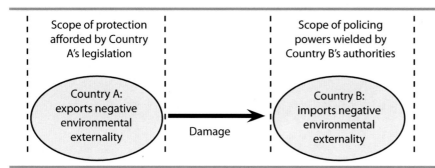

Figure 8.3: In the absence of cross-border oversight, Country B can neither sanction polluters nor fully protect its population

This contention highlights a whole set of other problems relating to the definition of jurisdictions, or the extent to which one state has the right to decide – often without consent – that it can and should oversee behaviour affecting the common good but occurring outside of its national borders. In some cases, a cross-border environmental oversight function of this kind will fit seamlessly into existing regional arrangements, like when the European Commission created the 'Guarantee of Origin' concept to track the transportation of electricity from renewable sources across the borders of member states, many of whom have a greater or less commitment to clean energy (Karmacharya and Vries, Laurens 2009). On numerous other occasions, however, territoriality constitutes a crucial dilemma, and one that – unless a political and legal

8

resolution is found – prevents governments with strong environmental protections from policing companies operating out of neighbouring countries where regulations are less stringent. The attraction of such 'pollution havens' will become too great for many managers, leading in the end to a proliferation of 'ecological dumping' strategies where the main logic guiding MNEs' production location decisions will simply be to minimise exposure to the long arm of a particular government's green sanctions by moving operations to locations where regulatory oversight is weak. Subsequently, this may very well spark a new **race to the bottom** goading desperately poor countries (or even less poor ones afraid of losing jobs) into sacrificing their ecological health to attract **foreign direct investment**. This 'beggar thy neighbour' attitude is not only unsustainable over the long run but also deeply unfair to the citizens of the poor countries forced to suffer from the pollution generated when they produce goods consumed by wealthy country citizens enjoying a pristine environment (Figure 8.4). There is a case to make, for instance, that China's worsening pollution situation is partially attributable to other countries' economic policy of allowing much global manufacturing to be located there (a decision for which China itself must clearly also take responsibility).

Race to the bottom: Where competition among disadvantaged producers forces them to accept lower returns for their services.

Foreign direct investment: Where a firm funds a permanent or semi-permanent physical unit abroad.

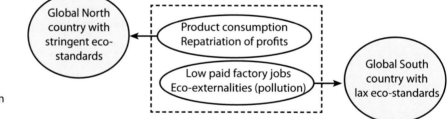

Figure 8.4: Distribution of benefits depending on regulatory stringency

The territoriality principle has long been a topic of debate. Philosophers have regularly toyed with concepts such as the 'common heritage of humankind', the idea being that certain amenities – such as clean air or water – are indivisible and indeed crucial to life on Earth. In this case and regardless of who is at fault for endangering natural amenities, the 'precautionary principle' dictates that a state would be neglectful if it did not do its utmost to protect them, even if this means operating outside its borders (which are, after all, largely artificial).

Key issue

... regardless of who is at fault for endangering natural amenities, the 'precautionary principle' dictates that a state would be neglectful if it did not do its utmost to protect them, even if this means operating outside its borders.

The problem is that actions of this nature might run foul of existing arrangements intended to smooth relations between nation-states. One example is embodied in the WTO principles of discrimination and reciprocity, where members are asked not to engage in policies benefiting local companies to the detriment of foreign rivals. This is often taken to mean that it is unfair for national governments to subsidise local infant industries. Yet without such subsidies, it might be impossible, for instance, to launch certain activities that are environmentally crucial – first and foremost being the clean energy sector that is struggling globally to attain the critical mass that would allow it to lower prices to levels where there will be sufficient demand to replace existing technologies (see Chapter 10). Similarly, some LDCs now require that any imports of energy-efficiency devices be accompanied by knowledge-enhancing technological transfers. As laudable as the proliferation of green science is, this demand can easily run foul of WTO measures aimed at protecting sellers' intellectual property rights (a measure that often works to the benefit of exporters from the world's older industrialised countries). Along similar lines, note some countries' practice of de-taxing green products to make them more competitive with their traditionally non-green rivals – a practice that the WTO might also find discriminatory.

A second obstacle relates to the UN principles of self-determination and non-interference in other countries' domestic affairs. At this level, producers from Country A required to pay a high price for carbon because their government wants them to change behaviour would be at a competitive disadvantage compared to rivals from Country B not facing the same requirements (for instance, because their government refused to sign up to a climate change protocol). In this case, Country A might consider it justifiable to impose fines ('countervailing duties') on imports from Country B, justifying this decision as a means of compensating for the competitive disadvantage bestowed unfairly on its national companies simply because their rivals from Country B have shirked their responsibility towards the environment. Unilateral measures of this kind – or other green stipulations, such as the requirement that labels detail imported goods' lifecycle assessment (LCA) or end-of-life decomposition properties – might be resented as a poorly veiled excuse for **protectionism**, however. Nor is it clear that the WTO would accept them. Numerous scholars have tried to come to grips with this category of problems, for instance by differentiating between whether an item's carbon footprint should be assessed at the level of its

> **?** When if ever is it fair to classify green subsidies as a form of hidden protectionism?

8

> ■ **Protectionism:** Where a national government adopts policies restricting foreign producers' access to its domestic market.

production processes, which can often be fragmented among different sites, or at the level of the finished product itself (Cottier *et al*. 2009). The difficulty is that such calculations can be both opaque and arbitrary.

In the end, the crux of the debate over the impact that trade (and its ancillary activity, foreign direct investment) have on the environment is the divergence in national environmental frameworks. The question then becomes what are the main factors affecting each country's specific behaviour in this area. For many scholars, the leading explanatory factor is the phenomenon of economic emergence or development.

■ Economic emergence and the environment

Ever since it was first enshrined in the 1987 Brundtland report, the term 'sustainable development' has been widely used to translate the sense that economic growth in the world's poorer countries needs to encompass more than economic priorities alone. During the early years of this doctrine, most attention seemed to focus on ensuring that the widest possible cross-section of the populations in question should enjoy the social benefits of development. As the ecological imperative has worsened, however, there seems to be greater concern nowadays with the environmental consequences of growth, as exemplified by the decision taken in 2007 to award a share of that year's Nobel Peace Prize to Intergovernmental Panel on Climate Change vice-chair Mohan Munasinghe in recognition of the **sustainomics** doctrine that he has formulated.

Sustainomics: Vision of economics in which the minimum requirement for the solutions on offer is that they be sustainable.

The starting point for analysing the relationship between national development and the environment is a well-established tool called the Kuznets curve (Figure 8.5). This states that countries produce relatively less pollution during the pre-industrial stage – with several studies showing that much of the world's population contributes little or nothing to total global greenhouse gas emissions (Satterthwaite 2009). Pollution then skyrockets during the early years of industrialisation as manufacturing activities expand without companies having the means or inclination to install anti-pollution devices. In the final stage of the curve, pollution levels fall to an intermediate level as companies in what have become newly industrialised economies accumulate the capital and technologies that will enable them to reduce the amount of pollution produced per unit of output. Citizens' expectations also change as income rises, often starting with a demand for cleaner drinking water followed by better air quality and culminating with an adoption of cleaner and more efficient sources of energy – a shift that reduces per-capita pollution even as per-capita energy consumption rises (Tierney 2009). A prime example of this transition is the way that many LDC households will abandon biomass-burning cooking stoves whenever the opportunity arises – a key shift given the older equipment's generation of vast quantities of the black carbon (soot) that has become the number two contributor to global warming-related greenhouse gases (Rosenthal 2009) and is largely responsible for the brown cloud of polluted air hanging over much of South Asia on many days (Fountain 2009).

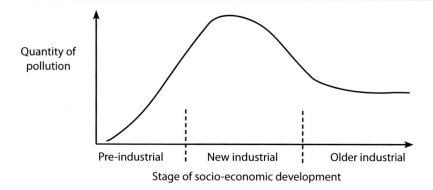

Figure 8.5: The Kuznets curve

The Kuznets curve makes sense intuitively and there is good empirical evidence backing it up: the monstrous factory pollution affecting many Chinese cities today; or the armies of desperate prospectors tearing up Zimbabwe's countryside in search of gold and diamonds, leaving in their trail devastated and polluted fields, forests and water sources (Mambondiyani 2008). What this does is to shift the debate towards how ethical it is for the older industrialised countries to demand that LDCs behave more sustainably when – as discussed throughout this book – the transition to greener practices requires large amounts of upfront capital that poor countries will not possess until they themselves have industrialised. In other words, forcing LDCs to adopt a green trajectory may be so costly that it prevents them from developing, condemning billions of desperate citizens worldwide to further crushing poverty. This is all the more unfair in that the eco-disaster facing the planet at present is largely due to centuries of environmental misconduct by the **Global North**, which stands accused of a 'drawbridge' attitude where rich countries refuse to extend to less developed countries the same growth opportunities as the ones they had.

■ **Global North:** Generic reference to the world's older industrialised nations. Sometimes referred to as the OECD countries.

8

Yet the severity of today's ecological imperative makes it just as inconceivable that emerging economics (led by the famous BRICs – Brazil, Russia and especially India and China) continue to deplete finite resources and generate pollution in the same way that the Global North did during its own development. In other words, at a certain level, traditional industrialisation trajectories and the environment agenda contradict one another. IGOs active in sustainability – led by the UNEP – have tried to resolve this dilemma by developing the concept of 'common but differentiated responsibilities'. This involves requiring lesser environmental action from LDCs (one explanation for the failure of the 2010 Copenhagen climate change conference) and, less contentiously, incentivising the Global North to subsidize emerging economies' greening processes. A range of tools exist towards this end. One is the Clean Development Mechanism (CDM) that came out of the 2007 Kyoto Protocol – a mechanism whereby industrialised countries' investment in other (often developing) countries' emission reduction efforts counts towards the fulfilment of their own targets. On the debit side, the CDM protocol excluded tropical deforestation, a serious oversight given that this causes about one-fifth of total global greenhouse gas emissions. Hence the work done by Brazilian Congressman Marco Santilli under the aegis of the UN's 'Reducing Emissions from Deforestation and Forest Degradation' (REDD) programme to structure a $500 million fund - $52 million of which comes from Norway alone, symbolically paid out of oil revenues – to reward countries cutting deforestation rates below their historical average (Downie 2009). MNEs active in resource extraction have a strong interest in monitoring developments of this sort to ascertain the effect on the overall economics in their sectors of activity.

> **?** Should LDCs be expected to have the same environmental responsibilities as wealthier countries?

At the same time, in a period of recession many OECD countries will be reluctant to fund environmental actions in the world's emerging economies, especially when the imbalances of the current global trading system mean that some of the largest capital surpluses in the world today are held by countries such as China that are still classified as LDCs (because so many of their citizens remain poor). Moreover, even where a country from the Global North does decide to help fund the green trajectory of one of its poorer neighbours, it is rare that the sums involved match the scale of the challenge. The logical conclusion is that the main catalyst for most LDCs' sustainable development will ultimately have to be internal. This raises both a practical question (whether an LDC government will legislate to raise environmental standards) as well as a business one (whether local companies might themselves take the initiative of embracing clean technology as a long-term commercial opportunity). After all, the Kuznets curve is not science, with a growing body of literature (Mukherjee and Chakraborty 2008; Barua and Hubacek 2008) starting to question the validity of its premise of a linear relationship between per-capita income and environmental behaviour. LDC managers do not necessarily have to exhibit the same ecological inertia as their OECD counterparts did in the past

> **?** Should OECD member states be asked to subsidise LDCs' greening costs?

> ... at a certain level, traditional industrialisation trajectories and the environment agenda contradict one another [but] LDC managers do not necessarily have to exhibit the same ecological inertia as their OECD counterparts did in the past.

Key issue

LDC companies taking the lead in the green economy?

Many LDC politicians and business leaders have expressed resentment at the way that the Global North's historical mismanagement of the global ecosphere restricts their development trajectories, with voices in countries such as India arguing that it is unreasonable to expect this emerging giant to eschew energy-intensive growth. At the same time, a growing number of Indian environmentalists have pointed out that irrespective of the origins of problems such as global warming, the country will suffer the effects (Himalayan glaciers shrinking, rising salinity of coastal water resources, heat waves) and therefore needs managers to migrate towards green business practices as soon as possible. To some extent, the rise of eco-entrepreneurship in LDCs is a matter of educating people about the unfeasibility of the status quo.

There is no question that green consciousness has already started to expand in the developing world (see Table 8.1). The already arduous circumstances reigning in many poorer countries – for instance, with half of humanity currently lacking access to any modern fuel sources – is likely to convince many LDC entrepreneurs that they have no choice but to industrialise along more eco-efficient lines. This is especially important given the widespread expectation that future energy shortages in the Global North will cause the older industrialised countries to drain whatever resources the LDCs are currently using (Ebenhack and Martinez 2009). Add to this concerns about the fairness of the globalisation model currently being pursued in much of the Global South – often characterised by a very small proportion of high

8

income citizens living in environmentally harmonious circumstances, as opposed to the huge numbers struggling to survive in crowded, smoggy cities lacking basic amenities such as clean water or air – and it becomes clear that it is in these countries' own interest to pursue greener industrialisation trajectories than their predecessors did.

Table 8.1: Longitudinal study of rise in concern for environmental problems, showing percentages who rate these as the top global threat (Pew 2007)

	2002 %	2007 %	Change		2002 %	2007 %	Change
United States	23	37	+14	Egypt	--	40	--
Canada	43	54	+11	Jordan	37	30	-7
				Kuwait	--	22	--
Argentina	28	53	+25	Lebanon	22	13	-9
Bolivia	39	42	+3	Morocco	--	31	--
Brazil	20	49	+29	Palestine	--	28	--
Chile	--	44	--	Israel	--	26	--
Mexico	34	45	+11				
Peru	37	55	+18	Pakistan	13	18	+5
Venezuela	20	42	+22	Bangladesh	28	30	+2
				Indonesia	26	32	+6
Britain	30	46	+16	Malaysia	--	37	--
France	29	52	+23	China	69	70	+1
Germany	27	45	+18	India	32	49	+17
Italy	39	51	+12	Japan	55	70	+15
Spain	--	46	--	South Korea	73	77	+4
Sweden	--	66	--				
				Ethiopia	--	7	--
Bulgaria	28	45	+17	Ghana	11	22	+11
Czech Republic	42	49	+7	Ivory Coast	16	14	-2
Poland	20	33	+13	Mali	--	19	--
Russia	40	43	+3	Nigeria	17	17	0
Slovakia	36	50	+14	Senegal	--	13	--
Ukraine	54	57	+3	South Africa	22	22	0
				Tanzania	20	24	+4
Turkey	22	27	+5	Uganda	8	22	+14

Some of the questions arising at this level include whether the new green activities will be brought into the Global South by MNEs coming from the Global North; whether home-grown companies will drive this process; or whether an intermediate solution can be found, for instance involving mixed funding from international bodies such as the World Bank or the UN's Clean Development Mechanism. One example of this kind of combined effort is the finance that these two institutions are jointly providing, for instance, for a $700 million 100 MW solar plant that Egypt is planning to build within a few short years near its Aswan Dam hydro-electric facility. Often, it is the amount of innovation involved in a particular clean energy project that will determine who might become its driving force. Where innovations are incremental in nature, larger MNEs are often in a better position to provide solutions since all they have to do is adapt their existing processes and products to the prevailing circumstances in the developing country in question. One example is the way that Swedish giant Electrolux was able to access the huge Chinese market once it had changed its basic washing machine product to a front-loading model that uses less hot water (a sparse commodity in many poorer communities). This was a small change that Electrolux, a long-established concern, could achieve without any major upheavals in its production process. Similarly, budding solar energy companies from the Global North might also view emerging markets as an appropriate launchpad for their new products, one example being the way that AES Solar Energy from the USA or Abengoa from Spain have worked with resource-poor countries like India to develop projects such as the 3000 MW combined solar panel and thermal power complex currently being built in Gujarat province (Leahy and Sood 2009). Where the cost of technological development is the main issue in a new product's rollout, the Global North's greater R&D capabilities gives their companies an advantage that will more than offset their relatively higher labour costs.

On the other hand, there are a number of factors that might limit Western MNEs' domination of the emerging green markets. Energy is viewed as a strategic input in any national economy, but the most direct way of motivating local entrepreneurs to develop clean energy is to enact dramatic carbon emission reduction targets and/or to mandate that a certain percentage of a country's total energy use must come from renewable sources – measures that some of the leading emerging economies have started to implement in recent years (Friedman 2010). Brazil, for instance, has become global leader in sugar-cane based ethanol production. India has plans to increase its total solar energy production capacity from 5 MW at present to 20,000 MW by 2020, with renewables scheduled to account for about 15 per cent of the country's total energy needs by that time. As for China, this enormous country recently replaced the USA as world leader in green energy markets, with 2009 private investments of $34.6 billion, almost twice the American total. Combined with the Beijing government's decision to ringfence upwards of one-third of the nearly half a trillion dollars in stimulus funds that it released in the wake of the 2008 credit crunch and allocate this colossal sum to clean energy, transportation and energy distribution infrastructure investments, and the question is no longer whether the Global North is going to dominate China in the new green markets but the other way around.

Conversely, OECD countries that have been reluctant to enact tough climate change standards due to fears that the associated costs may put their already more expensive local industries at a further competitive disadvantage might actually be doing themselves a disservice by not forcing managers to commit to one of the world's fastest growing markets. The USA, for instance, remains a powerhouse in (green) technological innovation but has started to fall behind both China (for solar panels) and Europe (for offshore wind turbines) in industrial production. Questions are now being raised over whether the American private venture capital model that presided over the birth of the computing industry is as effective as **state capitalism** in kick-starting the new eco-industries. In countries such France (see www2.ademe.fr) and above all Germany, the public sphere offers significant tax incentives and direct operational subsidies to support greening processes (see Chapter 4) – clearly a competitive advantage for the companies benefiting from such generosity. In the environmental sector as in most other sectors of activity, international business often starts and ends with a debate about the role of government.

State capitalism:
Where large swathes of market activities are undertaken by publicly owned enterprises.

■ Obstacles and pathways

1 Dispersed global value chains are vulnerable to rising fuel prices.

Explore 'nearsourcing' possibilities and 'multi-domestic' MNE configurations.

2 International variations in environmental reporting impede footprint monitoring.

Headquarters might develop group-specific analytical accounting systems.

3 Host countries diverge in their support for corporate greening initiatives.

Make 'regime arbitrage' ethical by negotiating a green 'race to the top'.

4 MNEs and domestic firms compete to dominate the budding clean technology market.

Possibility of strategic alliances/international joint ventures.

Case study: Chinese greens

It would be unbalanced to discuss China's progress towards becoming the world's largest producer of renewable energy without commenting on the truly terrible state of the country's ecosphere (Larson 2009), often characterised by lethal air quality, poisoned rivers, heat waves, dust storms and water shortages. This disaster stems directly from China's emerging role as the global centre for manufacturing, with recent studies finding that the vast majority of local air pollution is generated by factories serving export markets (Spencer 2007). This creates a difficult conundrum for local decision-makers fearful that the imposition of stricter environmental legislation will hamper wealth creation in a society where poverty remains the exception rather the rule. The lack of social consensus about sustainability (Chen et al. 2008) and the generally mediocre allocation of corporate resources to environmental responsibility (He and Chen 2008) raise doubts about what the Beijing government can actually do to force local industrialists to migrate towards greener practices. Changes have been made in recent years, including the decision to upgrade the State Environmental Protection Authority to ministerial status, replete with policing powers and the ability to lobby state-owned banks to lend money only to those companies that have achieved certain levels of eco-performance. What remains to be seen is the efficiency of such steps in the face of a structurally energy-intensive industry that largely relies on dirty coal – the only fuel source that is readily available in China.

Yet it is this very same resource availability constraint that has also driven China's remarkable recent penetration of the global clean energy sector. It is unclear whether the country's take-off can be best explained by state incentives to get companies to reduce air pollution in general (and carbon emissions in particular) or by managers' fear of resource depletion – probably a combination of the two. In any event, a great deal is being done in China at present to face up to the ecological imperative.

Some of this greening process has little or nothing to do with renewable energy and relates instead to current efforts to convert China's abundant coal supplies into cleaner energy (Wang and Xu 2008). A prime example is the work being done by a private company called ENN, whose previous specialisation was to provide natural gas to households or liquefied natural gas to filling stations. ENN is now looking to gasify coal and convert the resulting product into a fuel called dimethyl ester that produces neither sulphur dioxide nor soot when burned. The advantage of this strategy is that it mobilises existing infrastructure, with new technology simply being introduced at a more upstream level. An incremental approach of this kind is generally easier to implement.

At the same time, given the energy expended during coal gasification processes, the improvement in China's global environmental footprint might be marginal. Hence the country's impressive move into the renewable energy sector. Newspapers overflow nowa-

8

days with stories about this industry, usually involving state-owned power companies, often seeking to leverage the abundant sun and wind resources found in the vast expanses of West China's Gobi desert (Bradsher 2009). One town in this sparsely populated region, Dunhuang, has become the centre for renewable investment, hosting an immense wind power project with the capacity of 16 large coal-fired power plants – one of six such projects across the country. Indeed, China has started expanding its renewables capacity at such a rate that voices can already be heard expressing the fear that companies might be deliberately under-bidding their competitors for renewable power construction licences in the hope that once the project is theirs, they will be able to over-charge the customer (in essence, the govern-ment). Whereas China had originally planned for the installation of 5000 MW of wind power by year-end 2011, there has been such a rush that 30,000 MW is now being predicted. Such mass investment is justified to some extent by growing demand from the country's armies of urban dwellers, many of whom have started purchasing new, energy-hungry amenities. Add to this the Chinese government's ambitious renewables targets and the fact that the national banking sector is currently awash with cash and it is improbable that the boom will abate any time soon. In pure financial terms, the business may not make complete sense at present – with the development of a new 10 MW photovoltaic solar power plant in Dunhuang cur-rently being shelved until a rational pricing scheme can be worked out – but Chinese gov-ernment planners seem willing to accept that the possibility of short-term losses on new ventures is a price worth paying to kick-start the new sector. Given certain predictions that China will, at current rates of consumption, use up all of its coal resources in fewer than 50 years, this is clearly a risk worth taking.

Case study questions

1 What explains the dismal state of China's ecosphere?

2 What has the Chinese government done in recent times to improve the situation?

3 What is the outlook for ecology and management in China?

■ References

Barua, A. and Hubacek, K. (2008), 'An empirical analysis of the environmental Kuznets curve for water pollution in India', *International Journal of Global Environmental Issues*, **9** (1–2).

Boyce, J. (2004), 'Democratizing global economic governance', *Development and Change*, **35** (3).

Bradsher K. (2009), 'Green power takes root in the Chinese desert', 2 July, available at www.nytimes.com/, accessed 26 April 2010.

Brand, U., Görg, C., Hirsch, J. and Wissen, M. (2008), *Conflicts in Environmental Regulation and the Internationalisation of the State: Contested Terrains*, Routledge.

Carbone, V. and Moatti, V. (2008), *Greening the supply chain: preliminary results of a global survey*, ESCP-EAP Paris.

Chen, Y., Dutra, C. and Sanders, R. (2008), 'Institutional constraints on China's transition to sustainability', *International Journal of Green Economics*, **2** (2).

Cottier, T., Nartova, O. and Bigdeli, S. (eds) (2009), *International Trade Regulation and the Mitigation of Climate Change: World Trade Forum*, Cambridge: Cambridge University Press.

Downie, A. (2009) Heroes of the Environment: Marcio Santilli, 22 September, available at www.time.com, accessed 13th Decmber 2010.

Ebenhack, B. and Martinez, D. (2009), 'Before the peak: impacts of oil shortages on the developing world', *International Social Science Journal*, **57**, Supplement 1.

Epstein, M. and Roy, M. (1998), 'Managing corporate environmental performance: a multinational perspective', *European Management Journal*, **16** (3).

Fountain, H. (2009), 'Study pinpoints the main source of Asia's brown cloud', 23 January, available at www.nytimes.com/, accessed 22 April 2010.

Friedman, L. (2010), 'China leads major countries with $34.6 billion invested in clean technology', 25 March, available at www.nytimes.com/, accessed 22 April 2010.

Griffin, K. (2003), 'Economic globalization and institutions of global governance', *Development and Change*, **34** (5).

He, M. and Chen, J. (2008), 'Sustainable development and corporate environmental responsibility: A comparative study of Chinese and multinational corporations', *Industrial Electronics and Applications*, **1** (3–5) (3rd IEEE Conference).

Holtby, K., Kerr, W. and Hobbs, J. (2007), *International Environmental Liability and Barriers to Trade: Market Access and Biodiversity in the Biosafety Protocol*, Cheltenham: Edward Elgar Publishing.

Karmacharya, S. and Vries, L. (2009), 'A regional coordination framework for renewable energy policy in the European Union', *International Journal of Environment and Pollution*, **39** (1–2).

Larson, C. (2009), 'The great paradox of China: green energy and black skies', 17 August, available at http://e360.yale.edu/, accessed 23 September 2009.

Leahy, J. and Sood, V. (2009), 'India steps out of shade on solar power', *Financial Times*, 29 September, p. 11.

Levy, D. and Newell, P. (2004), *The Business of Global Environmental Governance*, Cambridge, MA: MIT Press.

Mambondiyani, A. (2008), 'Zimbabwe's desperate miners ravage the land', 3 November, available at http://e360.yale.edu/, accessed 23 September 2009.

8

Moore, S. and Wen, J. (2008), 'Business ethics? A global comparative study on corporate sustainability approaches', *Social Responsibility Journal*, **4** (1).

Mukherjee, S. and Chakraborty, D. (2008), 'Environment, human development and economic growth: a contemporary analysis of Indian states – including Kuznets', *International Journal of Global Environmental Issues*, **9** (1–2).

Newell P. (2005) 'The political economy of international trade and the environment', in D. Kelly and W. Grant (eds), *The Politics of International Trade in the 21st Century: Actors, Issues and Regional Dynamics*, Palgrave.

Pew (2007), 'Global unease with major world powers', 27 June, available at http://pewglobal.org/, accessed 25 May 2010.

Rosenthal, E. (2009), 'Third-World stove soot is target in climate fight', 15 April, available www. nytimes.com, accessed 28 January 2010.

Rowe, A. and Wehrmeyer, W. (2001), 'Why does the talk of positive environmental values not match the walk of environmental accountability in Shanghai?', June, available at www. commerce.adelaide.edu.au/, accessed 26 April 2010.

Satterthwaite, D. (2009), 'The implications of population growth and urbanization for climate change', *Environment and Urbanization*, **21** (2).

Sitkin, A. and Bowen, N. (2010), *International Business: Challenges and Choices*, Oxford: Oxford University Press.

Spencer, J. (2007), 'Chinese pollution rules target export industry', *Wall Street Journal-Europe*, 1 November.

Tierney, J. (2009), 'Use energy, get rich and save the planet', 20 April, available at www.nytimes. com/ accessed 26 April 2010.

Wang. M and Xu, D. (2008), 'Cleaner energy for China: An interview with the chairman of ENN Group', July, available at www.mckinseyquarterly.com/, accessed 26 April 2010.

Zhang, J., Guo, H., Li, B. and Wang, Wei (2009), 'The influence of financial situation on environmental information disclosure in China's chemical industry', *International Journal of Global Environmental Issues*, **9** (3).

9 Green Sectors for the Future

Learning objectives

After reading this chapter, you will be able to:

- Analyse the supply and demand factors influencing the future of agribusiness
- Identify stresses on global water resources
- Recognise the adjustments needed to implement green building principles
- Compare alternative transportation modes

■ Introduction

There are different ways of ascertaining entrepreneurial interest in green business opportunities. One is by monitoring patent registrations (see *Web Resource 9.1*), although questions remain about the comparability of national patent data and, above all, how much time it takes for a patent to become an industrial application. More generally, there are already several benchmark sources of information producing relatively exhaustive annual reports on global trading conditions in different green sectors. These include Pew Charitable Trust or Greenbiz.com in the USA; Carbon Trust in the UK; the United Nations Environmental Programme, etc. One of the clearest signs than a new industry has started to take root is the rigour and standardisation of its coverage in the media or academic circles.

Many commentators today are predicting that resource productivity will within a few short years become the main driver of global economic growth. The sectors concerned include 'the built environment, transport and industry, material productivity including steel, concrete and timber, chemistry, engineering, water efficiency and sustainable agriculture' (von Weizsäcker *et al.* 2009). The United Nations itself predicts that a global explosion in the number of green jobs, reaching as many as 20 million by the year 2030. Readers of this book will have noted that its author shares a similar vision.

At the same time and depending on how green business initiatives are being channelled, different rollout scenarios can be envisaged. A useful way of organising analysis in this regard is around the concept of sectors. These constitute the standard unit of study in most business economics since it is at this level that new technologies and managerial paradigms spawn new production organisations, achieve critical mass and ultimately diffuse. Altogether, these steps characterise the successive phases of a typical industrial revolution – which is how many observers view the present and future of the corporate greening process (Edwards 2005).

It is true that borders between sectors can blur, given that inventions associated with some areas of activity (i.e. lighting) will also have a direct impact on others (i.e. green buildings). In a similar vein, there is always a possibility of sector-based analyses being biased due to the variable speed with which different categories of actors migrate towards the ecological mindset. However, these hurdles are more than offset by the convenience of a sectoral structure. Moreover, this approach is also a good way of attending to the ecological prospects of what are arguably the most fundamental areas of economic initiative, to wit, the activities that cater directly to basic human needs: staples; and general living patterns. After that, the book's final chapter can focus on another key green sector – clean energy, arguably the main challenge in an ecologically constrained future – and explore the conditions determining entrepreneurial ventures in this field.

■ Staples

However far humankind has advanced over the millennia, a hierarchy of bodily needs must still be satisfied before other considerations can be addressed. This starts with food and drink, two elements without which life is impossible. The decision to use this text to focus on staples such as food and water is justified by the logic – detailed in Chapter 1 – that many business organisations underestimate the physicality of their circumstances, an ecological myopia that has led over the centuries to natural resources being undervalued (thus under-priced) in comparison with manufactured products or services. Thus, as the ecological imperative heightens and people realise the true value of the services rendered by a fully operative ecosphere, natural resources' relative prices can be expected to rise again (see Figure 9.1). This should benefit young managers with the foresight to build careers in basic commodities.

> ? How certain is it that the relative pricing of staples like food will rise in the coming years?

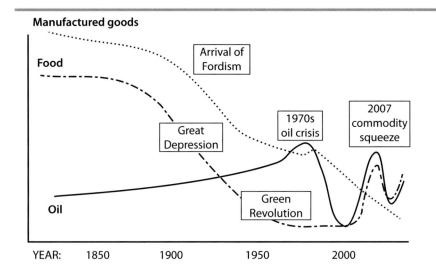

Figure 9.1: Relative pricing over time of different sectors

■ Agriculture

Green revolution: ■
International campaign
during the mid-20th century
to modernise agricultural
practices, particularly in
LDCs, through technological
and infrastructural
improvements.

Following the **Green Revolution** of the 1960s, the global food markets experienced nearly half a century during which sporadic starvation was increasingly restricted to populations in the so-called highly indebted poor countries (HIPC), with the rest of the planet enjoying increasingly abundant harvests and often a glut of food. Benefiting from technological advances and government subsidies, industrialised countries' output eventually exceeded total global consumption requirements, despite the world population having doubled between the 1970s and 2010 from 3 billion to nearly 7 billion inhabitants. The ensuing surpluses flooded most markets, putting downwards pressure on prices and forcing farmers to implement increasingly intensive agricultural methods to restore their profit margins. Of course, farmers from the developing world struggled to compete with their industrialised rivals' greater productivity, hampering many LDCs' development trajectories and aggravating tensions at the World Trade Organization (Sitkin and Bowen 2010). In more ecological terms, the overuse of fertilisers and pesticide has led to an impoverishment of arable land worldwide (see Chapter 3) – a vicious circle further aggravated by struggling farmers' tendency to no longer rest fields as rigorously as they should to replenish soil nutrients (Borlaug 2007). Combined with water stresses resulting from the over-exploitation of irrigation sources (and the recurrence of global warming-related droughts, most notably in Australia) and the emerging picture is one of a global agricultural sector whose short-term money focus is wreaking havoc on its long-term ecological health.

Key issue	... the emerging picture is one of a global agricultural sector whose short-term money focus is wreaking havoc on its long-term ecological health.

The year 2007 finally saw a reversal in the food markets' centuries-old trend towards higher surpluses and lower prices as shortages in basic commodities such as rice (still the staple for billions of citizens worldwide) caused food riots from Haiti to Bangladesh. To be accurate, this trend reversal was temporarily curtailed by the global recession of 2008–09, a turn of events that was much appreciated by consumers but also by the food processing and restaurant sectors, for whom food constitutes an input, thus a cost. It is also true that many experts continue to forecast years of plenty in the agricultural sector, basing this opinion on their hopes for rising productivity in South Russia's former collective farms and above all in Africa, where a modicum of technological progress and land reforms could readily produce much higher yields. Otherwise, it is also worth noting the way that a number of specialist MNEs such as Monsanto and Novartis have been promoting new and hardier **genetically modified (GM)** plant strains, ostensibly because of the positive effect on crop yields. Environmentally-minded NGOs such as Greenpeace criticise GM foods due to concerns about biodiversity – not to mention the semi-monopoly that GM foods give MNEs over crop seeds – but this perspective mainly resonates in the Global North's more politicised green subcultures. In the rest of the world, many farmers (and consumers) tend to focus on the fundamental problems of food availability and cost.

■**GM organisms:** Living entities whose biomolecular composition has been altered to induce certain characteristics.

However, there is an even stronger argument that the 2007 crisis was nothing exceptional but the start of a whole new dynamic in the agribusiness sector, one resulting from a perfect storm of ecological, economic and social conditions (Mathiason 2009).

? How do concerns about global food supply weigh against the ecological uncertainties associated with GM crops?

One new stress is encapsulated in the changing dietary requirements of emerging economy consumers who are now demanding large quantities of meat or dairy products. Calculated in terms of the ratio between the total energy required to produce such foods – feeding edible grains to livestock – and the energy derived from their consumption, this trend is a source of inefficiency and an explanation for some environmentalists' vegetarian leanings. It also adds to the detrimental effects of the wasteful food culture that has long reigned in the world's older industrialised societies, reflecting the richness of people's diet but also the common practice of affluent consumers buying (or supermarkets stocking) more food than they need, with surpluses simply being thrown away. Note that this practice has started to concern public authorities, many of whom respond by introducing municipal food composting schemes.

Future energy shortages (see Chapter 2) will harm agribusiness in many ways, starting with the price of most fertilisers, for which oil is a major component. Farmers have increasing cause to worry about energy price rises since these will affect much of their equipment, including the tractors, harvesters and other vehicles that farms use. There will also be a problem with the increased expense of transporting produce to market.

This latter issue also evokes what has become a major concern in modern agribusiness, to wit, the growing distance between where food

9

is produced and consumed. Agriculture is subject to many of the same globalisation trends as most other sectors, with countries increasingly encouraged by bodies such as the WTO to only produce classes of goods where they have a 'comparative advantage', while importing all other items. This has led to an international division of labour in the food sector, with a few big intermediaries dominating most global value chains – a quasi-oligopoly that has come under increasing criticism in recent years (Spurling 2008), if only for its social justice aspects. In addition, the professionalisation of most global food channels also means that consumers today are being encouraged to ignore whether a particular foodstuff is in season where they live. Indeed, it is in the interest of large supermarkets to amortise the long-distance supply chains that they have set up (see Chapter 8) by offering products all year long. The problem is that this system necessarily entails billions of 'food miles', placing further strain on global resources. As such, it is at odds with traditional localised **foodshed** production systems where consumers accept the specific constraints of their local ecosphere (Helenius *et al.* 2007) while adding to many governments' sense that agricultural free trade can be at odds with national security interests (Lang and Heasman 2004). Recent statistics have shown, for instance, that the UK is just 63 per cent self-sufficient in total food (DEFRA 2004). In other words, 37 per cent of the food that Britain consumes (and a much higher percentage in sectors such as fresh produce) is transported from abroad. Thus there is a clear link between a country's self-sufficiency and its vulnerability to external factors.

Foodshed: Concept of a food system as stretching from its original rural source to its urban marketplace.

? Are long distance food supply chains unsustainable?

Key issue

... a major concern in modern agribusiness [is] the growing distance between where food is produced and consumed.

A further factor undermining the equilibrium of today's globalised agricultural markets is intensifying competition for land resources. One example of this trend is the growing destruction of farmland in countries like China due to accelerating **urban sprawl**. Another is the way that a commodity such as palm oil, which is used as a major calorific source in many LDCs, has become unaffordable to poorer consumers because MNEs such as the Body Shop from the Global North now require it for cosmetic purposes (Bradsher 2008). Above all, there is the rise of **biofuels**, led by ethanol – which can be derived from cereals, beetroot and sugarcane (a major fuel source in Brazil) – and biodiesel, made from the vegetable oils extracted from crops such as colza and soy (see Table 9.1). The impending energy crisis, combined

Urban sprawl: Municipalities' extension towards their fringes, often leading to the development of previously rural land.

Biofuels: Energy sources derived from living organisms, often through the release of calorific energy previously stored via photosynthetic processes.

with air quality concerns about the further burning of hydrocarbons, means that many governments have adopted schemes such as the UK's Renewable Transport Fuel Obligation that lead to crops being diverted from the food chain for use as fuel. China, for instance, has set a target that upwards of 15 per cent of all domestic fuel consumption should come from crop sources within a few short years (Le Monde 2007) – an outcome that would involve a monumental reshaping of its agricultural landscape. Whereas grain farmers worldwide would benefit monetarily from this new demand for their output, other social categories would suffer – first and foremost being consumers unable to pay the higher food prices that would ensue. As some commentators have noted, there is something ethically dubious about diverting much needed food resources so that affluent people can continue their love affair with the automobile. Otherwise, in pure ecological terms, there are also concerns (www.biofuelwatch.org.uk/) that future practices in this area – with the International Energy Agency calling for a fivefold expansion in biofuel production by the year 2030 – will aggravate climate change, since many farmers will plant new crops in virginal fields, thereby releasing currently embedded CO2. Having said that, there is a small but growing niche in organic farm products whose production methods consciously adhere to recognisably sustainable principles (see *Chapter 9 online case study*). This latter category of farming remains very marginal, however.

	2008	2009	2010	2011	2012
USA	6,198	6,858	7,518	8,178	8,838
Brazil	4,988	5,238	5,489	5,739	5,990
China	1,075	1,101	1,128	1,154	1,181
India	531	551	571	591	611
Germany	319	381	444	506	569
World total	**16,215**	**17,574**	**18,934**	**20,293**	**21,653**

Table 9.1: World ethanol production forecast 2008–12 by country, in million gallons (available at www.marketresearchanalyst.com/, accessed 3 June 2010)

A number of sustainable agricultural policies have been proposed in recent years to face these challenges. Some highlight farmers' social protection, seeking to enhance their **resilience** to stresses by diffusing better technology and resource husbandry practices while encouraging crop diversification (ODI 2007) – a suggestion diametrically opposed to the monoculture cash crop specialisation often forced upon LDC farmers desperate for hard currency. Another category of policies tends to focus on farming techniques, either involving the development of nutrient-efficient plants capable of producing high yields despite severe ecological stresses (Fageria *et al*. 2008) or a reversal of the

Resilience: Concept increasingly used in environmental studies to refer to an entity's ability to withstand external shocks and continue to perform and/or survive.

9

traditional separation between rural farming and urban consumption. Interesting ideas in this latter area are offered by visionaries such as Dickson Despommier, whose 'vertical farm' or 'living tower' concepts encourage architects to design buildings with 'edible walls' that city dwellers can use to grow their own produce. If reproduced on a mass scale, this could go some way towards reducing the unsustainable accumulation of food miles that is a disturbing feature of modern agribusiness. City planners could also achieve similar results by creating 'transition towns' characterised by a seamless interpenetration of urban and agricultural land uses.

> **?** How feasible is city farming?

Key issue   ... reversal of the traditional separation between rural farming and urban consumption.

An ancillary benefit of having population centres control their own food supplies is tied to the concept of biodiversity. In today's international division of labour, specialised production centres seek economies of scale by growing vast quantities of whichever one of the vegetable, fruit and cereal – or livestock or fish – genuses or species fits best into their economic calculations (Spurling 2008). This impoverishes the diversity of life forms and exacerbates risks of blight, epidemic and occasionally extinction. Shortening production–consumption channels would hopefully have the opposite effect.

Of course, as always in green business, the main hurdle impeding migration towards a more sustainable organisation is cost. Some outlays would have to be made upfront, with the large MNEs that currently dominate the food sector having to rebuild their supply chains along more localized lines, often returning farming operations to the Global North where production costs are much higher. This raises the question of what might motivate companies to make such changes. Key in this respect is the public's attitude and specifically whether some parties' condemnation of the sector's currently unsustainable organisation will resonate as loudly as other parties' distress at having to pay more for food. Secondly, re-localising food production would create an opportunity cost as companies would lose out on the economies of scale that they currently realise by focusing agricultural production on as few mega-sites as possible. The contradiction is that small farmers who might be interested in positioning themselves in a sustainable niche may not have the resources to do so, whereas large conglomerates who can afford this change may lack the motivation.

■ Water

Like agriculture, the problems besetting the global water sector can be largely categorised as relating to supply and demand factors. In terms of the former, the main stress nowadays is the recurrence of global warming-related droughts. This is a worldwide phenomenon affecting all continents to a lesser or greater extent. The exact scenario for the future is difficult to determine since climate change is likely to translate into more rainfall in some places (which will reduce general awareness of the problem) and less in others (which will have the opposite effect). Clearly, any adjustment will be arduous – a prime example being the populations in northeast India who have little hope of replacing the traditional water sources that they lose as the Himalayan glaciers melt to cause monster floods that wash over their lands before running off into the Bay of Bengal. Similarly, it is difficult to see how the Chinese authorities can react to the drought conditions affecting the country's northern regions, which currently account for three-fifths of national crop production and two-fifths of its population (Wines 2009). Moving vast numbers of citizens due to changing weather patterns is clearly unfeasible.

Population growth and proximity to water supplies used to be correlated. The long-distance transportation of water supplies – involving the construction of aquifers and/or rise of a global market in bottled water now accounting for nearly 200 billion litres annually – seems to have loosened this connection, as witnessed by the population explosion in naturally arid regions such as the Southwestern United States' Sun Belt. On the other hand, dramatic water shortages in these regions have revealed the limitations of current migratory patterns. To support communities built in naturally hostile environments, many governments are starting to invest in desalination facilities, an industrial process that can be criticised because it is energy-intensity and causes damages to local wetlands (www.globalwaterintel.com/). Policymakers worldwide are frequently advised by bodies such as the International Water Association (www.iwahq.com/) to expend greater sums on water infrastructure, reducing losses from leaky delivery systems, protecting natural reservoirs from pollution and diffusing rainwater harvesting processes. This is especially crucial in LDCs whose development is often undermined by households' lack of access to potable water sources (www.wateraid.org/). Given the scale of the problem, however, there are serious doubts that simple efficiency measures will suffice. According to current estimates (McKinsey-WRG 2009) and all

9

else remaining equal, global water requirements are expected to rise from 4.5 to 6.9 trillion cubic metres by the year 2030 – a full 40 per cent above reliable supplies (see Figure 9.2). Thus – and as is so often the case in environmental matters – the only real hope for a more sustainable future is the moderation of demand. The complication for water companies is that on the face of things, this recommendation is not good for profits.

> ? What future for populations living in naturally arid zones?

Figure 9.2: Aggregated global gap between existing accessible, reliable supply and 2030 water withdrawals, in billion cubic metres (McKinsey-WRG 2009)

Total 4500	Total + 6900	2800		= 4200
Municipal/domestic 600	Municipal/domestic 900		+ 100	Groundwater 700
Industry 800	Industry 1500			Surface water 3500
Agriculture 3100	Agriculture 4500			
Existing withdrawals	2030 withdrawals	Basins with deficits	Basins with surplus	Existing, reliable accessible, sustainable supplies

Note as well that water is used for many commercial purposes, ranging from power generation (dams and hydroelectric power) to industrial cooling and cleaning. Above all, it is used for agriculture, which accounts for around 70 per cent of global water consumption. Thus, farming is the sector where the most can be done to increase water efficiency. This is a challenge, however, given the water-intensive nature of many crops – first and foremost being the genuses from which biofuels are derived (Evans and Cohen 2009). As so often in green business, the solution to one problem creates a new one.

Key issue

As so often in green business, the solution to one problem creates a new one.

A slew of urban and/or industrial initiatives have been launched to address this issue. Many revolve around green building techniques (Guevarra 2010) and are based on actions such as the installation of water supply control and repair systems, high efficiency fixtures (toilets, faucets) and smart meters monitoring total onsite use. More structurally, there is a sense that total urban consumption of water can be lowered if users move away from centralised systems (where water is pumped from stations via mega-conduits) and adopt a more localised, 'soft path' a pproach centred on rainwater harvesting systems that nowadays come in easy-to-install, pre-assembled off-the-shelf filtration and treatment packages (Steffen 2008). Also noteworthy are the measures taken by a number of industrial companies ranging from Coca Cola to RATP Paris Transit Authority to improve water efficiency (treatment of wastewater, recycling of runoffs, etc.). Unfortunately, there is often a sense that these steps deal with the symptoms of the problem rather than its causes.

■ Living patterns

After sustenance, the second basic human need is habitat, a broad concept that encompasses the different structures organising physical human interaction. This increasingly involves the living patterns of urban residents, who for the first time in history represent more than half of the world's population. Within this framework, there are two sectors of activity where green business opportunities seem to have expanded the most in recent years: construction; and transportation. As such, the decision to devote the remainder of this chapter to these two areas is justified by the strong possibility that – alongside the clean energy sector discussed in Chapter 10 – it is here that most green jobs will be created in the near term.

■ Green construction

The construction industry is comprised of myriad sub-sectors, each of which has its own environmental history. One example is the lighting sector (see *Web Resource 9.2*), which accounts in some countries for upwards of one-third of all electricity used in buildings (see UK Department of Business 2009 Energy Consumption update). Another is building materials, where researchers are actively developing substitute solutions such as reactive 'pozzolans' that can help to make concrete stronger and therefore use smaller quantities. Few companies are in a position to specialise in all of these competencies, meaning that construction projects are often driven by consortia comprised of partner firms. The question this raises is to what extent the different participants have similar environmental expectations or performance.

The first distinction to make in green construction is between the environmental profile of existing versus new buildings. Most developers nowadays are compelled by state authorities to apply green

9

CHP: ■————————————
Where heat waste created during energy or electricity generation processes is captured and used for heating, either on one site or across a wider area in 'district heating' systems.

construction principles either directly to the new structures that they are building (materials used, technology installed) and/or to its surrounding infrastructure (i.e. **CHP – combined heat and power**). These principles are relatively straightforward in new projects, where they generally equate to an upfront surcharge of between 2 and 10 per cent (Blackburn 2007) – an altogether acceptable price given the lower life-cycle operating costs from which future owners will benefit. However, retrofitting older units built to pre-ecological specifications is much more difficult, hence expensive. In this sector as in others, the more a green solution is applied *ex post facto* instead of being incorporated into the design process from the very outset, the harder it will be to implement.

Key issue	... the more a green solution is applied *ex post facto* instead of being incorporated into the design process from the very outset, the harder it will be to implement.

The principles underlying green construction are worth reviewing. Buildings have a significant environmental footprint during both their construction and operational phases. A leading concern in the former area is the production of traditional concrete, responsible according to some calculations for up to 5 per cent of total CO_2 emissions in countries such as the United States (Fountain 2009). Hence the ambitious work being done to develop a concrete capable of sequestering CO2 emissions. Irrespective of these laudable efforts, the reality is that unless building rubble is reconverted into new materials – as Texas IT company Rackspace famously did in the late 2000s when it converted a vacant shopping mall into its new corporate headquarters – construction work will always involve a net consumption of natural resources. Hence the move towards **biophilic** building designs using trees (www.wholetreesarchitecture.com/) or other natural elements such as roof gardens covered with plants to maintain temperature, produce oxygen and sequester carbon (Braungart and McDonough 2009). These are the kinds of measures that renowned landscape architect Ian Macharg refers to as 'design with nature', akin to the biomimicry approach discussed in Chapter 6. The goal here is to create a healthy environment healing the 'sick building' syndrome affecting many users. Similarly, there is a new emphasis on empowering buildings' occupants to control their micro-environments via thermostats or other tools instead of the heavy-handed practice of blasting vast quantities of heated or cooled

Biophilic: ■————————————
Postulate of a deep connection between humankind and biosphere.

air indiscriminately throughout the structure. Today's architects talk about humanising people's experience of being indoors.

The objectives at this level include better air quality, ventilation and filtration systems; toxin-free construction and cleaning materials (Friend 2009); optimised use of external daylight or internal design to reduce artificial lighting or heating needs; smart meters and other management systems to audit and reduce energy consumption (Hitchcock and Willard 2006); water-saving fixtures and landscaping; and initiatives reducing employees' commuter footprint (proximity to public transportation, changing rooms for cyclists, etc.) Most of these efforts feature in the holistic 'integrative' design approaches that constitute one or the other of the world's leading green building standards.

Indeed, strong codes have demonstrably been a real fillip for green construction, one example being the way in which per capita electricity consumption in California – where construction activities are strongly regulated – leveled out between 1979 and 2006 despite rising by 60 per cent in the rest of the USA (Schendler 2009). One benchmark in this area is a standard formulated by the United States Green Building Council (www.usgbc.org/) and widely referred to as LEED or Leadership in Energy and Environmental Design (see Figure 9.3). LEED covers a range of building projects (New Construction, Existing Buildings, Commercial Interiors, etc.) and includes a variety of performance levels. The top category is Platinum, which represents only 5 per cent of the more than 5000 LEED certified buildings worldwide – one signature example being the Engine Centre facility that a Pratt and Whitney/China Eastern Airlines joint venture has built in Shanghai. At least one-eighth of the structure's total energy needs come from renewable sources; energy-efficient and reflective windows and roofs work together to produce natural coolness; and water use has been cut by around 40 per cent (Greenbiz 2010b). Design features of this kind are particularly important in rapidly emerging markets such as China, which adds about 2 billion square metres of new buildings every year. The question then becomes which standards should be applied where.

9

The question then becomes which standards should be applied where.   **Key issue**

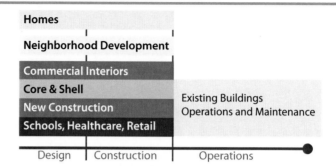

Figure 9.3: Structure of LEED green building certification programme (cf. www.usgbc.org)

The complication is that green building standards can vary widely, in terms of both performance – UK codes, for instance, accept that building leaks three times as much energy as their German equivalents would – and how rigorously certification is policed (Monbiot 2007). There has been a recent attempt to impose an International Green Construction Code based largely on Californian standards but allowing adaptation to local authorities' priorities and a site's objective building conditions (Greenbiz 2010a). Many European developers and architects work to BRE Environmental Assessment Method specifications (www.breeam.org/), although Italy's Green Building Council has recently decided to adopt LEED. Alongside these holistic codes, a number of targeted efficiency standards also exist, ranging from the increasingly popular Energy Star (and similar certifications discussed in Chapter 5) to building-specific codes such as 'Eco Balance'. Constructions worldwide are undergoing greening processes but to varying extents, with some projects involving simultaneous improvements in several areas (lighting, appliances, equipment, temperature control, etc.) and others being more narrowly defined – especially as the recession puts corporate budgets under pressure. A distinction should also be made between greening work done during a building's initial construction phase (the materials used, etc.) or subsequent operational phase (energy consumption, maintenance, cleaning, etc.). In construction as in other sectors, the relative novelty of many green activities means that there is still no agreement on what certain seminal terms actually mean. One consequence is the growing number of lawyers engaged in litigating building projects' compliance aspects (Armstrong 2010).

Yet there is no doubting the growing popularity of green building practices, despite the generally difficult economic conditions of the late 2000s. There are several reasons for rapid expansion in this sector, exemplified by the total of 135,000 LEED Accredited Professionals by year-end 2009, up from 77,000 just 12 months before (Greenbiz 2009).

On one hand, rising energy prices provide a strong market incentive, with recent statistics indicating that LEED buildings had saved about 300 trillion BTUs of energy by 2008, a number expected to rise to 1 quadrillion by 2020. This is because the proposal of an energy-efficient building is a strong sales argument for a developer seeking a commercial tenant in an era suffering from the overhang of previous bubbles. In a similar vein, many countries' 2009 economic stimulus packages contained retrofitting and weather-proofing provisions (involving commercial but also residential property, schools etc.) that raised questions about the role of the state in supporting the new sector's launch. The German government, for instance, has been famously proactive in green construction, exemplified by its decade-old CO_2 Building Rehabilitation Programme that spends about €1 billion annually to subsidise homeowners' greening initiatives (new boilers, insulation materials, solar panels, etc.). Note the positive knock-on effects of this policy for German companies ranging from eco-equipment manufacturers to consultancies specialised in drafting post-installation performance reports. German architects have also gained valuable experience in the cross-fertilisation of green techniques (Tobias 2010) – a specialist competency materialising in the low-tech **Passivhaus** building designs that have started to dominate in model green cities such as Vauban in Germany's Black Forest region, which has become something of a pilgrimage for green builders today.

> **?** What is the correlation between GDP growth and green building activities?

> ■ **Passivhaus:** Structure designed to reduce internal–external heat flows using triple-glazed windows and an airtight outer envelope. Contrast with hi-tech 'active' green structure that uses onsite renewable energy sources but needs pumps and motors to circulate heat (Steffen 2008).

All in all, an accurate macro-economic analysis of the cost of subsidising green building activities would include the policy's Keynesian multiplier effects as well as the opportunity cost of not advancing in cold weather countries such as the UK, whose ageing energy-inefficient housing stock is responsible, according to some analysts, for up to 60 per cent of the country's total building-related greenhouse gas emissions (Neale 2008). On top of this, there is also the possibility of using current building stock to host new clean energy systems (see Chapter 10), exemplified by the large solar arrays being installed on the rooftops of iconic buildings such as the Kaiser Permanente hospitals in Oakland (California), the Sears Tower in Chicago and even the White House, but also – and increasingly in Europe – on smaller public structures such as schools and town halls. Significantly, both the construction and energy sectors have a stake in such projects. The fact that multiple sectors have an interest in green construction further bolsters its future prospects.

9

■ Transportation

Localism: ■
Social/economic organisation emphasising the consumption of goods/services that have been produced locally.

Hinterland: ■
Regions surrounding a population centre and sustaining it with goods while relying on it as a trade hub.

Urban infill: ■
Policy of directing growth to undeveloped spaces within a metropolitan region's existing boundaries instead of expanding further on the fringes.

Brownfield sites: ■
Spaces that once hosted an industrial or commercial activity but are currently unused.

? How likely is it that major cities will stop encroaching on surrounding green spaces?

The outlook for green transportation can only be fully analysed in the context of broader issues such as population dispersion, migration patterns (particularly commuting), the shape of economic flows and general attitudes towards **localism**. Geographers tend to apply a **hinterland** concept when monitoring the relationship between a population centre and the regions with which it entertains regular relationships (economic or other). Clearly, the longer the distances covered by an economy's supply chains, the greater its transportation needs. The same can be said when commuters face long journeys on a daily basis, often because they inhabit a space characterised by 'extensive' land use. Macro-level responses to such circumstances might then involve public mass transit systems and above all **urban infill** policies directing further development to intra-mural **brownfield sites** instead of the municipality's fringes – as happens far too often in today's extensive growth model which had had the overall effect of augmenting transportation needs – thereby causing further pollution and resource consumption. Focusing on transportation modes exclusively without regard to more contextual factors necessarily limits the scope of analysis.

At the same time, transportation vehicles are still worth analysing in and of themselves for two reasons. Firstly, many companies' greening efforts have focused in recent years on vehicle technology – possibly because this is something that the private sector can control, as opposed to larger, more structural urban redevelopment projects that usually necessitate government intervention (note work being done by companies such as IBM to develop 'smart infrastructure' sensors and analytical software that optimise traffic flows). This distinction is actually quite important, since it is often at a more industrial level that young managers can expect greater green career opportunities. Secondly, transportation is a major source of pollution, accounting for over 23 per cent of global CO_2 emissions (see Table 9.2). As such, it represents the ecological front line for companies facing up to their environmental responsibilities. There is no doubt that fewer journeys by people and goods would mean less pollution – but until such mass behavioural change occurs, green business will want to focus on more achievable goals.

Air	130.2
Passenger cars	124.5
Two-wheelers	83.0
City bus	66.8
Rail	45.6
Maritime	43.1
Coach	34.3

Table 9.2: CO_2 emissions per passenger, grams per km.

Credit Allianz SE: available at http://knowledge.allianz.com, accessed 4 June 2010.

... it is often at a more industrial level that young managers can expect greater green career opportunities.

Key issue

Aviation

Flying is the mode of transportation that has received most criticism for its environmental footprint. Although it only accounts for 3 per cent of the global greenhouse effect at present, this proportion is predicted to at least double within a decade – in part because the gases that planes emit in the upper atmosphere tend to have stronger greenhouse effects. The **commoditisation** of flying for both business and leisure travellers means that passenger numbers have risen sharply in recent years despite higher ticket prices resulting from fuel inflation and the generalisation of airport taxes (see Chapter 4). Airline sector profitability does not entirely reflect this trend, since in addition to funding rising fuel costs operators must also fund enormous fixed assets and regularly struggle to adjust their capacities to demand variability. Add to this the extreme competition affecting the sector since its general deregulation – plus the rise of discount airliners – and the picture is one of a business whose future is anything but assured.

■ **Commoditisation:** Where goods are developed, processed and distributed according to an undifferentiated mass volume logic.

Airplane manufacturers (and their airliner customers) have placed their hopes in new passengers and new freight business from emerging Asian economies. As for concerns that passengers might stop flying due to carbon emissions, there is little sign of this happening, with many customers assuaging their guilt – if they feel any – by participating in tree planting carbon offset schemes (Neale 2008).

Lastly, some work is being done to increase jets' efficiency, which rose by 70 per cent over the past half decade (Carson 2009). Planes are unlikely to benefit from batteries' expected dominance as storage units because the power that they need to take off is generally greater than anything that batteries can supply. On the other hand, planes can be designed to become lighter and more fuel-efficient, and air-traffic

9

management can also be made more efficient. In addition, actors ranging from Boeing to Virgin Airlines have started testing biofuels, either alone or mixed with standard jet fuel. As aforementioned, however, this new solution creates a whole set of new problems regarding the ethics of diverting crops away from the global food chain so that people can continue to fly.

Railways

Like the aviation sector, railways require significant upfront infrastructure investments. Train itineraries are just as inflexible as planes, since they only offer 'port-to-port' links and require users to organise further connections from the arrival port to their final destination. On the other hand, trains perform astronomically better than planes in fuel-efficiency and carbon emissions terms, which may explain why the outlook for this sector is so much more positive.

Countries such as the USA where the rail network is relatively underdeveloped are experiencing a small boom in this sector. On one hand, trains are increasingly viewed as a more rational means to transport large passenger numbers, with the state of California, for instance, having recently voted to issue a bond to fund a fast train between the two population centres of Los Angeles and San Francisco – a corridor logic that is a cornerstone of President Obama's Green New Deal policy. The idea is that many citizens will stop flying or driving if links are established, possibly using a hub system, between intra-urban transport systems and inter-city fast train networks – the latter being a global activity dominated by industrialists from countries where integrated systems have already been established. Examples include Alstom for the French TGV, Hitachi for the Japanese 'Bullet Train' and Siemens for the German ICE (Siemens also makes the high-speed Velaro trains linking Moscow to Saint Petersburg in Russia). The Canadian company Bombardier is also a big name in this sector.

Secondly, there is a strong move afoot to transfer freight traffic from road to rail, despite the relative inflexibility of this latter mode. At the macro level, a shift of this kind would cause a huge reduction in fuel consumption and CO_2 emissions, although road provisions would still have to be made to transfer goods from freight depots to their final destination. Note that US tycoon Warren Buffett – convinced of the 'efficiency' of freight rail – has recently entered this sub-sector, spending $44 billion to acquire Burlington Northern Santa Fe, one of the country's largest freight railway operators. Similarly, the European

Union's 2003 Marco Polo programme provides financial assistance to improve the environmental performance of cross-EU freight transport. The train, the earliest mode of motorised transportation, also appears to be the one with the brightest future.

The train, the earliest mode of motorised transportation, also appears to be the one with the brightest future.	**Key issue**

Shipping

In terms of the per kilometre cost of transporting a given volume of goods, shipping is just as efficient a mode of transportation as rail and therefore an attractive alternative. The problem, of course, lies in this mode's very inflexible infrastructure and the even greater fixed costs involved in building port infrastructure and oceanworthy vessels. Shipping's inability to service the world's many landlocked destinations also undermines its universality, meaning that growth prospects in the sector, despite its comparatively low footprint, remain limited.

Still, some notable efforts are being made to further improve shipping's environmental performance. One involves raising 'Skysails' on motorised cargo ships to increase their relatively low travelling speeds – another one of shipping's comparative disadvantages – while cutting per-km fuel consumption by upwards of 20 per cent. Another involves the development of solar-powered navigation systems, with photovoltaic panels being laid out on ships' decks and energy stored in the lithium-ion batteries that are destined to become such a key feature of power storage in the future (see Chapter 10).

Road

Nowhere is this new battery-oriented motorisation logic more advanced than in the automotive sector – which can be subdivided into different categories, starting with freight and logistics, responsible for ca. 30 per cent of all transport emissions (Chapman 2010), and a proportion that is likely to fall given the sector's growing energy-efficiency focus. Above all, there is the passenger car sector, where several fully operative prototypes – famously led by the Toyota Prius – are already being widely marketed. The background to this transition is fuel prices' strong rise in recent years along with deteriorating driving conditions on increasingly congested networks. Secondly, passenger cars (which account by some calculations for 90 per cent of all urban journeys) are

9

> ? What percentage of car owners will drive electric vehicles by the year 2020?

responsible for 45 per cent of global CO2 emissions, a figure that could be cut by 70 or 80 per cent if citizens migrated to trains, trams or buses (Neale 2008). Under these conditions, it is more relevant to ask why consumers' take-up of zero or low emission automobiles has not been quicker.

At one level, the answer lies in the financial incentives that people need to migrate to modes that are less convenient and offer less privacy (buses also tend to be slower than cars, despite the growing number of dedicated bus lanes in many cities). Incentives include punitive sanctions such as **congestion charges** and higher fuel and road taxes but also positive measures such as subsidised public transportation. Public policy in this area varies widely, however, meaning that for most citizens, the advantage of forgoing passenger cars is not obvious given that public transit fares still seem high compared with the 'free' solution of simply driving away in one's car. Of course, cars are anything but free – they cost a lot to buy, operate and maintain (insurance, maintenance, fuel). Thus, the sector provides yet another example of consumers turning a blind eye to the total costs associated with a certain choice (car ownership, in this instance) and focusing instead on the short-term costs of the more ecological solution – a cognitive problem that is felt at every level of green marketing (see Chapter 7).

Congestion charge: ▪ Levy on drivers entering certain crowded city sections to dissuade them from doing so.

It is also noteworthy how many car advertisements still highlight petrol engines or at best 'mild hybrids' featuring a few incremental improvements. Moreover, even when consumers have heard of greener driving systems, they usually possess very little knowledge about it, with some confusion between Toyota or Honda's preferred petrol-electric hybrid solutions and Renault or GM's fully electric cars – a confusion that feeds into fears about performance (speed, durability, comfort and safety). Then comes the barrier of price, with green cars tending to cost at least 25 per cent more than non-green alternatives offering similar performance. This price differential is expected to last either until lithium-based battery technologies become cheaper and more efficient, or until oil prices skyrocket to such a point (estimated by some at $300 per barrel) that current petrol-based driving systems become prohibitively expensive. Lastly, there are fears about spare part stocks, and at a more fundamental level, the availability of electric recharging facilities. The sum total of these effects explains why despite all the publicity, green cars still account for such a small proportion of the international fleet of passenger vehicles.

At the same time, the very fact that the sector is taking so much time to develop might be viewed as an opportunity for graduates beginning their career. As with any infant industry, timing is a key question, with a consensus emerging that governments should intervene to accelerate the transition to green cars (Hensley *et al.* 2009). There are several justifications for this view. Firstly, the automobile industry and its supply chain are major employers, making their redesign along more sustainable lines a priority policy for many governments. Secondly and as aforementioned, there is a common perception that the electric battery industry will gain primacy as resource depletion hits traditional fossil fuel sources. Lastly, rapid car growth in emerging countries such as China – whose total fleet is predicted to rise from fewer than 50 million vehicles to more than 600 million within 50 years – will have very negative side-effects, not only locally (smog, congestion on roads ill equipped for such traffic) but also globally (CO_2 emissions). This is worrying for organisations such as the EU, whose recent strategy has been to convince car producers to voluntarily lower new vehicles' average CO_2 emissions, in part by gearing tax incentives towards this end.

... the automobile industry and its supply chain are major employers, making their redesign along more sustainable lines a priority policy for many governments.	**Key issue**

Manufacturers are also reshaping this new framework, in part by expanding the offer of all-electric models (see Box 9.1). The sector has attracted a number of new names as well, led by BYD, a growing Chinese firm that has leveraged its original competency in mobile phone batteries to become a world leader in electric cars. Enabling industries are also taking off, exemplified by an Israeli company called Better Place, whose mission is to install battery recharging points in neighbourhoods worldwide, thereby overcoming one of the main obstacles preventing a quicker migration to electric vehicles, to wit, fears over whether limited battery capacities will restrict driving ranges. Other greening efforts involve retrofitting existing automobile fleets so they can incorporate electric driving systems (Grove and Burgelman 2008); developing lightweight carbon fibre cars; and creating battery leasing arrangements to lower the surcharge that consumers face when operating an electrical vehicle. Lastly, there is even a concerted effort in some corners – such as SQbiofuels.com, a company from the environmentally ambitious US state of Oregon – to set up automobile fuel stations

9

dispensing biodiesel made from vegetable oil (mirroring Brazil's long established network of ethanol fuel dispensaries). The sheer number of initiatives underway intimates a strong need for young managers capable of carrying them to fruition.

Box 9.1: List of electric cars expected available by 2012 (www. greencarsite.co.uk)

Electric Mini E	Nissan LEAF, Nissan NUVU	Tesla S
Fisker hybrid	Pininfarina EV	TH!NK Ox
GEM Peapod	Porsche 911	Think City
Ginetta G50	Renault ZE	Toyota Prius (Plug-in)
Lightning GT	Smart EV	Vauxhall Ampera
Mitsubishi i	Subaru Stella / R1e	Venturi Volage
MIla EV	Tazzari Zero	

■ Obstacles and pathways

1 Global food supplies are falling in relation to population growth and demands.

   Vast opportunities in developing underused arable lands (Russia, Africa, etc.)

2 Many populations are suffering from water shortages.

   Investment in water efficiency/recycling to offset enormous current wastage.

3 Rising cost of building construction (materials) and operations (energy supply).

   Develop joint ownership arrangements with partners providing eco-solutions.

4 Rising fuel costs and congestion make for difficult driving conditions.

   Build energy-efficient public transit (small buses with hybrid driving systems, etc.)

Case study: Cybertran's foray into light rail

After graduating in 1980 from the University of California at Santa Barbara with a degree in environmental studies, Neil Sinclair spent the best part of two decades working on a variety of green campaigns, ranging from an opposition to offshore drilling that was the hallmark of his 1988 congressional bid, to a series of green transportation advisory roles during the 1990s (one of which culminated in a much-lauded electric bicycle hire scheme in the desert city of Palm Springs). Then in 1998, Neil joined CyberTran International (http://www.cybertran.com) a small San Francisco Bay Area start-up pursuing a vision of bespoken, ultra-light rail complementing the heavier passenger rail systems already operating in many municipalities worldwide. This new position seemed a good opportunity for Neil to implement the different green competencies that he had developed over the years.

CyberTran's business model is based on three basic concepts. The first is that the tendency in most Western countries to build urban habitats around expanded private vehicle use has created a dystopia where residents – especially lower and middle income categories that cannot afford to live in re-gentrified urban centres – spend more and more time stuck in traffic jams burning fuel, losing productive time and breathing unhealthy air. This spatial organisation is clearly untenable, meaning that many if not most societies are likely to harbour latent demand for improved public transportation provisions – a fundamental scenario that buttressed CyberTran founder Dr John Dearien's original confidence in the outlook for his chosen sector of activity.

Many mass transit systems suffer relatively mediocre take-up, however, in part because they often seem expensive to potential users compared with the ostensible cost of simply driving a car. The reality is quite different, of course, since the total cost of private vehicle ownership (acquisition, maintenance, insurance and fuel) generally far exceeds the total fares that commuters can expect to spend riding trains or taking buses. Given most individuals' aversion to short-term outlays, however – a psychological constraint highlighted throughout this book – anything that can be done to reduce the cost of public transportation should have a beneficial effect on user rates. This feeds into CyberTran's second business concept, since the company's ultra-light rail infrastructure is much cheaper to implement than heavier alternative solutions, a cost savings that can then be passed on to customers.

Lastly, many potential users are reluctant to accept the inconvenience of having to organise their daily journeys around the fixed schedules and stops that structure most underground or suburban mass transit systems. CyberTran's third business concept addresses this by proposing a fleet of self-directed pods (called 'trans') travelling across a network of small side tracks. The key to this system is advanced computer technology managing the 'trans' location and displacement to maximise availability. The analogy is that passengers will be able to request vehicles in stations as simply as people can call lifts in a building.

9

On the face of things, the sum total of these capabilities should have given CyberTran a relatively compelling sales proposition helping it to break into the market for public transportation systems alongside long-established multinational competitors like Canada's Bombardier, Germany's Siemens or France's Alstom. Yet for a number of reasons, progress has been difficult. Dr Dearien's death in 2004 was not only a personal tragedy but also a business problem – although Neil was able to step in as CEO, it is often difficult to replace the scientific knowledge and personal connections that a founder can bring to bear in an SME such as CyberTran. Indeed, the company's small size has been a hindrance at a variety of levels, first and foremost being its lesser access to the volume of equity funding that would help it to fully test, perfect and demonstrate the kind of experimental system that it is trying to market. When asked about this handicap, Neil prefers highlighting the flexibility advantage that SMEs have when it comes to implementing innovations, contrasting this with the innate conservatism of larger companies that may prefer, for short-term profitability reasons, to bury new and 'disruptive' technologies endangering their sunk investments. At the same time, there is no question that Neil has had to expend a significant amount of managerial time procuring the private and especially public funding needed to carry CyberTran through its introduction phase – a challenge given that the company's potential fund providers (and customers) are mainly public sector entities such as municipalities whose budgets were dramatically curtailed in the late 2000s due to the credit crunch-induced recession.

CyberTran's smaller size also means that it has to work hard to prove its technological and performance credibility. Interestingly enough, however, it is at this latter level that the company has progressed the furthest. Neil has put together an impressive dossier of letters from local, state and national politicians willing to express support for CyberTran, whose efforts they view as a perfect reflection of the kind of sectorial initiatives that President Barak Obama wants to support through his 'Green New Deal' stimulus package. The net result has been a serious expression of interest by a local municipality whose public transportation (and broader ecological) needs could be partially addressed via the functionalities that CyberTran offers. If a contract is signed, the company will finally have a launchpad not only for its own capabilities but also enabling it to highlight the profile of the sector that it is helping to create. Its trajectory might then resemble in certain ways the birth of the information technology sector, another industry where Bay Area start-ups have acted as a driving force. The question then becomes whether people in 30 years time will be speaking about CyberTran in the same tones as they use when discussing Apple or Intel today. As oil supplies deplete, the possibility is there.

Case study questions

1   Why and how did the focus of environmental activism evolve during the course of Neil Sinclair's career?

2   What is CyberTran's underlying business model?

3   What is the medium-term outlook for CyberTran and for its sector of activity in general?

■ References

Armstrong, J. (2010), 'The legal costs of going green', 11 January, available at www.dailyjournal.com/, accessed 29 September 2010.

Blackburn, W. (2007), *The Sustainability Handbook*, Earthscan.

Borlaug, N. (2007), 'A green revolution for Africa', *Wall Street Journal – Europe*, 29 October.

Bradsher, K. (2008), An Insatiable Demand, *The Observer*, 27 January, *New York Times* insert.

Braungart, M. and McDonough, W. (2009), *Cradle to Cradle: Re-Making The Way We Make Things*, London: Vintage Books.

Carson, S. (2009), 'How Boeing fights climate change', 23 May, available at http://online.wsj.com/, accessed 4 June 2010.

Chapman, S. (2010), 'Driving the green agenda forward', *MediaPlanet Guardian Insert*, May, p. 4.

DEFRA (Department for Environment, Food and Rural Affairs) (2004), *Agriculture in the United Kingdom 2004*, available at www.defra.gov.uk/, accessed 3 June 2010 .

Edwards, A. (2005), *The Sustainability Revolution: Portrait of a Paradigm Shift*, New Society Publishers.

Evans, J. and Cohen, M. (2009), 'Regional water resource implications of bioethanol production in the Southeastern United States', *Global Change Biology*, **15** (9).

Fageria, N., Baligar, V., and Li, Y (2008), 'The role of nutrient efficient plants in improving crop yields in the twenty-first century', *Journal of Plant Nutrition*, **31** (6).

Fountain, H. (2009), 'Concrete is remixed with environment in mind', 30 March, available at www.nytimes.com/, accessed 26 May 2010.

Friend, G. (2009), *The Truth About Green Business*, Upper Saddle River, NJ: FT Press

Greenbiz (2009), *Green Building Impact Report 2008*, available on www.greenbiz.com, accessed 4 June 2010.

Greenbiz (2010a), 'New construction code aims to unify green building standards', 15 March, available at www.greenbiz.com/, accessed 25 May 2010.

Greenbiz (2010b), 'Pratt & Whitney earns first LEED-platinum rating in China', 8 April, available at www.greenbiz.com/, accessed 25 May 2010.

Grove, A. and Burgelman, R. (2008), 'An electric plan for energy resilience', December, available at www.mckinseyquarterly.com/, accessed 17 April 2009.

Guevarra, L. (2010), 'Water-saving strategies to make every drop count', 25 March, available at www.greenbiz.com/, accessed 25 May 2010.

Helenius, J., Aro-Heinila, E., Hietala, R., Mikkola,M., Risku-Norja, H., Seppanen, L., Sinkkonen,M. and Vihma, A. (2007), 'Systems frame for multidisciplinary study on sustainability of localising food', *Progress in Industrial Ecology, An International Journal*, **4** (5).

Hensley, R., Knupfer, S. and Pinner, D. (2009), 'Electrifying cars: how three industries will evolve', June, available at www.mckinseyquarterly.com/, accessed 24 May 2010.

Hitchcock, D. and Willard, M. (2006), *The Business Guide to Sustainability: Practical Strategies and Tools for Organization*, London: Earthscan.

Lang, T. and Heasman, M. (2004), *Food Wars: The Battle for Mouths, Minds and Markets*, London: Earthscan.

9

Le Monde (2007), *Les biocarburants redessinent la carte de l'agriculture mondiale*, Special dossier, 3 April, pp. I–III.

Mathiason, N. (2009), 'Developed countries face threat of soaring prices and food shortages', *The Observer*, 1 November.

McKinsey-WRG (Water Resources Group) (2009), *Charting Our Water Future*, available at www.mckinsey.com/, accessed 4 June 2010.

Monbiot, G. (2007), *Heat: How We Can Stop the Planet Burning*, London: Penguin.

Neale, J. (2008), *Stop Global Warming: Change the World*, London: Bookmarks.

ODI (2007), 'Linking social protection and the production sectors', briefing paper, October.

Schendler, A. (2009), *Getting Green Done: Hard Truths from the Front Lines of the Sustainability Revolution*, New York: Public Affairs.

Sitkin, A. and Bowen, N. (2010), *International Business: Challenges and Choices*, Oxford: Oxford University Press.

Spurling, H. (2008), 'Our recipe for disaster', *The Observer*, 8 June.

Steffen, A. (2008), *Worldchanging: A User's Guide for the 21st Century*, New York: Sagmeister.

Tobias, L. (2010), 'Germany's insights on green building', 26 April, available at www.greenbiz.com/, accessed 26 May 2010.

UK Department of Business, Enterprise, Regulation and Reform (2009), *Energy Consumption in the United Kingdom*, available at www.decc.gov.uk, accessed 14th December 2010

Wines, M. (2009), 'Worst drought in half century shrivels the wheat belt of China', 24 February, available at www.nytimes.com/, accessed 4 June 2010.

von Weizsäcker, E., Hargroves, K., Smith, M., Desha, C. and Stasinopoulos, P. (2009), *Factor Five: Transforming the Global Economy through 80% Improvements in Resource Productivity*, London: Earthscan.

10 Clean Energy and New Ventures

Contents

Clean energy
Generation and transmission
Solar and wind – the main renewables

Launching new ventures
Funding
International outlook at year-end 2010

Learning objectives

After reading this chapter, you will be able to:

■ Weigh the factors driving renewable energy versus the obstacles that the sector faces

■ Adopt the perspective of potential investors considering green ventures

■ Determine the outlook for green ventures in a global economic context

■ Introduction

Previous chapters have discussed the many different ways in which the ecological imperative affects business operations. Since organisations' limited capacities force them to prioritise their workload, the question then becomes how companies should rank the different environmental challenges they face. As argued throughout this book, with managers generally operating under severe financial constraints, it is issues with a direct bearing on the bottom line that are most likely to receive immediate attention. In the field of Ecology and Management, this often means the supply and price of energy prices. The depletion scenario detailed in Chapter 2 forecast that energy costs will skyrocket in the near future as global supplies wane and demand accelerates. Add to this the costs that companies will bear as cap-and-trade carbon emission reduction schemes are implemented and it is no surprise that the fortunes of new clean energy ventures dominate the green business headlines.

> **?** Should energy be companies' green priority?

As often as not, the many millions of new 'green jobs' that most analysts are predicting do not actually refer to clean energy but to clean technology, involving the greening of existing industrial or service sector activities. Examples range from green construction (see Chapter 9) to energy consumption reduction devices, recycling measures and even process re-engineering – the latter being a market that has drawn particular attention in recent years from longstanding management consultancies such as KPMG and Accenture as well as new specialist advisors such as Carbon International. The present chapter, on the other hand, focuses specifically on the generation and distribution of renewable clean energy. This new sector currently generates an estimated $600 billion in revenues and employs 1.7 million people worldwide – or 2.3 million, including component manufacturers producing items such as photovoltaic cells for solar panels (TUC 2009). What is exciting for business students is the likelihood that these numbers will explode in coming years as the energy crunch hits global business. Joining a sector just before it takes off is a fantastic opportunity – as exemplified by the fortunes of those who were lucky enough to start a career in computers during the 1980s.

Key issue

Joining a sector just before it takes off is a fantastic opportunity – as exemplified by the fortunes of those who were lucky enough to start a career in computers during the 1980s.

Within the clean energy sector itself, a distinction should be made between efforts by new ventures and by older companies. Boeing, for instance, is a world leader in concentrated photovoltaic solar power technology; ABB has contracts to deliver photovoltaic solar plants; and Johnson Controls makes batteries for electric and hybrid vehicles. Not only does this influence total job creation in an economy – with older companies' green initiatives often involving a simple reallocation of workers previously employed in other functions – but it is also relevant to the issue of new ventures' longevity (see Figure 10.1). It might also be argued that larger firms have deeper pockets, which puts them in a better position to survive the cash shortages endemic to most infant industries' introduction phases. Start-ups, on the other hand, rely solely on entrepreneurs' resources or capital sourced from external providers such as venture capitalists. This argument can be turned around, however, since big companies' larger capital requirements forces them to seek funding from the financial markets, whose short-term focus generally means that new activities will have less time to justify themselves. Indeed, large energy companies may like trumpeting their devotion to clean energy but their new capital investments in this sector have been somewhat disappointing, given the resources at their disposal (Mouawad 2009). Large companies also tend to pursue more institutionalised paradigms. They also face significant 'sunk costs', meaning that managers may be more reluctant to try something new (Croston 2008). This is not to say that big established firms do not have a major role to play in the new clean energy sector – but it does explain why much of the impetus comes from start-ups.

> **?** What is the relative role of big vs. small companies in green entrepreneurship?

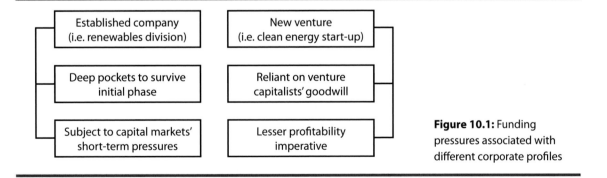

Figure 10.1: Funding pressures associated with different corporate profiles

10

■ Clean energy

In line with the green business principle that managers stand to benefit from greater knowledge of the physical environment within which they operate (see Chapter 1), it is appropriate for analysis of the clean energy sector to start with a review of the underlying science. This will involve a brief introduction to the generation and transmission of consumable energy, followed by a discussion of the two main sources driving this new industrial revolution – solar and wind power.

■ Generation and transmission

All economic activity is predicated on the expenditure of energy that has been captured and redirected in a way that creates a concentrated force. The animal (or human) forces driving pre-industrial economies drew strength directly from foodstuffs alone, via a slow and inefficient conversion process characterised by relatively little **energy density**. The advantage of the first industrial revolution was the appearance of a first reliable steam engine – developed by James Watt around 1770 and powered by having steam produced from combustibles such as wood or coal turn pistons inside of a cylinder – which uses its stroke action to generate highly concentrated **kinetic energy** capable of operating factory machinery. The problem with this system, however, was its comparative wastefulness, with the intermediation of machinery responsible for a great deal of **heat waste**. Hence the search for alternative modes of power generation.

For centuries, scientists had a basic understanding of electricity, which occurs when subatomic particles subjected to electromagnetic fields generate electric charges whose movement creates a current that can be used as a power source. The main challenge lay in capturing such energy flows – an outcome most famously achieved in the late 19th century by Thomas Edison, best known for his invention of the electric light bulb but who also registered countless other patents, most notably for an electricity distribution system. In turn, this paved the way for the power grids (see Figure 10.2) upon which most businesses and homes have relied for more than a century now.

Clearly, Edison's electricity grid is not the only way of transmitting energy – as exemplified by the vast network of service stations distributing petrol for internal combustion engine-propelled automobiles, or the pipelines delivering the natural gas used in so many buildings

Energy density: ■
Calculation of the volume of energy stored within a container of a given size.

Kinetic energy: ■
Energy wielded by an object in movement.

Heat waste: ■
Energy dissipating in heat form as the by-product of a chemical or mechanical action.

today for heating or other purposes. Moreover, there is some question about the efficiency of the grid approach, given the enormous amount of energy wasted when electricity is transmitted over long distances in its customary 'alternating current' form (with up to 40 per cent being lost according to some calculations). The problem is that the uneven global dispersion of factor endowments such as oil means that energy is often produced at a great distance from where it is consumed. Moreover, there is every chance that transmission distances will increase in the future as renewable fuels – often sourced from sparsely populated locations such as the Sahara, Gobi or Mojave deserts – account for a greater proportion of total energy production.

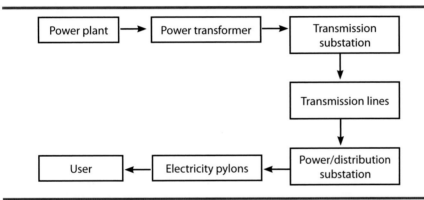

Figure 10.2: Schematic diagram of power grid

... the uneven global dispersion of factor endowments such as oil means that energy is often produced at a great distance from where it is consumed.

Key issue

Another problem is **intermittency**, a term that can mean different things. Firstly, it is difficult matching electricity supplies to demand levels that can vary considerably on a seasonal and even hour-to-hour basis. Power companies often try to solve the imbalance between 'baseline' and peak consumption by building added capacity in plants fired by conventional fuels and left in a 'part-loaded' state of readiness (Monbiot 2007). This is an expensive solution, although costs can be cut when smart grids (see Chapter 6) are used to direct supplies only where and when they are needed (or if temporary energy surpluses are not wasted but stored in devices such as batteries). Secondly, because of the intermittency of solar or wind sources, they often need to be supplemented by conventional fuels. These tend to be generated in large power plants that are few and far between, however, since each must be big enough to achieve economies of scale – a practical argument undermining many environmentalists' preference for micro-generation (see

■ **Intermittency:** Inconsistent behaviour. Energy from wind turbines or solar panels that only operate when the wind blows or the sun shines is, by definition, intermittent.

10

Chapter 2). As a result, the likelihood is that the electric grid approach, despite its imperfections, will survive for many years still.

Innovation efforts in this area have tended to focus instead on objectives such as increasing electric lines' efficiency by investing in high-voltage direct current; expanding **portability** through the miniaturisation of energy sources (i.e. laptop-sized solar panels using Solargorilla or Powertraveller technologies); and above all, innovating in the field of energy storage. A breakthrough in this latter area could help to kick-start a clean energy industry by solving the problem of renewable sources' intermittency, since the particular moment when energy is generated would no longer matter if it can be stored effectively (Luoma 2009). This explains the tremendous interest at present in battery technology. Current research in this field focuses on active materials such as lithium-ion that offer greater energy density and are capable of charging and discharging many times without losing too much power; super-sized batteries strong enough to run large automobiles (and even small electricity grids); and 'distributed' or 'flow' schemes that draw surplus energy accumulating in one section of a closed system, before storing it elsewhere for later usage. Future research may involve 'lithium metal-air' batteries such as IBM's PolyPlus, whose energy density is as explosive as petrol; two-way transfers between idled electrical vehicles and municipal electricity grids; 'ultracapacitor' devices; hydrogen fuel cells (see *Web Resource 10.1* for discussion of alternative clean energy sources); or air compression techniques. The growth prospects for all of these technologies depend on whether they can be made feasible at a competitive cost – and on how quickly first mover companies can impose their inhouse technology as an industry standard.

Portability:
Ease with which an asset, like an energy source, can be transported from one location to another.

? How might energy storage improvements tie into other green innovations?

■ Solar and wind – the main renewables

Following the 2009 Copenhagen Conference and given widespread fears of future energy shortages, a variety of more or less stringent modalities (see Chapter 4) are being used to expand the role of renewable energy. The European Union, for instance, has stipulated that these sources must account for 20 per cent of all final energy consumption by the year 2020, as opposed to 8.5 per cent in 2005. Note that in 2008 the EU's renewables industry employed something like 350,000 persons and produced ca. €40 billion in revenues– numbers that are bound to skyrocket as the new sector takes off. The same effects can be anticipated in the 24 US states that have already decided to impose renewables obligations – not to mention countries such as China, which is starting to dominate the global market for manufactured clean energy equipment. Elsewhere, the main catalysts for clean energy are subsidy mechanisms. A leading example is Germany, which offers generous feed-in tariffs to support green construction and has developed a number of large-scale solar arrays such as the 12 MW Gut Erlasee photovoltaic solar park in Bavaria. The net effect is that by 2008, 7.3 per cent of Germany's final energy consumption and 15.1 per cent of its total gross electricity consumption (vs. 6 and 12 per cent in 2006, respectively) came from renewable sources. Few if any other sectors of activity can match these impressive growth rates nowadays.

■ **Renewables obligation:** Requirement that a certain percentage of total energy production come from renewable sources by a certain deadline.

The following section analyses in detail the two main renewable clean energy sectors, to wit, solar and wind power. It excludes biofuels (see Chapter 9), a significant subsector in clean energy but one that remains subject to a great deal of controversy.

Before starting, it is important to specify that countries' variable endowment in sun and wind makes it hard to generalise about a global renewables market. Instead, the picture is one of differentiated national performances. (see Box 10.1). Certain aspects of this new industry have clearly globalised – specifically renewables equipment manufacturing, whose industrialisation has followed a relatively standard development path. Yet even this activity is affected by climate variations, since entrepreneurs located in countries with a particular natural resource (wind in Denmark, sun in China) will have an additional incentive to invest in a technology taking advantage of locally abundant factors. Moreover, above and beyond upstream operations, the clean technology sector is also associated with a number of downstream competencies, namely the installation of new equipment and its connection to local grids. These activities necessarily entail a local presence, however, although in some cases the MNE will pursue a vertical integration strategy, with a global equipment maker acquiring a local installer or vice versa (Pernick 2007).

? What are the arguments for and against vertical integration in the clean energy sector?

Note as well that the outlook for solar and wind differ somewhat. The solar sector, for instance, has historically attracted enormous investor attention, if only because the sun theoretically produces sufficient power to cover all of the Earth's total energy needs. At the same time, given the current state of technology, it is wind power that has come closest recently to achieving **grid parity** with conventional fuels (Luoma 2009). As a result, wind accounted in 2009 for more than half of global clean energy investment and installed clean energy capacity

■ **Grid parity:** Where energy from different sources costs the same to end consumers sourcing it via the grid.

10

(Pew 2010). This could soon change, however, as expected advances in solar technology drive production costs down in this sector.

Europe: Leading share of global financial investment in clean energy; Total of $43.7 billion, down from $48.4 billion in 2008

Asia and Oceania: Sharp rise in financial investment from $31.3 billion to $40.8 billion

China: 40% of global solar PV supply, 25% of global wind turbines (vs. 10% in 2007), and 77% of global solar hot water collectors

India: fifth worldwide in total existing wind power capacity; rapidly expanding rural renewables such as biogas and solar PV

North America: Investment down from $33.3 billion to $20.7 billion; but indications of renewed investment in 2010: solar arrays in California; wind arrays in Texas

South America: Investment down from $14.6 billion to $11.6 billion; Brazil produces virtually all global sugar-derived ethanol and has been adding new biomass and wind power plants

Middle East and Africa: Modest increase from $2.1 billion to $2.5 billion

Solar

Solar power refers to different processes, mainly silicon-based photo-voltaic (PV) cells that convert sunlight into electric current; and thermal captors, where mirrors called 'heliostats' collect heat that is then used for various purposes, including making steam to drive turbine generators. From a technological perspective, progress in this field will involve materials or designs that store heat or convert electricity more efficiently, such as roof tiles coated with thin, electricity-producing PV cells (c.f. www.srsenergy.com). Much attention has also been focused on parabolic systems that track the sun as it travels across the sky. In market terms, the key differentiation is between small home or commercial building installations and huge **solar arrays** using concentrator technologies – developed by companies such as Sharp Solar Energy, Emcore Semiconductors or Solfocus – to magnify the sun's effects. Target customers differ in each of these categories, with smaller installations being of interest to homeowners or developers (especially where the structures concerned feature large weight-bearing roof space) and larger arrays more of a focus for industrialists or utility companies.

Solar array: Large number of solar panels arranged in a way that maximises their thermal effects.

In the absence of government action, the solar sector's takeoff will depend on two factors: whether conventional fuel prices rise enough to spark a widespread search for substitutes; and whether technology advances sufficiently to make solar competitive. Chapter 2 spoke to the first condition. With regards to the second, many observers are already predicting that even without subsidies, solar's cost structure should approximate rival technologies within a few short years (Merfeld 2010), especially as knowledge spillovers from other industries mobilising similar skills sets – such as semiconductor chips – accelerate overall learning. For instance, the **nanotechnology** used to imprint memory on computer hard drives is similar to the one used in thin-film solar cells. This synergy may help to explain the prevalence of Silicon Valley computer firms in the budding solar sector (although leading Asian companies like Taiwan Semiconductor Manufacturing have also made a noted entry). The hope is that a combination of supply-side improvements and greater demand will enable production levels to achieve the critical mass beyond which economies of scale materialise, creating their own virtuous circle.

■ **Nanotechnology:** Study of matter on a very small atomic level.

? How prevalent are knowledge spillovers in green busness?

... takeoff [depends if] conventional fuel prices rise enough to spark a widespread search for substitutes; and whether technology advances sufficiently to make solar competitive.

Key issue

Some observers expect global installed solar capacity to rise from its current level of 10 GW to 200 GW or more by 2020 (Lorenz *et al.* 2008), with the fastest expansion occurring in sunny locales such as the Southwest USA, the Mediterranean and China and Japan – not to mention the Sahara desert, where a consortium led by German energy company RWE is looking to build a massive solar farm connected to Europe via underwater electric cables. What is unclear, however, is how future growth will break down between building-specific solar units and large solar arrays. The distinction is crucial, since there is no reason why the construction and utilities sectors should enjoy the same fortunes. Quite the contrary, whereas land use and financial constraints are likely to constrain future new build in the absence of government **weatherisation** subsidies (see Chapter 4), there is every chance that wholesale energy production will attract investment as traditional fuel sources deplete. This intimates that the focus of the new solar sector will tilt more towards mega-projects, such as the 2010 agreement between California company eSolar and China's Penglai Electric for the construction in the Mongolian desert of solar thermal

■ **Weatherisation:** Work done to improve physical structures' ability to withstand the elements while consuming a minimum of energy.

10

plants generating a total of 2 GW electricity – following another 2 GW PV solar plant project that China agreed in October 2009 (Woody 2010). A second growth area is likely to be comprised of opportunistic, 'roof space' projects. One recent example (Keeley 2008) was a €50 million deal where General Motors leased 2 million square feet at its Zaragoza automobile plant in Spain to a Franco-American consortium (Veolia Environnment and Clairvoyant Energy) that bought 85,000 lightweight PV panels from Energy Conversion Devices to produce 12 MW of electricity. Typically, the main hurdle facing projects of this nature is the capital expenditure, which often daunts customers despite the demonstrably beneficial effect on long-term operational costs. To overcome this barrier, a number of solar companies have devised arrangements interlinking customers' short and long-term interests, one example being SunEdison's willingness to take responsibility for the initial installation work as long as the customer signs a 20-year supply contract. By locking in flows, the company is selling solar energy rather than energy systems. Of course, this arrangement favours large providers with sufficient capital to afford outlays made upfront on customers' behalf – a condition that is always problematic in an infant industry.

Some managers have been so put off by this constraint that they have lost patience with the solar sector altogether. In early 2009, for instance, British oil company BP closed two solar cell manufacturing and module assembly plants near Madrid, along with a third module assembly plant in Maryland (USA). The MNE also brought a specialised division called BP Solar back inhouse, reflecting the comparatively unsympathetic attitude towards renewables held by former CEO Tony Hayward – who would later gain fame for his role in the 2010 Gulf of Mexico oil disaster. Otherwise and as outlined below, the sector's inability to sustain itself so far – due in part to an over-production of solar panels during the mid-2000s – means that enthusiasm has waned as cash-strapped governments have been forced to withdraw funds. This is exemplified by the dramatic demise of Puertollano, Spain's solar panel production centre, after state subsidies were slashed by one-third (Rosenthal 2010). Other factors shackling the solar sector's takeoff include anger at the competition for resources in desert environments – solar thermal processes typically consume a great deal of water (Woody 2009) – and criticisms of companies that publicise token solar projects to mask their overall environmental footprint. For example, Fred Pearce, the British greenwash specialist (see Chapter 7), has taken German energy company E.ON to task for seeking praise after installing 68 solar panels at its coal-fired power station in the English Midlands while neglecting to mention that the CO_2 benefits of this action were equivalent to at most one millionth of the plant's total greenhouse gas emissions. We may be witnessing the dawn of the solar industry, but it would be wrong to assume that everything is sunny in this area.

> **?** How long can and should clean energy entrepreneurs expect to wait for payback?

Wind

The situation for wind power is similar to solar insofar as both currently account for at best a few percentage points in most countries' energy mix; both are currently experiencing impressive growth rates and both continue to face a number of stumbling blocks. Windmill technology has been around for many years and is based on the simple idea that strong winds pushing blades attached to a tower create mechanical energy that a generator converts into electrical energy (see Figure 10.3). Improvements can always be made in different components' costs and performance, with an estimated half of wind turbines' total capital cost involving the infrastructure (foundations and cables), one quarter the tower and turbine and one quarter the gearbox and associated parts (BWEA 2009). It is worth noting that aside from the cables connecting turbines to the grid (an aspect requiring some understanding of electronics), the primary skill set required by wind technology is mechanical in nature – a knowledge base that is well established and widely dispersed worldwide. Thus, success in this sector is predicated less on advanced science and more on financial and human capital (i.e. the need for trained installers). This makes wind less esoteric – and more competitive internationally – than solar.

At the same time, there are serious questions about the maximum potential of wind power, if only because of small installations' poor cost/benefit ratio. Wind investments can only be justified if the chosen locations both benefit from strong average speed winds and are sufficiently close to users to avoid the loss of too much energy during transportation. Advances in weather forecasting can reduce errors in site selection (Obersteiner and Bremen 2009) and optimise the location of large wind farms but it is rare that perfect conditions exist in municipal areas, if only because such habitats have often been specifically chosen because they offer protection from the elements. All in all, whereas the future of industrial wind projects as a complementary energy resource is promising, a number of observers have already concluded that micro-wind turbines mounted on individual households'

10

rooftops waste resources (MacKay 2009). However, companies still explore the latter market, for instance by proposing silent turbines to alleviate the noise pollution that homeowners often associate with this technology (Eisenberg 2009). Yet without government assistance – and given the difficulties of erecting turbines tall enough to capture strong winds without damaging the structure of the household roofs upon which they sit – the prospects seem limited.

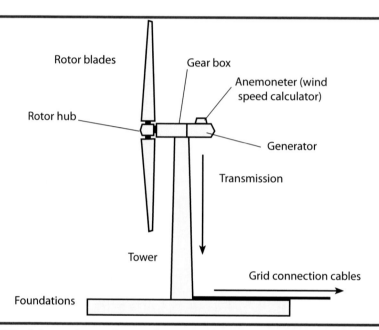

Figure 10.3: Schematic diagram of an electricity-generating wind turbine

Wind farms located on urban peripheries or in the countryside also face a number of obstacles, starting with frequent opposition from authorities who hesitate to give planning permission for projects that alter local scenery, kill birds, etc. A distinction should be made between complaints from residents who do not require the extra power and are unhappy that their neighbourhood is being appropriated to serve distant, energy-wasteful populations, versus **NIMBY** interests who consume great quantities of energy but simply refuse to have it produced locally. The political balance of power between these and other constituencies varies globally and goes some way towards explaining the potential for wind arrays in different regional markets.

NIMBY: ■⎯⎯
Not In My Back Yard. Where individuals avail themselves of the outcomes of an activity but do not wish to be directly confronted with the operations required to produce it.

Key issue

... the balance of power between .. constituencies goes some way towards explaining the potential for wind arrays in different regional markets.

Other, more technical factors include the disadvantage of building very tall structures that necessarily require deep foundations, an engineering feat that increases wind projects' upfront costs and makes the sector generally more reliant on external fund providers such as banks or investors. The intermittency of wind – and frequent lack of correlation between different sites' wind speeds – means that developers are often advised to build a multitude of arrays at a distance from one another, with stormy conditions on one location counter-balancing calm weather at another. This too raises overall costs, since each site will require its own grid connections and also because the project as a whole needs a larger land purchase.

Despite these constraints, recent years have witnessed a large number of wind farm investments globally – with the leading country in this sector, Denmark, well on the way towards achieving its goal of deriving half of its total electricity consumption from wind power alone within 20 years. Other interesting regions include Eastern Africa, exemplified by a recent project to build a 300 MW wind farm in the desert near Lake Turkana in North Kenya. This area suffers from remoteness, meaning that it is expensive to transport the energy produced here, plus maintenance and security conditions are difficult. However, it does enjoy very high average wind speeds, explaining hopes that wind power will account for at least 12 per cent of Africa's total energy need within a decade (Rice 2009). In terms of the wind turbine manufacturing industry, the UK has hosted a great deal of activity in recent years, for instance with Japanese MNE Mitsubishi's announcement in February 2010 that it would be building a £100 million wind turbine factory here. This came on the heels of similar announcements by other companies interested in the British offshore wind sector (see *Chapter 10 online case study*) or the highly publicised November 2008 alliance between Swedish company Vattenfall and Scottish Power Renewables, a subsidiary of Spain's Iberdrola Renovables, the world's largest wind operator. Last but not least, the United States is also becoming increasingly active in this industry, particularly along a north-south wind corridor stretching through the middle of the country, where Texas oil entrepreneur T. Boone Pickens has invested ca. $2 billion buying land and purchased 700 wind turbines from General Electric – the biggest single turbine order in history (Friedman 2008). Of course, mega-entrepreneurs of this ilk are probably accustomed to such mega-deals and possess the relational networks enabling the associated fund-raising.

10

This may explain why large corporate renewable divisions appear to be taking over from SMEs as the main drivers in both wind and solar, one example from summer 2010 being the way that small British turbine manufacturer Clipper Windpower was forced to seek equity from global MNE United Technologies Corporation because the former had insufficient reserves to survive the sector's liquidity-consuming take-off phase. The relationship between company's size and its access to funding is a key factor in determining the trajectory of a new sector such as clean energy.

■ Launching new ventures

Like all infant industries, clean energy has been hampered by high start-up costs, insufficient economies of scale and immature technology. Unlike most earlier industrial revolutions, however, the sector's takeoff phase had the bad luck of coinciding with a deep downturn in the international economy, triggered by the 2008 credit crunch. One of the effects of this crisis has been a restriction on the amount of capital available to entrepreneurs. This is a severe handicap in a new industry – external capital is the lifeblood of start-ups that do not yet benefit from sufficient demand to be self-sustaining. In analytical terms, the lesson is that the outlook for this and other new sectors can only be judged accurately in light of the financial and macro-economic conditions surrounding their birth.

■ Funding

Clean energy's first funding channel, in visibility if not volume terms, is comprised of government investments and incentives coming in the form of grants, subsidies, production tax credits or cheap loans. Although many countries have devised packages supporting SMEs' actions in new green sectors – one example being the US Environmental Protection Agency's Small Business Innovation Research Program – larger companies with their streamlined procedures are generally in a better position to apply for public funds. This was particularly evident after the 2008–09 recession, when the G20 group of leading global economies allocated an estimated $184 billion in green stimulus funds – $67 billion in the USA, $47 billion in China – most of which is to be disbursed in 2011 (Pew 2010). An emblematic programme is China's 'Golden Sun' grant, which pays investors half the costs of installing new PV solar power plants. Note that smaller companies will be hard pressed to lead projects on this scale, with their involvement generally being limited to a subcontractor's role. At the same time, SMEs are often in a better position to benefit from the much smaller micro-investment packages that many local authorities have started to develop worldwide (community power generation schemes, etc.).

It is unclear how big conglomerates analyse the financial aspects of clean energy initiatives since projects of this kind are often aimed at improving the performance of their other business lines. Hence the idea that large companies' return on investment calculations might be improved if their green activities were treated as standalone profit centres – with one observer suggesting that companies establish notional 'trusts' comprised of all public (or other) funds dedicated to green projects (Schendler 2009). Note that governmental influence on green funding is not limited to direct financing facilities alone, since legislative decisions taken with a view towards achieving particular clean energy goals also affect the corporate bottom line. For instance, there is a question whether US utilities seeking to satisfy local renewables obligation must necessarily own green power plants themselves or if it suffices that they source their energy from qualified providers via long-term so-called **offtake** power purchase agreements. Thus, clean energy funding is more than a series of ad hoc financial transactions and can only be analysed accurately within a wider conceptual framework.

> **?** Should returns on green investments be analysed in isolation or in the context of other corporate activities?

> **■ Offtake contract:** Where a utility or other energy buyer commits to buying the energy output from the project for a sufficiently long period of time to justify the original investment in plant capacities.

... large companies' return on investment calculations might be improved if their green activities were treated as standalone profit centres.

Key issue

The second clean energy funding channel, comprised of private sector providers of capital, is also influenced by the public channel insofar as investors interested in the new industry will clearly be reassured when governments are strongly committed to it. This is particularly true for financial investors such as hedge funds or private equity who might otherwise be daunted by the low profit margins typical of industries like clean energy that are still in their infant phase. Note also that the stock market's general enthusiasm for clean energy shares can vary sharply from one quarter to another, often for irrational market sentiment reasons. For instance, solar shares from China (Yingli Green energy) to Germany (SolarWorld or Q-Cells) plummeted during the first five months of 2010, only to recapture the lion's share of their losses by June of that year (FAZ 2010). Given its still developing profile,

10

the sector is subject to greater market volatility than some of its more longstanding counterparts. Conversely, short-term subjectivity will be less of a factor for investors who focus on lasting industrial goals. An example of the latter category is General Electric, which has stated that the purpose of its total $160 million investment in 20 green ventures before 2009 was to harness newcomers' breakthrough technologies and link them to its own portfolio of competencies (Gunther 2009). GE also requires profitability from its stakes but probably on a lengthier timescale than pure financial investors would do. What this reveals is the impossibility of analysing funding behaviour without understanding the specific goals of the parties involved.

The rise of 'socially responsible investing' (SRI) as an asset class has created a whole framework for some green investments – albeit ones that generally have greater relevance to established companies' energy efficiency efforts than to new ventures' capital needs. With 'eco-efficient' or 'environmentally stable' companies often outperforming standard market indices (Derwall *et al.* 2005; Krosinsky and Robins 2007), SRI is an expanding field that currently accounts for an estimated 8 per cent of global managed investment funds. This percentage varies enormously, however, and can exceed 20 per cent in countries such as the UK, where a great deal of publicity is given nowadays to green investment vehicles including the Guinness Alternative Energy Fund, the Jupiter Ecology Fund or Foreign & Commonwealth's Global Climate Opportunities Fund. Today, most large companies are screened to see whether their practices fit a given investor group's ethical requirements. This has underpinned the establishment of a number of well-known 'screened indexes' such as the Domini400 Social Index, the Dow Jones Sustainability World Index and the FTSE4Good Index. Companies listed on these indexes are deemed to conduct themselves in a sustainable manner, usually on the basis of their triple bottom reporting or compliance with GRI guidelines (see Chapter 5).

Similarly, ethical ratings agencies and non-governmental organisations such as CERES, the Carbon Disclosure Project or the UNEP Finance Initiative work alongside today's investors to pressure companies into improving their environmental performance, governance and disclosure. The idea here is that full understanding of a company's financial potential is only possible if its environmental activities are brought into the equation (one reason why Britain's Lord Stern has been advocating credit ratings systems based on companies' carbon profiles). Expressed in financial terms, this means that companies that attract investors due to their high environmental governance standards and low legal liabilities will find it easier to attract funding and lower their overall cost of capital. The complication is that some investors seem more attuned to clean energy behaviour than others. For instance, because many European investors are demonstrably more sensitive than their US counterparts to the risks associated with carbon emissions (disrupted supply chains, recurrence of natural catastrophes, costly regulatory compliance, etc.), the two markets can vary widely in their valuation of clean energy ventures, complicating **fair value** calculations for stocks in this sector. The risk is that the resulting confusion will lead to a recurrence of price bubbles, adding to market volatility and dampening overall investor enthusiasm. An example of the inconsistent nature of market valuations is the way that many solar stocks traded at extremely high price-earning ratios in 2007 – at a time when few of the companies involved had proved their viability – but experienced even greater falls than the general market index did by 2010, even as some were starting to achieve self-sustaining profitability. The clear lesson is that financial investment in the clean energy sector is not guided by rational thinking alone.

> ■ **Fair value:** Estimate of what a good is worth objectively, irrespective of potential buyers and sellers' interests or sentiments.

> **?** How rational are most clean energy investments?

... companies that are attractive to investors due to their high environmental governance standards and low legal liabilities will find it easier to attract funding.

Key issue

Because the diversification of funding sources spreads risk and alleviates the investor disaffection from which an infant industry such as clean energy tends to suffer regularly – a serious hurdle given the massive sums needed to meet global (clean) energy needs – there has been a recent trend towards co-investment projects combining government monies with bank funding and private equity. One example is the hybrid arrangement agreed for a huge wind farm in Lincolnshire that British energy company Centrica started operating in October 2009 and where the choice was made to call upon a whole range of fund providers to avoid any one having to put up too much capital. At the same time, some financial institutions have made a strategic choice to commit to clean energy and are purposefully seeking to expand their presence in this sector. One example is San Francisco bank Wells Fargo (Guevarra 2010), whose environmental loan and investment portfolio has grown in recent years by a factor of six to reach a total of $6.2 billion, split between green construction (52 per cent), renewable energy projects (30 per cent) and green or clean tech firms (18 per cent). The vehicle that

10

Asset financing: ■
Where the borrower offers
the lender a contingent
equity position in an asset in
order to collateralise a loan.

Initial public offering: ■
Where a firm floats shares
on public financial markets
for the first time in order to
expand its capital base.]

bankers clearly prefer in this area is **asset financing**, which amounted to more than 80 per cent of all clean energy equipment and generating capacity funding in 2009, totalling $95 billion in deals worldwide, first and foremost involving onshore wind projects. Far behind this, the sector's second leading source of finance comes from **initial public offerings** and assimilated capital market issues. However, largely as a reflection of general stock market weakness, global capital from this latter source fell from $23 billion in 2007 to $12 billion in 2009 (Pew 2010).

Last but not least, the smallest source of clean energy funding is venture capital (VC) – a variant of private equity finance – which plummeted in 2009 to a mere $6.4 billion. Even so, entrepreneurs are visibly intrigued by VC. Since the computer revolution of the 1980s, the relationship between high-tech start-ups and venture capitalists has been widely hailed as a key driver of innovation in the modern era. In reality, this is largely an American funding mechanism, with other economies – led by China, which in 2009 became the world's top investor in clean energy – tending to prefer more institutionalised channels. VC firms invest their or their customers' funds in small companies in the hope these will turn into the Microsofts or Apples of tomorrow. The subsectors that are fashionable in any one year will often vary, with 2009 having shown signs of growing interest in energy storage and grid technologies alongside a few signs of impatience with the solar panel business – possibly due to the fact that relatively few solar start-ups have qualified for introduction to a stock exchange, which is how venture capitalists usually make their profit. Clean energy's lengthy introduction phase means that the sector is of greater interest to long-term investors interested in positioning themselves in the industries of the future as opposed to short-term speculators more focused on immediate returns. This compartmentalises the sector's investor base and influences green entrepreneurs' funding quests.

? Is venture capitalism as
optimal way of funding
the new clean energy
sector?

Key issue

... [clean energy] is of greater interest to long-term investors interested in ... the industries of the future as opposed to short-term speculators.

Recent years have also seen the development of 'green accounting', which tries to ensure that a company's financial statements internalise all of its environmental activities' positive and negative externalities. As demonstrated in Chapter 2, however, accurate quantification is almost impossible in situations where one party accrues the financial benefits from green actions and others assume the burden (see *Web Resource 10.2*). Thus, instead of framing funding appeals in emotional terms speaking to clean energy's widely acknowledged higher purpose of reducing negative macro-economic externalities, today's green entrepreneurs are expected to develop a business case when publicising their projects (Laszlo 2008). This is yet another sign of the sector's normalisation.

■ The international outlook at year-end 2010

There is no question that the outlook for clean energy entrepreneurship was brighter during the 2007 energy crisis, when skyrocketing prices made the search for alternatives seem like an absolute imperative, as opposed to a few years later, when most of the world was suffering from the effects of a deep recession. In all business but particularly in an infant industry such as clean energy, entrepreneurial actions will always be judged in light of their vulnerability to a fast changing world. As the first edition of this book is being written towards year-end 2010, it seems a good idea to conclude with a review of trading conditions as it comes to press.

In 2008, the global market for low carbon environmental goods and services was estimated to be worth around $3 trillion globally, with Asia accounting for slightly more than one-third of this total and Europe and North America for slightly less apiece (Jha 2009). As always, there is some vagueness associated with the term 'low carbon' and it is crucial to specify that renewable business in the strictest sense of the term is currently deemed to account for just a few percentage points of the total low carbon market (with the exception of a very few countries – mainly in Scandinavia – where the number is as high as 40 per cent).

There are various ways of apprehending the new industry's global expansion. Simply monitoring current installed capacity in renewable energy necessarily over-emphasizes the larger economies. To get a more dynamic picture of market trends, analysis of current stocks should be complemented by flows data. Table 10.1 combines these two categories to reveal one country where high current capacity is complemented by rapid expansion – China.

10

Table 10.1: Renewable energy capacity and five-year growth in different countries (Pew 2010)

Top 10 in renewable energy capacity (2009)	(GW)	Top 10 in five-year growth in installed capacity (2004-09)	(%)
United States	53.4	South Korea	249
China	52.5	China	79
Germany	36.2	Australia	40
Spain	22.4	France	31
India	16.5	India	31
Japan	12.9	United Kingdom	30
Rest of EU-27	12.3	Turkey	30
Italy	9.8	United States	24
France	9.4	Canada	18
Brazil	9.1	Rest of EU-27	17

This shift in global leadership is unsurprising, given that China's annual investment in clean energy was nearly twice as much as the USA in 2009 and easily three times as any one EU member-state. Of course, when all EU investments are combined they easily come top of the table, translating Europe's high per capita green investments. In turn, this reflects the willingness of several mainly Western European countries, along with emerging giants such as China, Brazil and increasingly India, to establish carbon reduction, energy efficiency and/or renewable energy targets; monitor companies' environmental performance; and/or subsidise clean energy production. As stressed throughout this book, clean energy (and more broadly, green) entrepreneurship occurs within a context that is partially determined by political action. US clean energy entrepreneurs will therefore have been reassured by President Barack Obama's overt support for the sector, epitomised in the July 2010 announcement that his Administration would be offering $2 billion in loan guarantees to bolster both Abenoga Solar's construction of the world's largest solar thermal plant in Arizona, and Abound Solar Manufacturing's production of thin-film panels in Colorado and Indiana. The birth of a new industry is partially a question of technology and finance, but also of confidence in a vision.

Key issue

The birth of a new industry is partially a question of technology and finance, but also of confidence in a vision.

The final element in this equation is timing, since it clearly makes more financial sense to invest in a sector just before it takes off rather than having to wait long years for payback. Unsurprisingly, the fall in oil prices since their 2008 peak meant that within a year, wind and especially solar power looked expensive, thus non-competitive, in relative terms. With the global supply of venture capital also dwindling, a number of clean energy projects had to be mothballed, culminating in many of signature firms laying off workers. The sector continued to expand (especially wind power), but at a slower rate. Clearly, clean energy entrepreneurs would have had to be very courageous to choose this moment to engage their resources.

Yet by late 2009/early 2010, there were strong signs that the industry growth rate was returning to previous highs. A central explanation is that energy prices had started to creep up again, largely because economic activity in the BRIC group of leading emerging economies remained strong even as the older industrialised countries faltered. Otherwise, new social constituencies in the Global North were also starting to invest in renewable energy sources on a mass scale – one example being the particularly fast growth in solar and wind installations in farming communities all across the world's older industrialised nations. During the first three quarters of 2009, total 'non-hydro green power generation' actually gained market share across all categories (see Table 10.2), having risen by 9 per cent year-on-year even as total electricity generation fell. Normally this reversal in fortunes would have been treated as a signal for renewed investment, but enthusiasm was tempered by fears about cash-strapped governments' inability to provide much needed direct or indirect **bridge funding**. Over the long run, it is the interaction between energy prices and available funding that will determine the long-term prospects of clean energy entrepreneurship.

■**Bridge funding:** Loans granted for the express purpose of allowing borrowers to survive a temporary period of financial deficit attributable to a particular cause.

	Solar	Wind	Biofuels
Brazil		11.9	61.8
China	8.0	71.1	N/A
Germany	44.3	31.2	N/A
France	19.2	63.3	8.1
Spain	60.6	34.2	N/A
USA	17.4	43.1	22.1
UK	1.9	57.1	10.6

Table 10.2: Leading G-20 country profiles, percentage breakdown in renewable investments (available at www.pewglobalwarming.org/, accessed 10 July 2010)

10

■ Obstacles and pathways

1 Return costs on solar arrays can be prohibitive.

Seek economies of scale through vertical integration or, conversely, alliances with large-scale panels manufacturer.

2 The intermittency of solar and wind power limits generalisability.

Increase investment in power storage technologies.

3 The payback on clean energy projects is very long and puts off investors.

Appeal to industrial stakeholders and seek ancillary aids (tax equity, etc.)

4 The potential for renewable energy is restricted by a country's factor endowments.

Concentrate investment on factor(s) that abound locally.

Case study: Birthing green energy ventures

After graduating from Hastings College of the Law in 1986, Jill Feldman's first position in San Francisco's legal community saw her develop a specialisation in equipment leasing contracts. One of her clients at that time made many leasing investments as the tax owner of wind, biomass, hydroelectric, solar and landfill gas energy projects. These transactions were structured as the sale and lease-back of operating renewable energy projects or as a construction loan followed by a sale and lease-back transaction. Little did Jill realise at the time how important this competency would become to her subsequent career.

In the late 1990s, Jill joined Morrison Foerster (http://www.mofo.com/), a large and highly respected international law firm with a focus on high-tech start-ups, initial public offerings, intellectual property rights, corporate finance and high stakes litigation – all of which explains the important role that the firm has come to play as a bridge between the Silicon Valley investor community and the growing number of clean energy entrepreneurs seeking venture capital to fund their projects. By 2010, Jill found that an increasing proportion of her time was being spent on green projects, and more specifically on developing legal structures enabling her clients to extract the kind of investment returns from renewable energy ventures that take advantage of their tax or investment positions while protecting the safety and soundness of their returns.

Jill's work is helping to bring critically needed debt and equity investments into green energy projects. The cost of current technology and relative pricing levels have made it difficult for renewable power sources (wind and especially solar) to compete with energy projects that use conventional carbon-based fuels. Given the investors' profitability imperative, this means that renewable energy ventures are only likely to receive significant seed capital if the government offers sufficient incentives to bridge the profitability gap. Such incentives can be in the form of a 'carrot', such as a tax break for a renewable energy project, or a 'stick', such as a tax or penalty on ventures exceeding a specified carbon footprint. In the current US system, such incentives often take the form of tax credits and, in certain circumstances, government grants that substitute for tax credits or state-mandated renewable portfolio standards requiring utility companies to purchase a certain percentage of their energy needs from renewable energy sources. Jill works to identify which parties are likely to benefit from a project's different revenue streams (such as proceeds from federal and state tax benefits, proceeds from sales of electricity, or proceeds from sales of assets) and creates joint venture structures that allocate income in the manner best suited to the different types of investors in a renewable energy project. She is also mindful of creating debt and equity structures that enhance the finaceability of a renewable energy project and protect all relevant stakeholders, including equity investors, tax investors, project finance lenders, EPC (engineering, procurement and construction) contractors, equipment suppliers, insurance providers, maintenance suppliers, electricity purchasers and parties that provide other credit support and services to a renewable energy project. Jill's skill set goes beyond the consideration of legal issues to include parties' investment and tax issues, risk appetite and desire to engage in 'social good'. This forces Jill to transcend purely legalistic assessments of a particular venture's feasibility, thus to take a broader overview. As highlighted throughout this book, environmental business is first and foremost predicated on a holistic and multidisciplinary understanding of the world.

Where intellectual property rights are vital to a new green venture's potential, Morrison Foerster has a number of specialists who are capable of judging the scientific and economic applicability of critical patents and intellectual property rights. Jill and her colleagues will generally only get involved in ventures whose technology is vetted and found to be sound, and where all patent and intellectual property rights have been assigned to the company to avoid intellectual property battles with other possible claimants. Then there is the question of the balance of power between hopeful green entrepreneurs and the investment partners that they are seeking to attract. After an initial wave of investor enthusiasm peaked in early 2008 – at a time when many viable projects seemed to have few problems accessing funding – the bubble burst as the effects of the credit crunch began to bite. Nowadays, many potential equity and debt investors are looking to only support start-ups that have already attracted substantial equity investments or benefited from some form of US Department of Energy funding. In part, this is because such companies have already received a stamp of approval from the investment community or governmental sources. Confidence in a new venture is to some degree a subjective assessment, and the more potential investors hear favourable opinions about a possible company or project, the likelier they are to overcome their professional scepticism.

10

As a niche specialist, it is in Jill's interest to keep a close eye on all the elements determining her client's investment decisions. Asides from consulting a wide range of professional contacts, she and her research assistants access data sources such as Bloomberg New Energy Finance (http://bnef.com/free-publications/press-releases) and the National Renewable Energy Laboratory (http://www.nrel.gov). In 2009, this latter source sponsored a Renewable Energy Project Finance Tracking initiative that studied 132 renewable energy projects completed in 2009. It also listed two main obstacles to renewable energy ventures' development: difficult access to 'tax equity'; and the need to demonstrate a strong 'offtake' contract. A renewable energy project can have a useful life of 20 years or more, meaning that the developer must find a utility or other energy purchaser willing to purchase the electricity output for a similarly long period. In an era of great financial and economic uncertainty, such customers are hard to find. Despite general optimism about renewable energy's future – and the impressive knowledge being accumulated by specialists such as Jill Feldman – the new sector still faces challenges inhibiting its rollout. It is one thing for green production to make sense for the environment. It is quite another for it to make business sense.

Case study question

1 What specific role has Jill Feldman played in the development of California's clean energy industry?

2 What are the different considerations that legal experts like Jill must take into account when structuring clean energy deals?

3 In light of Jill's experience, what are the clean energy sector's prospects?

■ References

BWEA British Wind Energy Association (2009) *Powering a Green Economy: Wind, wave and tidal's contribution to Britain's industrial future*, available at www.bwea.com, accessed 12 June 2010

Croston, G. (2008), *75 Green Businesses You Can Start to Make Money and Make A Difference*, Irvine, CA: Entrepreneur Press.

Derwall, J., Guenster, N., Bauer, R. and Koedijk, K (2005), 'The eco-efficiency premium puzzle', *Financial Analysts Journal*, **61** (2).

Eisenberg, A. (2009), 'Bringing wind turbines to ordinary rooftops', 14 February, available at www.nytimes/, accessed 10 May 2010.

FAZ (2010), 'Anleger entdecked die Solarwerte wieder', *Frankfurter Allgemeine Zeitung*, 24 June, p. 19.

Friedman, T. (2008), 'Texas to Tel Aviv', 27 July, available at www.nytimes.com/, accessed 1 July 2010.

Guevarra, L. (2010), 'Wells Fargo green financing surges to $6.2 billion', 22 March, available at greenbiz.com, accessed 6 June 2010.

Gunther, M. (2009), 'How and where GE is placing its cleantech bets', 20 October, available at greenbiz.com, accessed 6 June 2010.

Jha, A. (2009), 'Natural power unleashed', *Technology Guardian*, 9 July, p.1.

Keeley, G. (2008), 'GM installs world's biggest rooftop solar panels', *The Guardian*, 9 July, p. 27.

Krosinsky, C. and Robins, N. (2007), *Sustainable Investing: The Market Beating Strategy for the 21st Century*, London: Earthscan.

Laszlo, C. (2008), *Sustainable Value: How the World's Leading Companies Are Doing Well By Doing Good*, Stanford, CA: Greenleaf Publishing.

Lorenz., P., Pinner, D. and Seitz, T. (2008), 'The economics of solar power', June, available at www.mckinseyquarterly.com/, accessed 2 June 2010.

Luoma, J. (2009), 'The challenge for green energy', 3 July, available at http://e360.yale.edu/, accessed 20 June 2010.

MacKay, D. (2009), 'Saving the planet by numbers', 23 April, available at http://news.bbc.co.uk/, accessed 20 June 2010.

Madigan, P. (2009), 'Wave and tidal: growth in 2009', *BWEA Real Power*, Issue 16, April–June, p. 21.

Merfeld, D. (2010), 'Why it's time to take solar seriously', 6 April, available at http.greennbiz.com, accessed 20 June 2010.

Monbiot, G. (2007), *Heat: How We Can Stop the Planet Burning*, London: Penguin.

Mouawad, J. (2009), 'Oil giants loath to follow Obama's green lead', 7 April, available at www.nytimes.com/, accessed 28 June 2010.

Obersteiner, C. and Bremen, L. (2009), 'Influence of market rules on the economic value of wind power: an Austrian case study', *International Journal of Environment and Pollution*, **39** (1–2).

Pernick, R. (2007), *The Clean Tech Revolution: The Next Big Growth and Investment Opportunity*, Collins.

Pew Charitable Trusts (2010), 'Who's winning the clean energy race? Growth, competition and opportunities in the world's largest economies', available at www.pewtrusts.org/, accessed 26 April 2010.

Rice, X. (2009), 'The greening of Africa: Kenya outlines plan for continent's biggest windfarm', *The Guardian*, 28 July, p. 15.

Rosenthal, E. (2010), Solar Industry Learns Painful Lessons in the Spanish Sun, *The Observer – New York Times* insert, 4 April, p. 5

Schendler, A. (2009), *Getting Green Done: Hard Truths from the Front Lines of the Sustainability Revolution*, New York: Public Affairs.

TUC (Trade Union Congress) (2009) *Unlocking Green Enterprise: a Low-carbon Strategy for the UK Economy*, London: Impetus Consulting.

Woody, T. (2009), 'Solar power ignites a war over water', *The Observer — New York Times* insert, 1 November, p. 5.

Woody, T. (2010), 'Forget Red China. It's Green China these days – at least when it comes to making big renewable deals', 11 January, available at www.grist.org/, accessed 26 April 2010.

10

Glossary

Note. The number at the end of each entry refers to the first chapter where the term can be found.

Altruism: Sense of greater concern for the welfare of others than for one's own immediate (material) self-interest. (7)

Anthropocentric: View that humans are the central feature of all existence. (1)

Asset financing: Where the borrower offers the lender a contingent equity position in an asset in order to collateralise a loan. (10)

Balanced scorecard: Strategy tool used to measure performance based on a range of financial and non-financial parameters. (5)

Best practice: Optimal performance becoming a benchmark for actors pursuing a similar line of activity. (3)

Biodegradable: Molecular compounds whose residues merge harmlessly into the surrounding environment once they have decomposed. (1)

Biodiversity: Extent to which genuses of living organisms vary within a given ecosystem. (2)

Biofuels: Energy sources derived from living organisms, often through the release of calorific energy previously stored via photosynthetic processes. (9)

Biological nutrients: Natural inputs into the production process. (6)

Biomass: Raw materials derived from recently harvested plants and used for energy or heating purposes. (2)

Biophilic: Postulate of a deep connection between humankind and biosphere. (9)

Biosphere: Sum total of factors on Planet Earth that make it possible to sustain life. (1)

Biota: Living organisms in a particular biosphere at a given period of time. (3)

Brand tribes: Communities of consumers defined by their shared loyalty to (and often experiences with) a brand. (7)

Bridge funding: Loans granted for the express purpose of allowing the borrower to survive a temporary period of financial deficit attributable to a particular cause. (10)

Brownfield sites: Spaces that once hosted an industrial or com mercial activity but are currently unused. (9)

Carbon emission trading schemes: Mechanisms whereby participants receive (or buy) initial permits enabling maximum carbon emissions over a specific period of time. Such allocations can only be exceeded by purchasing fellow participants' unused permits. Conversely, unused permits can be resold for a profit, providing an incentive to emit less carbon. (1)

Cascade: Flow via a series of discrete steps. (5)

Clean energy: Energy captured, distributed and used in a way characterised by a minimal environmental footprint (mostly involving renewable sources).. (4)

Clean technology: Set of industrial principles where energy or power are generated in an environmentally friendly manner. (6)

Climate change: Lasting variation in temperatures and weather. (1)

Closed loop: System whose existing components suffice for its continued functioning, i.e. which requires no further inputs. (1)

CHP Combined heat and power: Where heat waste created during energy or electricity generation processes is captured and reused for heating purposes, either on one site or across a wider area in so-called 'district heating' systems. (9)

Code of conduct: List of rules detailing accepted behaviour within an organisation. (5)

Commoditisation: Where goods are developed, processed and distributed according to an undifferentiated mass volume logic. (9)

Congestion charge: Levy on drivers entering certain crowded city sections to dissuade them from doing so. (9)

Corpocracy: Regime where power is wielded mainly and conceivably solely by and for corporate interests. (5)

Corporate responsibility: The idea that a company should ensure that all of its actions are both legal and ethical. (1)

Degradation of the biosphere: Where damage, often in the form of pollution caused by human activities, is done to the natural support systems sustaining life. (1)

Dematerialisation: Virtualisation. (6)

Demography: Study of population patterns (birth rates, mortality, migration, etc.). (3)

Disclosure: Provision of information. Often comes in a specified form complying with legal requirements. (5)

Disassembly: Act of breaking an item down into its component parts, usually at the end of its working life. (6)

Downstream: Later value chain activities relating to the interface between a company and its customers. (4)

Dystopia: Disturbing/nightmarish future – opposite of 'utopian'. (1)

e-waste: Electronic and electrical equipment that has been discarded, having come to the end of its useful working life. (5)

Eco-efficiency: Organisational process characterised by lower material and energy intensities, less toxicity, greater recyclability and maximal use of renewable inputs. (6)

Ecological deficit: Excess of human consumption of planetary resources over their natural regeneration. (1)

Ecological imperative: View that ecosystem protection is a priority for all social, political and economic endeavours and probably a sine qua non condition for the preservation of modern civilisation. Also known as the 'green' or 'environmentalist' agenda. (1)

Ecological inertia: Slower adaptation to environmental problems than would normally be expected using rational analysis. (4)

Ecological justice: Extent to which different segments within a society enjoy equal access to a sustainable environment. (4)

Ecological myopia: Unwillingness or inability to envision the long-term environmental consequences of one's own behaviour. (3)

Ecosystem: Sum total of living 'biotic' flora or fauna and inanimate 'abiotic' elements whose interactions enable life on Earth, often through the self-sustaining food chains that have evolved. (1)

Effluents: Outflows, runoffs or sewage from a transformation activity. (1)

Elasticity: Correlation between the movement of one variable, like price, on another, like supply or demand. 'Inelasticity' signifies that no such correlation exists. (2)

Embedded inputs: Total amount of energy or water consumed during the entire production process leading to the materialisation of a final product. (5)

End-of-pipeline: Total output following the completion of all transformation processes. (2)

End users: Ultimate customers of a product that is fully evolved and not destined for further enhancement. (2)

Energy density: Calculation of the volume of energy stored within a container of a given size. (10)

Energy elasticity: Relationship between changes in a country's economic expansion and its energy use. (2)

Energy-intensive: Description of activities requiring a higher than average injection of energy resources. (2)

Energy productivity: Quantity of outputs produced with fixed level of inputs. (2)

Energy security: Confidence that a country (or company) can source the energy it needs to achieve its ambitions. (2)

Environmental footprint: The measurable effects of an activity on the ecosphere. (1)

Environmental management system (EMS): 'Framework through which [a company's] environmental performance can be monitored, improved and controlled' (see http://www.envirowise.gov.uk). (5)

Externalities: Impact of a transaction on a third party. (3)

Fair trade: Markets organised to ensure that the producer receives a living wage, even if this involves consumers paying more than the market minimum for the good in question. (8)

Fair value: Estimate of what a good is worth objectively, irrespective of potential buyers and sellers' interests or sentiments. (10)

Feed-in tariffs: Sums that a utility (often supported by the state) pays to private parties producing and selling their own renewable energy. (4)

Finite: A quantity characterised by limited total supply. (1)

Food miles: Distance a foodstuff has travelled from its place of production to its place of consumption. (6 & 8)

Foodshed: Conception of a food system as stretching from its original rural source to its urban marketplace. (9)

Foreign Direct Investment (FDI): Where a firm funds a permanent or semi-permanent physical unit abroad. (8)

Frictional costs: Costs relating to the transfer of economic actors from one sector to another, often because the former has faltered due to the arrival of new technology. (8)

Genetically modified (GM) organisms: Living entities whose biomolecular composition has been altered to induce certain characteristics. (9)

Global governance: Where regulatory and supervisory functions are fulfilled by authorities whose responsibilities supersede national borders. (4 & 8)

Global North: Generic reference to the world's older industrialised nations. Sometimes referred to as the OECD countries. (8)

Green chemistry: Where companies develop and apply natural compounds producing certain performance attributes while avoiding the bio-hazards associated with traditional industrial compounds. (3)

Green marketing: Where companies offer products or services that are largely defined by their environmental benefits. (7)

Green premium: Surcharge paid for a green product over a non-green product offering the same functionalities. (7)

Green redemption: Where a company that once suffered from a reputation of environmental destruction restores its brand image through green (marketing) actions. (7)

Green Revolution: International campaign during the mid-20th century to modernise agricultural practices, particularly in LDCs, through technological and infrastructural improvements. (9)

Green sacrifice: Actors' willingness to renounce personal material advantage in favour of ecological benefits enjoyed by the wider community. (1)

Greenhouse effect: Condition where heat (often in light form) entering a partially hermetic environment is prevented from dissipating. (3)

Greenwash: Where companies' advertising overstates the extent of the environmental activism. (7)

Grid: Interconnected power supply infrastructure bringing energy from the location where it is generated to the sites where it is consumed. (4)

Grid parity: Where energy from different sources costs the same to end consumers sourcing it via the grid. (10)

Habitat: Where a population normally lives. (2)

Halo effect: Where a company gains marketing goodwill in certain areas because consumers appreciate its actions in others. (7)

Heat waste: Energy dissipating in heat form as the by product of a chemical or mechanical action. (10)

Hinterland: Regions surrounding a population centre and sustaining it with goods while relying on it as a trade hub. (9)

Holistic: View that a system is defined by the interactions between its components rather than by their sum total. (1)

Initial public offering: Where a firm floats shares on public financial markets for the first time in order to expand its capital base. (10)

Intangibles: Immaterial, non-physical assets such as patents or brand image. (8)

Intergovermental organisation: International body created by nation-states, often for coordination purposes, to deal with cross-border issues. (8)

Intermittency: Inconsistent behaviour – energy from wind turbines or solar panels that only operate when the wind blows or the sun shines is, by definition, intermittent. (10)

Internal waste tax: Invoicing system where the different entities comprising a multidivisional company pay notional fines for the waste they produce. (8)

Kinetic energy: Energy wielded by an object in movement. (10)

Knock-on effect: Where events occurring at the upstream level of a sector's value chain affect its downstream phases. (6)

Licence to operate: Permission to engage in a productive activity. (4)

Lifecycle assessment: Analysis of an asset's total value including acquisition price, performance and residual value. (4)

Lifecycle costing: Total cost of an item once all expenditures are accounted for, particularly relating to the minimisation of its environmental footprint (pollution permits, disposal, safety measures). (6)

Lightweighting: Engineering initiatives aimed at reducing the mass of materials comprising a manufactured item. (6)

Localism: Social/economic organisation emphasising the consumption of goods/services that have been produced locally. (9)

LOHAS: Acronym for Lifestyles of Health and Sustainability, a market segment focused on health and fitness, the environment, personal development, sustainable living, and social justice, c.f. http://www.lohas.com/. (7)

Market failure: Inability of a market system to achieve an optimal outcome (allocation of resources, accurate pricing, etc.). (4)

Metrics: Indicators chosen as measurement instruments. (5)

Micro-generation: Production of power from small, local sources. (2)

Monoculture: Where an agricultural production region specialises in a single plant genus instead of diversifying. (8)

Moral hazard: Where incentives are skewed so that a party is motivated to take a risk because it does not suffer the consequences if things go wrong.

Nano-technology: Study of matter on a very small atomic level. (10)

Nearsourcing: Where a company moves to procure supplies from a provider located in relative proximity instead of at a great distance.

Neo-liberal: Belief in a minimal interference of government in the economy. (2 & 8)

NIMBY: Not In My Back Yard. Where individuals avail themselves of the outcomes of an activity but do not wish to be directly confronted with the operations required to produce it. (10)

Non-governmental organisation: Civil society associations created to deal with specific issues or promote a particular ethos or policy. International NGOs usually focus on problems that are cross-border in nature. (5)

Non-product ratio: Percentage of inputs that are transformed over the course of a production process into waste. (6)

Offtake contract: Where a utility or other energy buyer commits to buying the energy output from the project for a sufficiently long period of time to justify the original investment in plant capacities. (10)

Opportunity cost: Cost of not doing something. (5)

Organic: Grown without any synthetic additives. (7)

Outsourcing: Where a company buys supplies that it needs for its products or services from an outside company instead of making them itself. (8)

Paradigm: Worldview, general philosophy. (4)

Passivhaus: Structure designed to reduce internal–external heat flows using triple-glazed windows and an airtight outer envelope. Contrast with hi-tech 'active' green structure that uses onsite renewable energy sources but needs pumps and motors to circulate heat (Steffen 2008). (9)

Pathogen: Agent causing disease in a living organism. (3)

Planned obsolescence: Where companies design products to wear out prematurely so that consumers are forced to buy replacements. (2)

Portability: Ease with which an asset, like an energy source, can be transported from one location to another. (10)

Precautionary principle: Philosophy that when faced with an indeterminate choice, the best option is the one that minimises potential risks. (4)

Protectionism: General policy where a national government adopts policies restricting foreign producers' access to its domestic market. (8)

Public goods: Goods that are 'rivalrous' but 'non-excludable', meaning that (1) their consumption by one party will prevent others from enjoying them, yet (2) no one can be excluded from their use. (4)

Race to the bottom: Where competition among disadvantaged producers forces them to accept lower remuneration for their services. (8)

Regime arbitrage: Where multinational enterprises put pressure on a national government to relax regulations under threat of investing elsewhere. (8)

Relative price: Value attributed to one category of asset compared to another. (4)

Renewables obligation: Requirement that a certain percentage of total energy production come from renewable sources by a certain deadline. (10)

Resilience: Concept increasingly used in environmental studies to refer to an entity's ability to withstand external shocks and continue to perform and/or survive. (9)

Resource depletion: Exhaustion of irreplaceable stocks of raw physical commodities consumed as a result of human activity. (1)

Retrofitting: Adjoining new technological features on old platforms. Often refers to modernisation of building stock. (5)

Reverse logistics: Where a company organises shipment channels enabling the return of its used goods for recycling purposes. (2)

Sequestering: Containing an unwanted substance so that it does not permeate and damage the surrounding environment. (3)

Slurry: Liquid thickened by the solid particles that it has accumulated, often after use as a cleansing agent. (3)

Smart grid: Energy distribution network that uses information technology to optimise power allocations and reduce wastage. (6)

Social marketing: Commercial efforts by companies to affect consumers' behaviour in a way that will enhance the broader social good. (7)

Solar array: Large number of solar panels arranged in a way that maximises their thermal effects. (10)

Stakeholder: Anyone affected, however indirectly, by an organisation's actions. Often understood to include employees, local governments, suppliers, consumers and host communities. (5)

State capitalism: Where large swathes of market activities are undertaken by publicly owned enterprise. (8)

Stewardship: Idea that one entity has a practical if not moral obligation to take responsibility for another. (1)

Stressor: Any agent disturbing the biological processes of another. (3)

Sunk costs: Sums already invested in assets that cannot be sold off. (4)

Sustainability: Capacity for survival for unlimited period of time through infinite repetition of existing regulation mechanisms - or adoption of new ones – enabling adjusting to changing external circumstances. (1)

Sustainomics: Vision of economics in which the minimum requirement for the solutions on offer is that they be sustainable. (8)

Sustenance: Factors supporting the existence of life. (1)

Symbiosis: Interdependent relationship. (6)

Synthetic: Human-made. The opposite of natural. (3)

Technical nutrients: Synthetic inert inputs into the production process. (6)

Throughput: Holistic overview of elements in all of their different stages as they transit through a transformation process. (3)

Toxicity: Extent to which an agent causes harm to different living organisms. (3)

Triple bottom line: Idea that firms should report not only financial but also social and environmental outcomes; formulated by John Elkington in 1994. (5)

Upgradeability: Ease with which an object can accommodate modernisation. (6)

Upstream: Early value chain activities undertaken when processing or transforming a product or service. (2)

Urban sprawl: Municipalities' extension towards their fringes, often leading to the development of previously rural land. (9)

Urban infill: Policy of directing future growth to undeveloped spaces within a metropolitan region's existing boundaries instead of expanding further on the fringes. (9)

Utilitarian: Designed solely to fulfil a practical function. (6)

Value chain: The succession of acts that successfully add value to an item as it is transformed from a raw material or input stage to a finished product or service. (2)

Venality: Willingness to sell one's services for a material reward. (1)

Vertical integration: Where a firm controls, and/or moves towards controlling, both the upstream and downstream sides of its value chain. (2)

Virtual: Intangible replication of reality. (6)

Weatherisation: Work done to improve physical structures' ability to withstand the elements while consuming a minimum of energy. (10)

Zeitgeist: Dominant paradigm at a particular moment in history. (1)

Index